328.73073
R618v

D0435581

APR   2011

Lincoln Branch Library
1221 E. 7 Mile
Detroit, MI 48203

APR 2011

VOTE
THIEVES

RELATED TITLES FROM POTOMAC BOOKS, INC.

Counting Every Vote: The Most Contentious Elections in American History
—Robert Dudley and Eric Shiraev

*The Cure for Our Broken Political Process: How We Can Get Our
Politicians to Resolve the Issues Tearing Our Country Apart*
—Sol Erdman and Lawrence Susskind

Getting Immigration Right: What Every American Needs to Know
—David Coates and Peter Siavelis, eds.

Congress at War: The Politics of Conflict Since 1789
—Charles A. Stevenson

The Faith Factor: How Religion Influences American Elections
—John C. Green

VOTE THIEVES

THIEVES

Illegal Immigration, Redistricting, and Presidential Elections

Orlando J. Rodriguez

Potomac Books, Inc.
Washington, D.C.

Copyright © 2011 by Orlando J. Rodriguez

Published in the United States by Potomac Books, Inc. All rights reserved. No part of this book may be reproduced in any manner whatsoever without written permission from the publisher, except in the case of brief quotations embodied in critical articles and reviews.

Library of Congress Cataloging-in-Publication Data
Rodriguez, Orlando J.
  Vote thieves : illegal immigration, redistricting, and presidential
elections / Orlando J. Rodriguez.
     p. cm.
  Includes bibliographical references and index.
  ISBN 978-1-59797-671-8 (hardcover : alk. paper)
  1. United States—Emigration and immigration—Government policy. 2.
Illegal aliens—United States. 3. Illegal aliens—Suffrage—United States.
4. Apportionment (Election law)—United States. 5. Elections—United
States. I. Title.
  JV6493.R63 2011
  328.73'073455—dc22
                                                        2010048988

Printed in the United States of America on acid-free paper that meets the American National Standards Institute Z39-48 Standard.

Potomac Books, Inc.
22841 Quicksilver Drive
Dulles, Virginia 20166

First Edition

10 9 8 7 6 5 4 3 2 1

For Shirley Akers,
who cared when no one else did.

Contents

Preface

The United States is being yanked, pulled, and twisted repeatedly as the nation struggles in 2011 with both heightened political turmoil not seen since the Civil Rights Movement of the 1960s, and severe economic hardships not felt since the Great Depression of the 1930s. Add to these problems the end of a questionable war in Iraq and an ongoing war in Afghanistan. Furthermore, the country's ugly history of racism is resurfacing, as some Americans fear that their African American president (who placed the first Hispanic female judge on the U.S. Supreme Court) threatens their way of life. The media and politicians exacerbate the situation and vie for the public's attention with ever more outrageous headlines on illegal immigrants, anchor babies, birthright citizenship, healthcare reform, Muslims, birthers, the Tea Party, or whatever new spin will yield the highest ratings or most media exposure.

What is happening? Essentially, the United States is experiencing growing pains. The country is transforming from having a relatively uniform culture into the most culturally and ethnically diverse society in human history. There is also a demographic rift as populations in the North and Midwest become older, while the South and West remain young. The corresponding political landscape is changing unevenly across the country, which has spawned a loud and strong resistance among those who fear change the most. In 1787 the framers of the Constitution could not have foreseen an America so culturally and regionally diverse. Nor would they recognize an America that is much more democratic than they allowed for in their original constitution.

The United States Constitution was written for a society of the late 1700s and has been amended twenty-seven times to both rectify faults and reflect more enlightened morals. In particular the expansion of voting rights has been an ongoing struggle. Only after a civil war was slavery eliminated and African American males given the right to vote. Women did not obtain voting rights until 1920. Then in 1971 the voting age was lowered to eighteen for all citizens. The struggle to expand voting rights was necessitated by a Constitution that lacks an incentive for voter participation. There is not a right to vote among the Constitution's fundamental Bill of Rights.

Another amendment to the Constitution is needed now to ensure that the House of Representatives reflects the wishes of voters as cultural and regional diversity increase. Moreover, this amendment is also needed to rectify a constitutional flaw known to the framers. Otherwise, the country will remain politically polarized, either culturally, or regionally, or both, and Congress will remain unresponsive to the wishes of the majority of citizens.

Vote Thieves proposes that we base congressional apportionment on the number of voters that participate in federal elections—voter-count apportionment. In 1941 Laurence Schmeckebier, Ph.D. and an expert on congressional apportionment, wrote, "It is therefore recommended that there be adopted a constitutional amendment providing that apportionment be based on votes cast."[1] Schmeckebier wanted to penalize southern states that had disenfranchised blacks and southwestern states that had disenfranchised Hispanics. Schmeckebier reasoned that apportionment based on votes would create an incentive for states to enfranchise all eligible citizens.

Voter-count apportionment will reward states for increasing voter participation. It will penalize states that tolerate voter disenfranchisement—like Florida on Election Day in 2000. States will not gain additional representation from illegal residents. Voter-count apportionment will have a moderating influence on today's ultra-partisan and divisive politics. Political competition will increase and lessen the need for term limits. There will be fewer "safe" seats in the House of Representatives, and congressional representatives will become beholden to voters—not their political parties.

Vote Thieves advocates for a cause that is common to the tenets of liberals, conservatives, and moderates alike: that one person's vote be equal to another's and that government reflects the will of the governed.

1

APPORTIONMENT

The Consequences of Counting Everyone

The admission of slaves into the Representation when fairly explained comes to this: that the inhabitant of Georgia and S. C. who goes to the Coast of Africa, . . . shall have more votes in a Govt. instituted for protection of the rights of mankind, than the Citizen of Pa. or N. Jersey who views with a laudable horror, so nefarious a practice.

—Gouverneur Morris, Delegate from Pennsylvania,
Constitutional Convention, August 8, 1787

Vigilantes on the Mexican Border: A Dilemma for Republicans

Members of American vigilante groups on the U.S.-Mexico border typically identify with the far-right faction of the Republican Party. This creates a dilemma for Republicans as well as business owners and corporations that willingly hire illegal immigrants because they want cheap labor. While vigilantes are vocal, businesses contribute heavily to the Republican Party. In short, the activities of vigilantes might reduce the supply of cheap labor that enables businesses to increase their profits. This makes it difficult, if not impossible, for Republicans to have an immigration policy that would be supported by all factions within the party.

Congress has 435 representatives in the House of Representatives (House), which are reallocated among the fifty states every ten years following a decennial census. This process is called reapportionment and assigns representation to states based on the size of the entire population—including illegal immigrants—as counted by the most recent census. The last round of reapportionment occurred in December 2010 following the 2010 census. Ten years earlier, after reapportionment in 2000, three states received additional representatives because of their population of undocumented residents: California (three), Florida (one), and North Carolina (one). After reapportionment in 2010, California and Texas will each likely gain two additional congressional representatives because of their population of illegal residents. If vigilante groups reduce the number of illegal border crossings, it could result in fewer representatives in states with large populations of undocumented Mexicans—such as California, Arizona, and Texas.

Even Republicans who condemn illegal immigration find it hard to turn down the added congressional representation that comes with illegal immigrants. Tom Feeney, a Republican and former Florida Congressman, condemns illegal immigration.[1] However, in 2007 Feeney supported Florida receiving additional congressional representation because of its population of illegal aliens. "I am sort of ambivalent, not in the sense that I don't care, but that I could see arguments for both sides . . . anything that helps Florida gain a relative advantage is a good thing and I would be biased in favor of."[2] Feeney's comments came after he had co-sponsored House Bill 839 in 2006, which expressed support for the Minuteman Project—a vigilante group working to reduce illegal immigration along the U.S.-Mexico border.[3] Feeney's comments illustrate the dilemma illegal immigration creates for Republicans. The party needs to appease their anti-immigrant constituents without doing harm to business owners that benefit from illegal workers.

Republican Candice Miller of Michigan might differ with fellow Republican Feeney of Florida. Miller has sponsored bills in Congress to exclude the illegal population from apportionment. After reapportionment in 2000, the population of illegal residents in states such as California, Arizona, Texas, and Florida caused Michigan to lose one representative.

If the activities of border vigilante groups reduce the number of illegal immigrants entering the United States, it would reduce the population of undocumented residents in immigrant destination states. This has the potential to reduce the number of congressional representatives in these states. After the 2010 elections, Republican congressional representatives were in the majority in six of the top ten immigrant destination states including Arizona, Georgia, Florida, Illinois, Nevada, and Texas. Democrats were the majority in the other four top immigrant destination states of California, New Jersey, New York, and North Carolina.

Vigilante groups on the U.S.-Mexico border claim they are patrolling the border because the federal government has failed to stop illegal immigration. Furthermore, about 65 percent of illegal drugs sold in the United States enter the country from Mexico.[4] From 2006 to mid-2010, about 23,000 people had been killed in drug-related incidents in Mexico, including engagements with the Mexican military.[5] The Mexican military was enmeshed in a civil war, fighting Mexican drug gangs in the northern Mexican states bordering the United States. In March 2010, drug smugglers killed Robert Krentz, a prominent cattle rancher from southeastern Arizona, after they crossed onto his land from Mexico. Two months later in May, the Obama administration announced it would send as many as 1,200 additional National Guard troops to border areas to police against drug smugglers.

Bob Maupin, who lives near the border in southern California says, "A vigilante is, by definition, a citizen upholding the law in the absence of law enforcement. That's the way we out here look at it."[6] The prevalence of illegal crossers has increased dramatically since the early 1990s according to Maupin's neighbor Lorna House. "I had eighteen of them walk by my little fenced-in yard yesterday, and they gave me this sneer and look and kind of grin, like, 'You can't do anything.'"[7]

A mixture of patriotism and an intense dislike of foreigners motivate vigilantes. The Southern Poverty Law Center described the vigilante group Ranch Rescue as a group that "conduct[s] paramilitary operations and equip themselves with high-powered assault rifles, handguns, night-vision devices, two-way radios, observation posts, flares, machetes, all-terrain vehicles, and trained attack dogs."[8] Some of the vigilante groups have drawn interest from other groups with known racist ideologies such as the Ku Klux Klan and David Duke's National Organization for European American Rights.[9]

The most visible vigilante group is the Minuteman Project, which claims to be nonracist. However, statements from some of their volunteers run counter to the group's public persona.[10]

The group instructs volunteers not to interact with suspected illegal crossers and not detain them in any way.[11] Volunteers contact the U.S. Border Patrol when they spot illegal crossers. The Minuteman Project claims they have been responsible for the capture of thousands of illegal border crossers. The U.S. Border Patrol has reported that volunteers with the Minuteman Project have disrupted the work of border agents by inadvertently tripping sensors along the border.[12] However, some Border Patrol agents admit that the Minuteman Project has helped to reduce the number of illegal border crossings.

Law enforcement officials worry that vigilante groups may start with good intentions but evolve into nefarious organizations. American vigilante groups have existed along the Mexican border since the Mexican-American War ended in 1848. From 1848 to 1928, vigilantes lynched nearly six hundred Mexicans in the United States.[13] American mobs would disregard the legal process and take Mexicans from police custody and lynch them.[14] Mexican victims of lynching were typically poor working-class persons of mixed Anglo, Indian, Spanish, and African race.[15] American vigilantes considered these Mexicans racially inferior.

The last recorded lynching of a Mexican immigrant in the United States was in 1928. However, in 1972 in southern Texas, Kenneth Adami was convicted of murdering five undocumented Mexicans he found in his hunting shack.[16] Adami admitted the killings were "kind of coldblooded." Nine years earlier in 1963, Adami had been convicted of killing his neighbor for leaving a gate open. Adami spent twenty-seven years in prison for killing the five immigrants and was released in 2001 at the age of eighty-eight.[17] In 1976 in Douglas, Arizona, cattle rancher George Hanigan and his sons tortured three Mexican men who had crossed the border illegally.[18]

The history of the Texas Rangers (Texas State police, not the baseball team) provides a good example of how vigilante groups can advance beyond their original purpose. The Texas Rangers were formed in 1823 as a paramilitary force by American settlers, in the Mexican province of Tejas, for protection against Indian raids. The Rangers became a government organization in 1835 when Texas—Tejas—fought for independence from Mexico. After Texas declared independence from Mexico in 1836, the Texas Rangers played an active role in intimidating Mexican ranchers into selling their property. Rangers told Texans of Mexican origin, "If you are found here in the next five days you will be dead."[19] Mexican land owners were forced to sell their lands to Anglo settlers for a pittance: "Texas Rangers, in cooperation with land speculators, came into small Mexican villages in the border country, massacred hundreds of unarmed, peaceful Mexican villagers and seized their lands. Sometimes the seizures were accompanied by the formality of signing bills of sale—at the point of a gun."[20]

Walter Prescott Webb, historian of the Texas Rangers, wrote, "[i]n the orgy of bloodshed that followed, the Texas Rangers played a prominent part, and one of which many members of the force have been heartily ashamed."[21] Texas Rangers would also ride into Mexico to capture black slaves who had escaped into Mexico via the "Little Underground Railroad," which ran from central Texas into Mexico.

The Texas Rangers were reorganized in 1919 because of their partisan involvement in elections. The organization continued to operate above the law and there were several attempts to abolish the Rangers after 1920. In 1974, the U.S. Supreme Court ruled that the use of the Texas Rangers as strike breakers against farm workers had been unconstitutional.[22] The history of violence against people of Mexican heritage provides the core concern regarding the activities of vigilantes on the U.S.-Mexico border.

The long history of vigilante groups along the Mexican border is characterized by activities that are illegal and immoral by contemporary standards. Today, vigilante groups operating along the border fall into legal gray zones. Vigilantes are considered private citizens and their border-related activities are constrained by state laws, which vary among the four border states. Texas, New Mexico, and Arizona do not allow citizens to arrest illegal border crossers.[23] In these states, vigilantes can only inform the U.S. Border Patrol of persons they see crossing the border. In California, citizens can arrest suspected illegal border crossers but cannot use unreasonable force and must deliver the offenders to law enforcement authorities without delay. Citizens who violate these rules are subject to criminal penalties, and illegal aliens crossing the border can sue members of vigilante groups for assault, battery, or inflicting emotional distress.

Consider the case of Casey Nethercott, formerly with the vigilante group Ranch Rescue. In 2003 Nethercott, an ex-felon, was arrested for allegedly assaulting two Salvadorans who had illegally crossed the Mexican border into the United States.[24] Nethercott was given a five-year prison sentence because he had been in possession of a gun, which is illegal for former felons. The consequences worsened for Nethercott when the Salvadorans filed a civil lawsuit against him. Nethercott did not respond to the lawsuit and the court decided in favor of the Salvadorans, who were awarded Nethercott's ranch.

In a separate incident in November 2006, a jury in Arizona ordered vigilante Roger Barnett to pay $100,000 in damages to a group of five Mexican Americans whom Barnett unlawfully detained at gunpoint.[25] Barnett allegedly pointed an assault rifle at three young girls and threatened to kill them. The five Mexican Americans were on a hunting trip on Arizona public lands that Barnett leased for grazing. Barnett told the media, "Humans. That's the greatest prey there is on earth."[26]

Starting in the late 1990s, the United States federal government targeted border enforcement at areas along the Mexican border where most illegal crossings occurred. These areas included San Diego, the Rio Grande valley in Texas, and El Paso. In San Diego, about 6,000 illegal immigrants tried to cross into the United States every night.[27] Mexicans then moved their crossing locations to dangerous remote areas such as the Sonora Desert of southwestern Arizona. The chances of dying from drowning, heatstroke, or dehydration during an illegal crossing doubled.[28] Between 1998 and 2003, nearly 1,900 Mexicans died trying to cross the border illegally into the United States.[29] A thirty-one-year-old illegal migrant stated, "We know there are dangers. There are snakes, you run out of water, somebody can come and kill you. . . . It's what you have to do if you want to get ahead."[30] In 2008 the U.S. Border Patrol found the bodies of 390 illegal migrants who died attempting to cross into the United States.[31] Illegal immigrants have been found dead in truck trailers and railroad cars.[32] In the early 1990s before border enforcement increased, a Mexican wanting to cross into the United States illegally would pay about $150 to a smuggler—also known as a coyote.[33] By 2004 the cost had increased to as much as $2,500, but this did not reduce the number of illegal crossings.

The volunteer organization No More Deaths (NMD) embodies the antithesis of the border vigilante groups. NMD aims to reduce the number of deaths among illegal border crossers in the southern Arizona desert. The group mans camps in the desert where illegal crossers get food, water, and medical attention. In 2009 Walt Staton, a seminary student and volunteer with NMD, was sentenced to 300 hours of community service for leaving clean water along known migrant trails in the Buenos Aires National Wildlife Refuge.[34] (A court found Staton guilty of littering.) Other volunteers who have left water in the desert have been similarly charged.[35]

The U.S.-Mexico border is the most crossed political boundary in the world. In 2008, over 200 million people crossed the border legally.[36] Nearly 45 million of the crossings were pedestrians. In 2008 the U.S. Border Patrol apprehended nearly 725,000 people trying to cross illegally into the United States from Mexico.[37] Because reliable estimates do not exist, the real numbers are likely much higher.[38] In comparison, about 62 million people crossed the U.S.-Canada border legally in 2008. Such a high level of exchange of peoples between the United States and Mexico calls into question the significance of the political boundary that separates the two countries.

The movement of people across the U.S.-Mexico border has gone through cycles of enforcement and indifference. Historically, when the United States wanted cheap Mexican labor, border enforcement was lax. In contrast, when Mexicans were unwelcome, border enforcement increased—or appeared to increase. During the 1920s, over 600,000 Mexicans entered the United States.[39] Then during the Great Depression, over 450,000 Mexicans either left voluntarily or were deported.

Today's undocumented immigrant is in an economic and political predicament similar to that of slaves before the Civil War. Unlike slaves, most immigrants come to the United States voluntarily and can leave when they want. However, like the slave, undocumented immigrants are exploited by their employers and have no political power. Like the slaves, undocumented immigrants influence representation in Congress because everyone, including illegal aliens, is counted in apportionment.

Noncitizens, both legal and illegal, provide extra voting power to voters, as explained by law professor Grant M. Hayden, "resident aliens now lack the right to vote in most every jurisdiction in the country. They are, however, included in the population base for reapportionment purposes, which gives their citizen neighbors [voters] a little extra voting power."[40] This results in increased representation for voters in congressional districts that have large numbers of illegal immigrants.[41] Excluding illegal immigrants from the apportionment basis does not undermine their representation in Congress, as illegal residents cannot vote and therefore are not a tangible constituent group.[42] Professors Garcia and Sanchez write in *Hispanics and the U.S. Political System: Moving into the Mainstream,* "If an individual or group does not vote, or votes at very low rates, their input into the behavior of public officials will be minimized."[43]

The real concern is that illegal aliens distort the political power of citizens who do vote. Former Chief Justice Earl Warren of the U.S. Supreme Court stated in 1964 "the right of suffrage can be denied by a debasement or dilution of the weight of a citizen's vote just as effectively as by wholly prohibiting the free exercise of the franchise."[44] This occurs with the current method of apportionment, which dates to the 1787 Constitutional Convention in Philadelphia. Congressional districts with large populations of nonvoters, including illegal aliens, overweigh the voting power of voters in that district.

The Cruel Compromise on Apportionment

The framers of the Constitution made a mistake and trusted that a future generation of Americans would rectify what they had done—or had failed to do. Delegates to the Constitutional Convention in 1787 could not agree on a just method of assigning congressional representation to individual states. They adopted a stopgap and expedient solution. The framers agreed to disagree and moved on to other issues, but they expected apportionment would be revisited. Gouverneur Morris said at the Constitutional Convention in 1787: "If we can't agree on a rule [apportionment] that will be just at this time, how can we expect to find one that will be just in all times to come? Surely those who come after us will judge better of things present, than we can of things future."[45]

James Madison warned Americans that states would purposefully swell their populations with the aim of increasing their congressional representation and gaining control of Congress: "it is of great importance that the States should feel as little bias as possible, to swell or to reduce the amount of their numbers."[46] This constitutional flaw is known as apportionment of the House of Representatives.

The Constitution of 1787 was nothing if not a compromise. The Constitution was crafted as a means to an end with the North giving many concessions to entice the South to join a more interdependent Union. George Mason said in 1788, "the northern states agreeing to the temporary importation of slaves, and the southern states conceding, in return, that navigation and commercial laws should be on the footing on which they now stand."[47] There were two highly contentious issues at the time. The first was deciding the form of government. Some delegates such as Alexander Hamilton wanted a strong "national" government that would do away with state governments. Alexander Hamilton was considered a monarchist who wanted a government structured similar to the British system. In opposition, most delegates sided with George Mason, who feared a national government would be authoritarian and no different than being ruled by the British Parliament. Less populous states had the added concern that they would be excluded from the political process by the more populous states.

The framers settled on the Connecticut Compromise, which created a bicameral legislature composed of the Senate and the House of Representatives. This was a "federal" government that obtained its power from the states. The states would remain self-governing. The Senate would provide for equal representation among all states—regardless of population—with each state having two senators. In contrast, representation in the House would vary by state. This was the basis for the second most contentious issue, how to allocate representation in the House. This process is known as apportionment.

Adopted in 1781, the Articles of Confederation were the precursor to the Constitution. The Articles based apportionment—representation—on the value of land in each state. In practice, the states did not assess their lands as required and thereby avoided paying taxes to Congress. A later proposed amendment to the Articles required states pay taxes to the federal government based on the population in each state. Each slave would count as three-fifths of one person. While this was a practical solution, it never became part of the Articles.

In 1787 the Constitutional Convention revisited the issue of apportionment. The debates were messy and divisive. After heated discussions for and against various alternatives, the framers agreed to use population as the basis for both taxation and apportioning representation in the House. States with larger populations would pay more taxes and have more representatives than states with smaller populations. Apportionment would count everyone—except Indians.

Northern states had larger populations and southern states feared this would mute their political power in the House. Northern states wanted to exclude slaves from apportionment but southern states demanded slaves be included. William Davie, a delegate from North Carolina, insisted that North Carolina would never join the new Union unless each slave was counted as at least three-fifths of a person. The South prevailed and a compromise was reached—the Three-Fifths clause. Law professor Sanford Levinson explains, "slaves would have been better off with the North's rule [not being counted], however much it formally denied their membership in the polity."[48]

Slave states had initially sought to count each slave as a whole person. This would have maximized the population count in the South, resulting in the largest possible representation for southern states. Southern politicians admitted their intent to offset the larger population in northern states. William Davie made this intent clear in the summer of 1788 in North Carolina. "It became our duty, on the other hand, to acquire as much weight as possible in the legislation of the Union; and, as the Northern states were more populous in whites, this only could be done by insisting that a certain proportion of our slaves should make a part of the computed population."[49]

Conversely, northern states did not want slaves counted in any manner, as this would increase representation for southern states. Added to the jumble of concerns, residents of some northern states believed blacks, including free men, were not the equal of whites, and should be counted as less than one whole person. These differing viewpoints resulted in adoption of the Three-Fifths clause as a compromise.

Anti-Federalists were a group of advocates against adoption of the Constitution as it was written in 1787. They thought the Constitution failed to represent the people adequately. The Anti-Federalists pointed to slavery and apportionment as one of many failings agreed to at the Constitutional Convention in Philadelphia. In 1787, Anti-Federalists argued that counting slaves in apportionment buttressed slavery:

> By this mode of apportionment, the representatives of the different pans
> of the union, will be extremely unequal: in some of the southern states,
> the slaves are nearly equal in number to the free men; and for all these
> slaves, they will be entitled to a proportionate share in the legislature —
> this will give them an unreasonable weight in the government, which
> can derive no additional strength, protection, nor defence [sic] from the
> slaves, but the contrary. Why then should they be represented?[50]

Ironically, counting the slave population in southern states worked to prolong slavery as this gave slave states additional representation in Congress. Slaves could not vote and therefore had no say in how Congressmen from southern states would vote.

The Three-Fifths clause influenced congressional apportionment after the first census in 1790. There were fourteen states with a total population of 3.7 million.[51] Just over 18 percent of the country's population were slaves. Virginia had the largest number of slaves, nearly 300,000, which was more than the entire population of eight other states. Northern states had over 40,000 slaves, except for Massachusetts and Vermont, which did not have slaves.

The inclusion of slaves had a significant affect on the geographic distribution of power in Congress. Northern states gained one additional representative (from fifty-six to fifty-seven) because of the slave population, while southern states gained an additional fourteen representatives (from thirty-five to forty-nine). This gave southern states a net gain of thirteen representatives. In 1850, sixty years later, slave states had a net gain of forty representatives.

Apportionment provides states their political power in the House of Representatives. While apportionment is based on the entire population, only the voting population elects representatives. As argued by the Anti-Federalists in 1787, there is little benefit to a person to be counted in apportionment but not allowed to vote. Recently this issue arose again as a failure of the founding fathers. "They were blind to the claims of women and slaves and native Americans to equal participation in the electoral process—without votes, how could these groups protect themselves?"[52]

In 1787 the criteria for determining voter eligibility were narrow and voting rights varied between states. White males who were Catholic, Jewish, or Quaker could not vote in some states, yet, they counted for apportionment. Slaves and free blacks could not vote. Women lacked voting rights, yet, they counted for apportionment.

The basis for apportionment has not significantly changed since 1787, except for the elimination of the Three-Fifths clause in the fourteenth amendment in 1868.[53] In hindsight, this aided segregationists in southern states after the slaves were freed. Southern whites gained even more representation in Congress by counting blacks as whole persons—as long as blacks were kept from voting. In 1787 southern states had wanted to count slaves as whole persons.

Southern states intimidated blacks to keep them from voting until the Civil Rights movement of the 1960s. Mechanisms of disenfranchisement included segregation, poll taxes, and literacy tests, all of which quashed the political power of blacks with no detrimental consequences to whites.

The election of the president is also linked to apportionment via the Electoral College. The number of representatives apportioned to a state directly corresponds with the number of votes that a state is allocated in the Electoral College. Apportionment thus influences both the executive branch of government—the president—and the legislative branch, which is Congress. In this way, slaves played a crucial role in the election of presidents Thomas Jefferson and John Quincy Adams.

Slaves Elect Two Presidents

Thomas Jefferson was elected president in 1800 because slaves in the South were counted in apportionment but did not vote. As law professor Sanford Levinson stated in 2002, "Thomas Jefferson would not have prevailed over John Adams in 1800 had he [Jefferson] not benefited from the Electoral College 'bump' provided by the slaves."[54] Again in 1824, John Quincy Adams was elected president because slaves in the South were counted in apportionment but did not vote. Similarly in 2000, George W. Bush was elected president due to the disenfranchisement of thousands of African Americans in Florida, which had the fourth highest number of electoral votes.

John Adams was the incumbent in the presidential election of 1800 but he received fewer electoral votes than the challengers and was not re-elected. Thomas Jefferson and Aaron Burr tied with each having won seventy-three votes in the Electoral College. However, Adams would have won outright except for the Three-Fifths clause, which boosted the number of Electoral College votes from southern slave states for Jefferson and Burr.

The Constitution stipulated that the House had the power to elect the president in the event of a tie in the Electoral College. In the House, support for Burr was strongest among northern states, while support for Jefferson was strongest among southern slave states. On February 17, 1801, Jefferson won the House vote on the thirty-sixth ballot having obtained support from the majority of southern slave states. Delegates from South Carolina and Delaware did not vote. Burr became vice-president.

Jefferson was a Virginian that owned slaves. This certainly influenced representatives from the southern slave states that voted for him. In contrast, Burr received electoral votes from New Hampshire, Massachusetts, Rhode Island, and Connecticut, which were northern anti-slavery states. Burr's own view of slavery was inconsistent. Burr had sponsored legislation to eliminate slavery when he was a member of the New York State Assembly. However, like Jefferson, Burr owned slaves.

Thus, in 1800 the slave population unintentionally elected slave owners Jefferson and Burr to the presidency and vice-presidency. The incumbent, John Adams, deplored slavery and never owned slaves. Ironically, Adams was defeated by the additional political weight given to southern slave states by the slave population via the Three-Fifths clause.

In 1824 the slave population was again instrumental in electing a president. This time there were four candidates in the general election. They were Andrew Jackson, John Quincy Adams, William Crawford, and Henry Clay. Andrew Jackson won the general election with the most popular votes and a corresponding ninety-nine votes in the Electoral College. Jackson was a southerner from Tennessee and had widespread support from southern slave states. He benefited from the Three-Fifths clause as fifty-five of his electoral votes came from slave states.

In 1824 the Constitution mandated that Jackson needed at least 131 electoral votes to be elected president, but he had only ninety-nine. As in 1800, selection of the president shifted to the House of Representatives. The House would select the president from the three candidates who had obtained the most electoral votes. This included Jackson, Adams, and Crawford.

After much political intrigue, John Quincy Adams (son of the second president John Adams) was elected. Similar to events in the 2000 presidential election, Jackson (like Gore) had won the general election but Adams (like Bush, son of the forty-first president George H. W. Bush), who had fewer popular votes, became president. Adams was selected over Jackson due to an endorsement from Speaker of the House Henry Clay. Adams later appointed Clay as Secretary of State. Jackson was outraged and believed Clay had betrayed the American people. "So you see," Jackson cried, "the Judas of the West [Henry Clay] has closed the contract and will receive the thirty pieces of silver. . . . Was there ever witnessed such a bare faced corruption in any country before?"[55]

If not for the Three-Fifths clause, the list of candidates sent to the House would have included Clay instead of Crawford. Clay had served as Speaker intermittently from 1811 to 1825. His tenure as Speaker of the House is the second longest. He was well respected by members of the House as evidenced by the election of Adams after Clay's endorsement. If Clay, not Crawford, had been the third candidate, it is likely that his fellow members in the House of Representatives would have elected Clay president.

The election loss of John Adams in 1800 and the win of his son John Quincy Adams in 1824 are steeped in irony. Both candidates were impacted by the Three-Fifths clause—John Adams lost because of the Three-Fifths clause but his son John Quincy Adams won because of it.

In 1800 African Americans were denied voting rights because they were slaves. The result was the election of Thomas Jefferson as president instead of incumbent John Adams. Similarly, in 1824 John Quincy Adams was elected president in part because slaves were denied voting rights yet counted in apportionment. In 2000 history was repeated when George W. Bush was elected president, instead of Al Gore, due to the large number of African Americans who were denied their voting rights in Florida.

The presidential elections of 1800 and 1824 are prime examples of unintended consequences that are possible when nonvoters are counted in congressional apportionment. Counting slaves in apportionment also resulted in the deaths of Native Americans during their westward march on the Trail of Tears.

Removal of Native Peoples

Including slaves in apportionment had yet another unintended conse-quence—the Indian Removal Act of 1830 was passed. This law allowed for Cherokee Indians from northern Georgia to be forcibly relocated to the Louisiana Territory—a forced march that would come to be known as the Trail of Tears. Nearly 5,000 Cherokee died in the migration. Historians have placed most of the blame on then President Andrew Jackson who was from Tennessee and a slave owner, but he was not solely responsible. The states of Georgia, Alabama, Mississippi, and Tennessee would benefit the most.

In 1829 whites began mining gold on Cherokee lands near Dahlonega, Georgia. Settlers rushed into Cherokee tribal lands in what history recalls as the Georgia Gold Rush. Within one year, about 3,000 white men were illegally digging for gold on Cherokee lands. Nearly thirty years earlier, in 1802, the federal government had agreed to acquire title to all Indian lands in Georgia—including Cherokee lands—but had not done so. After gold was discovered, Georgia could wait no longer for the federal government to fulfill its pledge to purchase the titles to Cherokee land. The state of Georgia be-lieved it had to act to have legal authority over gold miners and settlers who had illegally moved into the lands of the Cherokee Nation.

In December 1829 the state of Georgia passed legislation that placed the lands of the Cherokee Nation under the jurisdiction of Georgia's laws. The Cherokee Nation ceased to be an independent sovereign nation separate from Georgia. Georgians viewed this as consistent with the United States Constitution, which did not allow a sovereign state to exist within another state: "No new State shall be formed or erected within the Jurisdiction of any other State; nor any State be formed by the Junction of two or more States, or Parts of States, without the Consent of the Legislatures of the States con-cerned as well as of the Congress."[56] The state of Georgia wanted both sov-ereignty and ownership of all Cherokee lands.

In Congress Wilson Lumpkin, a representative from Georgia, sponsored the Indian Removal Act. The law called for the removal of all Indian tribes from southern states. The law gave then President Andrew Jackson the power to negotiate treaties to relocate native peoples west of the Mississippi River. Indians would receive property rights in the Louisiana Territory in exchange for their current tribal lands in the South. Tribes would be relocated west of the Arkansas Territory to an area that would later become the Oklahoma Territory. Indians could remain in the South but they would be subject to state laws. Indian tribes would have no legal status.

In 1830 Congress passed Representative Lumpkin's Indian Removal Act on a close vote: 102 "for" and ninety-seven votes "against." Slave states cast sixty-six votes in favor of removal. Southern states derived twenty-two representatives from the slave count and the Three-Fifths clause. Without the slave count, southern states would not have had enough votes to pass the Indian Removal Act.

For the South, there was an additional benefit to the removal of Indians. Apportionment excluded the Indian population, which made Indians of no political benefit to southern states. In contrast, new settlers on former Indian lands would increase the number of congressional representatives apportioned to the southern states. The *Southern Patriot* newspaper in Charleston, South Carolina, reported in 1830, "One of the reasons why certain people of the north are so strongly opposed to the Indian emigration . . . is that it will give the southern and southwestern states [Louisiana, Mississippi, and Alabama] . . . an influence in the councils of the Nation which they do not now possess, while their territory is inhabited by savages."[57]

Indians were not citizens and were an obstacle to increasing the number of southern congressional representatives. The rules of congressional apportionment created an incentive to relocate them to a territory that was not represented in Congress.

The Indian Removal Act called for the voluntary relocation of native populations, but only a minority of native peoples left their tribal lands by choice. Southern state governments and settlers intimidated Indians until they abandoned their tribal lands. The Indian Removal Act intended to provide tribes with money by selling their lands—at a fair price—before their removal. These monies would be used by the Indians to aid in relocating and settling in their new lands. But the outcome was much different. Indians became destitute, without property, and unable to care for themselves before leaving the South. This caused the death of many Indians during their march west. They were sick, starved, and lacked needed clothing to protect themselves in the winter. Many lost the desire to live after leaving their tribal lands in the South. General Parsons wrote to the U.S. Secretary of War regarding the Creek Indians: "How the Indians are to subsist the present year, I cannot imagine. Some of them are sustaining themselves upon roots. They have, apparently, very little corn, and scarcely any stock. The game is gone, and what they are to do, God only knows. Nothing can preserve their property, or their existence, other than their immediate removal to the country designed for them."[58] Colonel Abert also wrote to the U.S. Secretary of War about the plight of the Creek Indians, "You cannot have an adequate idea of the deterioration which these Indians have undergone during the last two or three years, from a general state of comparative plenty to that of unqualified wretchedness and want."[59]

Settlers easily defrauded native peoples. Federal government agents, contracted to help the Indians, cheated them. Most Indians lacked an understanding of business transactions and the monetary value of land. The significance of property rights was strange and unfamiliar to them. In another letter to the U.S. Secretary of War from General Parsons and Colonel Abert concerning the Creek Indians in 1833, "Their helpless ignorance, their generally good character, (for they are a well disposed people), instead of establishing claims upon good feelings, seem rather to expose them to injuries. Their weaknesses receive no compassion and their very helpless ignorance but renders them more liable to wrongs."[60]

White settlers destroyed Indian villages and crops to force Indians off their lands. Settlers further impoverished the Indians by selling them whiskey, which was new to native peoples, and which led to oftentimes disastrous consequences. The Creek Nation wrote to the U.S. Secretary of War in 1831: "They bring spirits among us for the purpose of practicing frauds; they daily rob us of our property; they bring white officers among us, and take our property from us for debts that were never contracted. We are made subject to laws we have no means of comprehending; we never know when we are doing right."[61]

At the request of President Andrew Jackson, Francis Scott Key, who penned the words of *The Star Spangled Banner*, went to Alabama in November 1833 to ascertain the state of affairs between the Creek Indians and whites. About the Creek Indians Key reported, "I met crowds of them going to Columbus with bundles of fodder on their heads to sell, and saw numbers of them in the streets there where they exchanged everything they carried for whiskey."[62]

The federal government negotiated treaties that required the surveying of tribal lands before relocating tribes. Nonetheless, whites moved into tribal lands before the surveys were completed. Settlers paid Indians a fraction of the value of their land. State governments encouraged settlers to continue. Colonel Abert wrote about the Creek Indians in a message to the U.S. Secretary of War in 1833, "The free egress into the nation by the whites; encroachments upon their lands, even upon their cultivated fields; abuses of their person and property; hosts of traders, who, like locusts, have devoured their substance and inundated their homes with whiskey, have destroyed what little disposition to cultivation the Indians may have once had."[63] John Hogan wrote to President Andrew Jackson in 1836 regarding the Creek Indians, "A greater mass of corruption perhaps, has never been congregated in any part of the world, than has been engendered by the Creek treaty in the grant of reservations of land to those people."[64]

Among the southern tribes, a mixed blood Indian frequently ruled a tribe. Some mixed blood Indians made decisions that would benefit themselves without regard for their full blood cousins. Mixed blood chiefs often accepted bribes from the federal government in exchange for support of treaties, which were unpopular among the full blood members of the tribe. Chiefs Greenwood LeFlore, Nitakechi, and Mushulatubbe accepted bribes of additional lands in Mississippi in exchange for their support of removal. These chiefs remained in Mississippi while their tribes relocated to the Louisiana Territory. In exchange for his support of relocation, Greenwood Leflore, a mixed blood Choctaw chief, received an additional $100 from the federal government to pay for his daughter's education.

Georgia, Alabama, and Mississippi did not abide by the treaties negotiated by the federal government and there were not enough federal troops to protect all the tribes from settlers. The federal government could do little to force states to comply with the terms of federal treaties. The federal government had authority to negotiate treaties but could not enforce them. The obstacle was states' rights, which superseded the U.S. Constitution. The federal government could protect the Indians and abide by its treaties only after the tribes relocated. There were no state governments to challenge federal authority in the Louisiana Territory. Hence, the federal government did not want to delay the removals. In a message to Congress in 1832, President Andrew Jackson remarked that once removal was accomplished, "there would then be no question of jurisdiction to prevent the Government from exercising such a general control over their affairs as may be essential to their interest and safety."[65] General Parsons and Colonel Abert wrote to the U.S. Secretary of War in 1833 concerning the Creek Indians: "We see no remedy to their condition but in emigrating west; and it would be better for them to abandon their lands for nothing (as they are now said to be doing) and to move, than to remain under their present circumstances."[66] The Choctaw, in Mississippi, was the first tribe relocated under the Indian Removal Act of 1830. The first group of Choctaw migrated west in the fall of 1831.

In May 1838 the period for the voluntary departure of the Cherokee from Georgia expired. Only 2,000 Cherokee had left, while about 15,000 remained in northern Georgia and eastern Tennessee. Gen. Winfield Scott, commander of federal troops on Cherokee Nation lands, began the forced removal of the remaining Cherokees. Georgia militia rounded up the Cherokees with rifles and bayonets. The militia burned Cherokee homes and stole their livestock. The Georgia militia held the Indians in stockade forts. One month later, on June 18, 1838, Gen. Charles Floyd, commander of the Georgia militia, reported that all Cherokees still in Georgia were prisoners in stockades. The population count was about 13,000. The last group of Cherokees started their westward migration in December.

The Cherokees of northern Georgia suffered the most of the four tribes during the migration to the Louisiana Territory. About 15,000 Cherokee left the South but only 10,000 arrived at their new lands. Nearly 5,000, or one in three, died on the 800-mile march from northern Georgia to the Louisiana Territory. History remembers their migration as the Trail of Tears.

The Indian Removal Act of 1830 passed Congress because the slave count had apportioned an additional twenty-two representatives to slave states.

The Fourteenth Amendment: A Missed Opportunity

Women are the reason congressional apportionment is based on total population instead of the number of voters. More specifically, in 1866 men wanted to keep women from voting, which resulted in Section 2 of the fourteenth amendment that bases apportionment on total population. One Congressman did not want to grant voting rights to women because "it would enfranchise wenches."[67]

The women's suffrage movement had supported the abolition of slavery since before the Civil War. Suffragettes had expected to be given the right to vote along with emancipated blacks after the Civil War. Over 10,000 letters were sent to Congress supporting women's right to vote before adoption of the fourteenth amendment.[68] Women felt betrayed when white males extended voting rights only to black males in the fourteenth amendment in 1868.

When the fourteenth amendment was being drafted in 1866, congressional representatives Robert Schenck (R-Ohio), Thaddeus Stevens (R-Pennsylvania), and John Broomall (R-Pennsylvania) proposed that apportionment should be based on the number of voters in each state.[69] Republicans assumed freed slaves would vote for the political party that abolished slavery—Lincoln's Republicans—and wanted to ensure that the former slave states would allow blacks to vote. Republicans believed southern states would do whatever was necessary to keep their former slaves from voting. Democratic Sen. "Pitchfork" Ben Tillman (South Carolina) would later say regarding black male voters: "We have done our level best. We have scratched our heads how we could eliminate every last one of them [blacks]. We stuffed ballot boxes. We shot them. We are not ashamed of it."[70]

Voter-based apportionment would have penalized states that disenfranchised blacks. Intimidation and discrimination against blacks in the South may have been avoided if the fourteenth amendment had based apportionment on the number of voters.

Republicans controlled Congress and wanted to reduce the number of congressional representatives from the South, which was predominately Democratic. Republicans believed the former slave states would lose fifteen representatives to the North if Congress enacted voter-based apportionment.[71] But there was a political complication. At that time, white females accounted for over 50 percent of the white population in the Northeast but less than 30 percent of the white population in the West.[72] If apportionment were based on voters, it would have excluded women from the apportionment count, because women lacked the right to vote. Excluding New England's female population from apportionment would have caused states in New England to lose four representatives. Voter-based apportionment would not pass in Congress because representatives from New England would vote against it.

An alternative would have been to enfranchise women and thereby maximize a state's voter count for apportionment. However, the white male Congress was unwilling to extend voting rights to women. Representative James Blaine (R-Maine) thought voter based apportionment evil because it "would cheapen suffrage; would cause an unseemly scramble to increase voters, and the ballot, which cannot be too sacredly guarded, would be demoralized and disgraced everywhere."[73]

A two-part solution was reached. The entire population would be counted in apportionment as stated in the first sentence of Section 2 of fourteenth amendment (ratified 1868): "the whole number of persons in each State, excluding Indians not taxed." Indians have been counted in apportionment since 1940 when the Attorney General of the United States ruled that there were no longer any "Indians not taxed."[74] The ensuing second sentence was meant to deter southern states from disenfranchising former slaves, "But when the right to vote at any election for the choice of . . . Representatives in Congress . . . is denied . . . or in any way abridged . . . the basis of representation therein shall be reduced . . . in such State."

States that disenfranchised voters would be penalized by having congressional representatives taken away. In theory it appeared to be a good compromise. However, in practice it has been a failure. The penalty has been ignored for over 140 years, resulting in the widespread disenfranchisement of African Americans, Mexican Americans, and other minority groups. In particular, southern states, which for nearly 100 years openly disenfranchised African American voters, never lost representation. The same is true for western and southwestern states that disenfranchised Americans citizens of Asian and Mexican ancestry.

After the Civil War and adoption of the fourteenth amendment, blacks in the South were politically worse off than before because the former slaves were then counted as whole persons—not three-fifths of one: "after emancipation ex-slave states would be entitled to count all inhabitants at five-fifths, whether or not freedmen could vote. Emancipation thus ironically threatened to increase the South's clout in future Congresses (and electoral colleges)."[75]

Former slave states would gain an additional thirteen representatives by eliminating the Three-Fifths clause and counting everyone (excluding Indians not taxed) in apportionment.[76] Southern slave states would have more representation in Congress after the Civil War than before the war. Penalties for disenfranchisement in the fourteenth amendment were not enforced, which "allowed Southern whites not only to keep blacks from voting but in effect to vote for them."[77]

In 1941 The Brookings Institute released a book titled *Congressional Apportionment* written by Laurence Frederick Schmeckebier. In his book, Schmeckebier suggested apportionment should be based on the number of voters as had been originally intended in 1866. He saw it as a way of penalizing southern states for disenfranchising blacks. Jim Crow laws and intimidation had kept blacks from voting ever since federal troops left southern states after the Civil War. After reapportionment in 1940, blacks accounted for about twenty-one congressional seats in the former slave states, however, only 3 percent of eligible African Americans in southern states registered to vote.[78] Between 1903 and 1953, about 15 percent of roll call votes in the House were altered by seats detained from the population of southern blacks.[79] Professor Richard Valelly states, "white supremacist interests were not only entrenched but overrepresented."[80]

The fourteenth amendment based apportionment on total population to eliminate any incentive to extend enfranchisement to minorities and women. It worked. It took another fifty-two years for women to get voting rights, while minorities were disenfranchised until the Voting Rights Act of 1965. What would have been the impact on women and minorities if voter-count apportionment had been adopted in 1868? The fourteenth amendment still fosters disenfranchisement.

In the presidential election of 2000, Florida disenfranchised over 100,000 voters—mostly African Americans. Florida would have had congressional representatives taken away if the fourteenth amendment were enforced. However, after reapportionment in 2000 Florida gained two additional congressional representatives.

The Decennial Census: A Flawed Count for Apportionment

Thomas Jefferson directed the first decennial census in 1790. He and President

Washington believed the 1790 census had undercounted the nation's population. Nevertheless, the results were used as the basis for apportionment of Congress and taxation of states as mandated by the Constitution. Law professor Grant M. Hayden highlights many of the flaws inherent in today's decennial census count, saying that,

> census numbers are far from perfect. The census overcounts [sic] some populations, undercounts others. . . . As a result, areas with large numbers of people missed by the census, often with large minority populations, are numerically underrepresented. And even assuming a perfect decennial census, those numbers only provide a snapshot of a dynamic demographic process. The census numbers rapidly become outdated as people are born, die, and move.[81]

The decennial census has a history of dubious counts with undercounts being the norm. The 1970 census undercounted the nation's population by over 5 million.[82] Nearly 8 percent of blacks were missed while only 2 percent of whites went uncounted. There were fifty-two lawsuits filed against the U.S. Census Bureau challenging the counts from the 1980 census. Most of the lawsuits came from state and local governments claiming undercounts of minorities and hard-to-count populations.[83] The 1990 census missed over 4 percent of blacks and Native Americans, 5 percent of Hispanics, and more than 2 percent of Asians.[84] In comparison, less than 1 percent of non-Hispanic whites were undercounted. In total, the 1990 census missed about 4 million American residents.

Census 2000 missed over 6 million residents and double counted about 3 million residents resulting in total errors of nearly 10 million. The 2000 decennial census undercounted blacks by over 2 percent, Hispanics by nearly 3 percent, and Native Americans by nearly 5 percent. The largest undercounts were in California and Texas, which are the two most populous states and have the largest population of undocumented residents. These two states were home to 40 percent of undocumented residents in the country in 2009.[85] Because of their large populations, California and Texas have the largest congressional delegations with a total of eighty-five representatives after reapportionment in 2000 (one in five seats).

The 2010 census was expected to have a lower rate of participation than the 2000 census.[86] Minorities, particularly undocumented Hispanics, are some of the least likely to participate.[87] Illegal residents fear that responding to the census would result in being deported. Democrats are more likely to participate then either Republicans or Independents. Older people are more likely to participate, as are people with college educations and higher incomes. Ironically, people living in low-income areas are less likely to participate even though they benefit the most from federal programs linked to census population counts.

Decennial census undercounts have tangible effects on where federal monies are spent. States with the largest undercounts in Census 2000 may have lost $4.1 billion in federal funding between 2002 and 2012. Undercounts disproportionately shortchange metropolitan areas with high population densities. The fifty-eight most populous counties may have lost about $3,000 per person during the ten-year hiatus between the 2000 and 2010 censuses.

The National Research Council (NRC) reported that data, including citizenship status, from the Census 2000 long-form "were no better and in some cases worse than in previous censuses."[88] The NRC recommended that the Census Bureau inform users to be cautious when interpreting long-form data.[89] After the 2000 census, the State of Utah sued the U.S. Secretary of Commerce (the Census Bureau) claiming the method used by the Census Bureau to account for residents in non-responding housing units was flawed. Utah had lost a congressional seat to North Carolina by a population count of less than 1,000 during reapportionment in 2000. The U.S. Supreme Court ruled in favor of the Census Bureau.[90]

The decennial census has a history of being politicized. The most reprehensible incident occurred with the decennial census of 1840. That census included a question on the number of people in the household who were "insane and idiotic." Data from that census suggested that blacks in the North had higher rates of insanity than blacks in the South. However, the data were found to be erroneous because they had been collected using a poorly designed two-sided questionnaire with eighty columns worth of questions. Nonetheless, slave states used these data to argue that freedom made blacks insane, and therefore, blacks were better off as slaves.

The 1920 census showed America's population, and political power, shifting from predominately white rural areas to urban areas having large numbers of immigrants and minorities. Congressional representatives from rural areas derailed the 1920 reapportionment to stall their loss of political power to urban areas. Congress ignored the 1920 census and reapportionment did not take place again until 1930.

Just before the 2010 census, the Republican National Committee (RNC) mailed a fundraising letter to homes to collect survey information and solicit donations.[91] The envelope had the words "Census Document Registered To" stamped on it, and the letter included a "census tracking code" and "census certification and reply." Democrats and Latino leaders believed Republicans were trying to confuse the public and take advantage of media hype surrounding Census 2010.[92] Republicans claimed the mailing was not meant to mislead and was clearly marked as a RNC mailer. Ricardo Ramirez, Democratic National Committee Spokesman, said of the mailer, "These deceitful tactics are nothing new from Republicans," as Republicans had done a similar mailer ten years earlier before Census 2000. Soon after the RNC mailer incident, Representative Carolyn Maloney (D-New York) introduced the *Prevent Deceptive Census Look Alike Mailings Act* (H.R. 4621) to end deceptive use of Census Bureau "look alike" mail.

Congressional investigators created a list of the thirteen most urgent issues for president-elect Barack Obama after his election in November 2008.[93] Census 2010 was on the list. The eight-year administration of outgoing president George W. Bush, along with the Republican controlled Congress, had intentionally, or by neglect, impaired the functioning of the U.S. Census Bureau. None of the senior managers at the agency had experience running a national census. Demoralized workers at the Census Bureau had suffered through nearly eight years of politically motivated management and three directors.

As of this writing, whether the Obama administration was able to repair the damaged agency and conduct a reliable census in 2010 will not be known until after final tabulations are obtained. Regardless of its accuracy, the next round of reapportionment will be based on whatever data were obtained from Census 2010.

Why Is This Important? Apportionment Still Reflects American Society of 1787

The United States was not a true democracy either before or after the Constitutional Convention in 1787. Only a small fraction of the country's inhabitants—white male landowners of a certain age—had the right to vote and participate in government. George Washington was not elected president by the American people but by a small cadre of Americans. The current method of congressional apportionment continues to reflect the elitist and patriarchal views of the framers in 1787.

Arguably, the most controversial compromise of the Constitutional Convention in 1787 was the accommodation on slavery. Congressional representation—apportionment—was at the core of this appeasement. The framers of the Constitution agreed to include slaves in the apportionment count to entice southern states to remain in the Union. As slavery expanded into new states, the slave count disproportionately increased the political power of white males in the South.

The slave population affected nearly half of all roll call votes in the House of Representatives between 1795 and 1861. The Three-Fifths clause caused many bills to pass that otherwise would have failed, and vice versa. The Federalist Party disappeared early in the country's history because of the slave count. In 1800 the House of Representatives selected Thomas Jefferson as president because of the slave count. The removal of Indians from southern states took place because of the slave count. Tribal lands were seized and thousands of Indians died in a forced migration. Would the Civil War have taken place if these Indian lands had remained closed to settlement? More than 600,000 died in the American Civil War. The effect of the slave count, and apportionment, on the early history of the United States cannot be overstated.

The framers of the Constitution used total population as a basis for apportionment because counting people was the most practical method for taxing the states. Prior attempts to tax states based on the value of property failed when states refused to assess their property. Apportionment also became the basis for taxation.

On December 6, 2005, the House Subcommittee on Federalism and the Census Bureau met to discuss changing apportionment to include only citizens as called for in House Joint Resolution 53 (H.J.R. 53) sponsored by Representative Candice Miller (R-Michigan). Several experts testified before the subcommittee, which focused on the pros and cons of changing apportionment to a basis of citizens. However, the subcommittee should also have discussed the pros and cons of the current basis for apportionment. Comments from members of the subcommittee and presenters showed a blind support for the status quo on apportionment and a lack of knowledge on the damage the current method of apportionment has had on American society.

Committee member Carolyn Maloney (D-New York) said that changing apportionment to include only citizens "would be the second amendment in our history which did not expand individual liberties."[94] Representative Maloney's comments ignore that the fourteenth amendment set apportionment to a basis of total population because men did not want to grant women voting rights. In 1866 Congress feared that setting apportionment to a basis of voters would result in expanding voting rights to women. Representative Maloney supports the current basis of apportionment, which delayed women's suffrage for over a half a century, taking a position that is contrary to the goals of the women's suffrage movement of the 1880s.

The constitutional amendment sponsored by Representative Candice Miller would require the Census Bureau to differentiate citizens from non-citizens. Professor Kenneth Prewitt, director of the Census Bureau from 1998–2000, testified that "Responses to a citizenship question cannot be validated on a case-by-case basis . . . litigation over the accuracy of the count separating citizens from non-citizens is certainly a possibility."[95] Basing apportionment on the number of citizens is impractical because the Census cannot accurately count citizens separate from non-citizens.

Nina Perales, of the Mexican American Legal Defense and Education Fund (MALDEF), testified in favor of maintaining the current basis for apportionment: "Section two was adopted to override the infamous 'three-fifths' rule by which slaves were not counted as full persons for the purpose of apportionment . . . Congressional representatives serve all individuals in their district."[96] When slaves were counted in apportionment, it resulted in additional representation for the slave owner. American history clearly proves that being counted does not guarantee being represented. Perales ignores the history of disenfranchisement that Mexican Americans suffered through before the Voting Rights Act of 1965. Being counted in apportionment did not guarantee Mexican Americans would get to vote, and it did not stop vigilantes from lynching Mexicans. In 1866 Republicans in Congress wanted to change apportionment to a basis of voters to ensure that freed blacks in the South would get to vote. Instead, total population became the basis for apportionment, and women, blacks, and Mexican Americans were disenfranchised.

Representative Linda Sánchez (D-California) also testified in favor of the current method of apportionment, saying, "Amending the Constitution to only count U.S. citizens for congressional apportionment is too reminiscent of the shameful days in American history when African Americans were counted as three-fifths of a person, and women were denied the franchise."[97] Representative Sánchez's argument ignores that freed blacks became worse off politically after the fourteenth amendment was adopted. By counting blacks as whole persons, but not allowing them to vote, it further increased congressional representation for the former slave states. Southern whites had more political power in Congress after the Civil War than before, and blacks suffered because of it.

Lawrence Gonzalez, of the National Association of Latino Elected and Appointed Officials (NALEO), testified against H.J.R. 53, which would base apportionment on the number of citizens. Gonzalez said, "one out of two of the nation's legal permanent residents eligible for U.S. citizenship were Latino—4.2 million."[98] Gonzalez discounts that apportionment based on the number of citizens, or voters, would create an incentive for states to encourage the federal government to turn those 4.2 million Latinos into citizens. The current method of apportionment provides no such incentive.

During the hearing, Representative Candice Miller explained the link between illegal immigration and congressional representation: "In a very twisted way, it also gives states an incentive—that may or may not be acted upon—to create a situation where illegal immigration is tolerated, accepted, or even encouraged."[99] In 1788 James Madison made a similar argument that basing apportionment on total population would cause the most populous states to "have an interest in exaggerating their inhabitants."[100]

The current basis for apportionment—total population—creates an incentive for states to either encourage or tolerate illegal immigration. It distorts political representation and provides an incentive to maintain a permanent underclass of residents with no political influence.

The framers of the Constitution knew their compromise on apportionment was imperfect. They expected a future generation of Americans to fix apportionment and remove that vestige of slavery from the Constitution. Nearly 225 years have passed since the Constitution was written, and it has been corrected to abolish slavery and extend voting rights to women and minorities.

It is time to correct apportionment.

2

REDISTRICTING

When Representatives Pick Voters

Drawing lines for congressional districts is one of the most significant acts a state can perform to ensure citizen participation in Republican self-governance.[1]

—U.S. Supreme Court Justice Anthony Kennedy,

LULAC v. Perry, 2006

Kidnapping, Packing, and Cracking

"Congressmen are more likely to die or be indicted than they are to lose a seat [in Congress]."[2] It is not by chance, nor is it a coincidence, that incumbents in the federal House of Representatives are habitually re-elected every two years. Law professor Nathaniel Persily wrote in 2002, "Current rates of House turnover may equal historic rates of turnover in the Politburo [former Soviet Union]."[3]

Every ten years, following the decennial census and reapportionment, states redraw congressional districts—redistricting—with the most recent iteration taking place in 2011 and 2012. Elections for the new and redrawn districts will take place in November 2012. The House will reflect the changes in January 2013 when the 113th Congress begins.

During redistricting incumbents have the opportunity to redraw their districts and cherry-pick voters who will re-elect them. The process resembles a pick-up football or basketball game. The incumbent is a captain who gets to pick the players for their team; however, there is a twist to the rules. The incumbent gets to pick all the players for their team first and the challenger gets whatever players remain. It is a foregone conclusion that the incumbent will pick the best players. The process of redistricting is referred to as gerrymandering and dates to 1810–1811 when Elbridge Gerry, governor of Massachusetts, purposely delineated a congressional district just so an incumbent from his party would be re-elected. A political cartoon outlined the district boundaries to look like a salamander, hence the term *gerry*mander.

Continuing with the team analogy, some argue that gerrymandering sends the strongest teams to Congress to represent local interests. Others counter that gerrymandering is unfair because only the strongest players get representation. It boils down to a matter of opinion. People who believe the House should be divided into either winners or losers will likely support gerrymandering. There is also the perspective that the majority party has the "right" to gerrymander to its benefit—regardless of the outcome. In contrast, people who believe the House should represent the full spectrum of American society will likely oppose gerrymandering. John Adams believed Congress "should be an exact portrait, in miniature, of the people at large, as it should think, feel, reason and act like them."[4] If the House reflected America in 2008, then 220 representatives would be women, 214 would be men, 326 would be white, 67 would be Hispanic, 54 would be African American, 19 would be Asian, and 3 would be Native American.[5] However, current circumstances are much different.

Redistricting occurs every ten years following the decennial census and reapportionment. States with more than one congressional representative must redraw their congressional districts so all districts within a state have equal populations. The process is inherently political and partisan. Both Republicans and Democrats are well aware of the importance of controlling the drawing of district boundaries. Mark Braden, an attorney for the Republican Party says: "How you draw the line has a huge impact on who sits in legislative chambers."[6] Gerald Hebert, a lawyer for Democrats, suggests an even greater impact: "You can actually rig elections in such a way that you can produce an electoral outcome almost regardless of what happens on Election Day."[7]

The U.S. Constitution does not specify how states should assign congressional representatives to local populations. When the Constitution was adopted, five states used at-large elections to pick their representatives to the House.[8] Not until 1842 did Congress enact legislation requiring states to use single-member districts for electing representatives. However, a handful of states ignored the law and Congress continued to accept representatives from states with at-large elections. The U.S. Supreme Court ended at-large elections for congressional representatives with a series of rulings in the 1960s. Now, all states use single-member districts to elect their representatives to Congress. This does not apply to states such as Delaware and Montana, which have only one representative each.

The Supreme Court has been hesitant to interfere in redistricting and adheres to its 1986 ruling in *Davis v. Bandemer*,[9] which limits its involvement to cases where there is "continued frustration of the will of a majority of the voters or effective denial to a minority of voters of a fair chance to influence the political process."[10] The wording is intentionally vague and reflects the court's reticence to get involved in political issues. As recently as 2006, the Supreme Court ruled in *LULAC v. Perry*[11] that partisan gerrymandering is acceptable as long as other restrictions, which the court did not clarify, are not violated in the process. A study presented at the National Academy of Sciences in 2005 states, "Courts have reached a muddled set of legal standards for drawing nonwhite-majority districts."[12]

In 1946 U.S. Supreme Court Justice Felix Frankfurter said, "Courts ought not enter this political thicket."[13] He was referring to redistricting. The Court has allowed gerrymanders that are politically biased because the judiciary is hesitant to interfere in political matters that are the purview of the legislative branch of government. Typically, state and federal courts have imposed redistricting plans when state legislatures have been unable to reach a consensus or in response to violations of the Voting Rights Act that adversely affect racial minorities.

The redrawing of congressional district boundaries is the responsibility of state legislatures—not Congress. The process varies among the fifty states. In some states only the House of Representatives is involved while other states also require their Senate's approval. In some states the governor can veto the redistricting plan while in other states the governor is excluded from redistricting. A few states rely on commissions that are supposedly impartial.

What typically happens in most states is that the political party that controls the state's legislature will draw boundaries to benefit its candidates, and its incumbents in particular. Incumbents select district lines for what may seem arbitrary reasons but are ultimately political machinations focused on getting re-elected. Bruce E. Cain describes several cases in *The Reapportionment Puzzle*.

In Bruce Cain's "The Give Me What I Need Only" scenario, an incumbent needed to add about 15,000 new constituents from other districts. They had to be people who were "acceptable" to him. In other words, people who would vote for him. The incumbent had recently had a falling-out with a minority community adjacent to his current district and did not want to include them in his newly redrawn district. He also found it difficult to communicate with young, college-age populations so they were excluded from his district. The incumbent wanted his redrawn district to look and think like him as much as possible.

Cain's "No Place Like Home" scenario illustrates what happens when an incumbent's residence is redistricted, forcing the incumbent to move if he or she wants to run for re-election. A Democratic incumbent in California had recently purchased a house and did not want to move. However, the population in his district had grown too large and the population needed to be shifted to surrounding districts. Unfortunately for the incumbent, the areas being shifted included his neighborhood. To stay in his house, the incumbent Democrat redrew his district by exchanging densely populated Democratic areas for sparsely populated Republican areas. In short, the incumbent made the district less safe for his own party because he did not want to sell his house. Ironically, this benefited voters because the new district would be competitive, however, the motivation was purely self-serving.

Cain's "Constrained from the Top" scenario features an incumbent whose last election was close, and redistricting could determine whether he would win the next round of elections. He had a diverse district consisting of both white working-class and wealthy suburban populations, and needed to add several thousand new residents. Fortunately for the incumbent, redistricting increased his support among potential voters by 3 percent.

Drawing a perfectly neutral or "non-gerrymandered" district is impossible. There is no perfect set of boundaries for congressional districts because all districts within a state must have equal populations. This requirement limits what would otherwise include a vast number of alternatives. Consequently, redistricting will always involve some level of gerrymandering. There are three main tactics to gerrymandering: kidnapping, packing, and cracking.

Kidnapping of districts involves redrawing district boundaries to force incumbents from the same party to compete for one district. In 2000 Republicans gained control of both the Pennsylvania House and Senate and consequently controlled congressional redistricting in 2001–2002. The Republicans redistricting plan caused Democratic incumbents to run against one another in two redrawn districts.[14] In 2000 the Pennsylvania congressional delegation to the House consisted of eleven Republicans and ten Democrats. After redistricting, Republicans had a twelve to seven edge over Democrats. The Pennsylvania redistricting plan included a loss of two congressional seats because of reapportionment in 2000. Similarly, in Michigan in 2001–2002, Republicans managed to redraw districts to force three pairs of Democratic incumbents to run against one another.[15]

Packing involves herding voters from one party into the same district. This limits the influence of their votes to one district. Packing results in overkill and wastes votes, because the majority party in the district has more than enough votes to win. Republicans often apply this strategy when redistricting communities of racial minorities, who tend to vote Democratic. Similarly, Democrats use a form of packing known as the cul-de-sac theory of districting. Democrats treat gated communities and neighborhoods with cul-de-sacs as Republican strongholds and combine them into as few districts as possible.

Gerrymandering also involves dividing geographic areas of homogeneous voters into separate districts in such small numbers that they do not influence the election. This is known as "cracking voters." Whereas packing creates homogeneous voting districts, cracking breaks these districts apart. In Maryland, Democrats controlled redistricting in 2001–2002 and added Democratic voters to the district of Republican Representative Constance A. Morella.[16] Democrats cracked the Republican voters in Morella's district. Morella subsequently lost re-election in 2002 to Democrat Chris Van Hollen.

The American Bar Association, which represents lawyers, believes that among the ills of gerrymandering is that it rewards incumbency, reduces competition, undercuts the responsiveness of elected officials, and discourages voter participation. Some politicians and scholars believe the effects of gerrymandering are overstated. But as Allan B. Moore states in the Harvard Journal of Law & Public Policy, "If gerrymandering were not so effective, why would it be so prevalent?"[17]

During redistricting in 2001–2002, 75 percent of competitive districts were transformed into partisan districts more likely to re-elect the incumbent.[18] Law professor Samuel Issacharoff writes, "The cost of gerrymandering is unfortunately the polarization of representative bodies and the increased distance of elected representatives from the median preferences of the voting public."[19]

Majority-Minority Districts: Minorities Are Made the Majority

In 1986 the U.S. Supreme Court ruled in *Thornburg v. Gingles*[20] that gerrymandering could not be used to "dilute" the votes of racial minorities, and that states must endeavor to create districts specifically for minorities (majority–minority districts). A majority–minority district is defined as one in which racial minorities account for over 55 percent of a district's population, but not necessarily its voters.[21] The ruling intended to provide minority populations the opportunity to elect someone of their choosing. The court's ruling was based on a 1982 amendment to Section 2 of the Voting Rights Act.

The court's ruling lead to the creation of several majority–minority congressional districts during redistricting in 1991–1992.[22] Creating majority–minority districts is akin to putting all your eggs in one basket. It is a form of gerrymandering known as "packing." Eighteen African American representatives and ten Hispanic representatives were added to Congress in 1993.[23] While most majority–minority districts elected Democrats, the broader nationwide effect on Democrats was negative.

When the 104th Congress was seated in January 1995, Republicans took control of the House of Representatives from Democrats for the first time since the 83rd Congress in 1953.[24] It cannot be definitively proved that majority–minority districts were to blame for the first Republican takeover of the House in over forty years. However, political pundits and scholars claim it was not a coincidence because the Democrats had wasted minority votes by over packing minorities into single districts. Subsequent research found that Democrats would likely win a district where minorities comprised only 40 percent of the population, which was less than the majority requirement established by the court.[25] Democrats did not regain control of the House until the 110th Congress was seated in January 2007 but lost control again in the 112th Congress in January 2011.[26]

The creation of majority–minority districts has been partially counter-productive for minorities, resulting in a Congress less focused on minor-ity issues. Majority–minority districts have resulted in minorities, and white Democrats, being herded into the same district. Republican whites then be-come the majority in the remaining districts. An increasing number of con-servative representatives—Republicans—have been elected to the House as the number of majority–minority districts has increased. As professor Franita Tolson states, "redistricting plans that create more African American leg-islative seats necessarily create more Republican seats, which come at the expense of white Democratic seats, thereby limiting minority influence to a few safe districts and minimizing it elsewhere."[27] Majority–minority districts have made it easier to create highly partisan districts, and have been partially responsible for a politically polarized House. Districts have become so differ-entiated by race that "candidates of both parties can secure voting majorities without appealing to biracial coalitions."[28]

Before the congressional elections of 1992, voters focused on the quali-ties of each candidate, not their party affiliation. Districts had both Republican and Democratic voters, which forced candidates to be less partisan and more open to compromise. This changed significantly after redistricting that fol-lowed the 1990 census. New majority–minority districts were represented primarily by Democrats, which allowed Republicans to tie Democratic ide-ologies to racial minorities. Increasingly, whites began to view Democrats as the party of racial minorities, and Republicans exploited the situation. As professors Barreto, Segura, and Woods suggest, "the vast majority of non-Hispanic white voters in America lives in jurisdictions where both the ra-cial and the partisan outcomes of legislative elections are rarely, if ever, in doubt."[29]

As districts became highly partisan, or homogeneous, congressional representatives became increasingly beholden to voters on the extreme right or left. The influence of moderate voters has diminished and with it the number of representatives elected to the House who are able to compromise has faded away. Representatives have lost touch with the thoughts of the broader electorate— moderate voters—and are attentive to only the extremes. Juliet Eilperin writes in *Fight Club Politics*, "the irony is that while many U.S. voters are more complex . . . sometimes their elected representatives are not."[30]

Centrists, typically from moderate districts, from either party are few and increasingly endangered. Party leaders demand that centrist representatives support highly partisan legislation. This puts centrists in a difficult predicament. They must pick between the demands of party leaders, who finance their re-election, or the voters who elected them because of their moderate views. Centrists who do not support the objectives of their party's leadership can expect retaliation. Christopher Shays (R-Connecticut) supported campaign finance legislation in opposition to the Republican leadership.[31] Shays was later denied the chairmanship of the House Committee on Oversight and Government Reform. Shays, a moderate Republican, understands the affect uber-partisanship is having on the House: "We're losing touch with what ordinary Americans are thinking."[32] Highly partisan congressional districts further aggravate personal relationships between congressional representatives, making compromise and dialogue unlikely. As Representative Collin Peterson (D-Minnesota) says, "Bottom line, the big picture is there are a hundred Republicans who never talk to Democrats on the floor, and a hundred Democrats who never talk to Republicans on the floor. . . . They don't know each other, they don't like each other, and they don't trust each other."[33]

Later in the 1990s, after creation of majority–minority districts, the court tempered its prior opinion on race-based districting. In a series of separate rulings, the court established that race could not be the "predominate" criteria in redistricting, which made an already murky redistricting process even less clear.

Minorities did not make significant gains in House seats following redistricting in 2001–2002.[34] In the congressional elections of 2002, the number of Hispanic representatives in the House increased by only three—from nineteen to twenty-two—while the population of Hispanics nationwide had increased by over 50 percent—nearly 13 million—since 1990.[35] Two additional Mexican American Democrats were elected in California and another Cuban American Republican was elected from Florida. All Hispanic representatives in the House were elected from majority–minority districts.[36] Why were so few Hispanics added to the House?

In 1984 professors Susan Welch and John R. Hibbing wrote, "in the U.S. House, Hispanics do not lack influence, they just lack the influence their numbers warrant."[37] This state of affairs has not changed. While the number of Hispanic representatives in Congress has increased, it has lagged the sizable increase in the population of Hispanic residents nationwide.

In 2008 over one-third of Hispanics were too young to vote and over one-fourth were not citizens.[38] These demographics result in low levels of voter participation, which minimizes the tangible influence that Hispanics can have on American politics. As professors F. Chris Garcia and Gabriel R. Sanchez write, "this limits the bargaining power of Latinos because elected officials may not be as responsive to individuals who cannot hold them accountable through voting."[39]

Majority–minority districts have increased the number of racial minorities in the House. These districts are important because they send representatives to Congress with life experiences that differ from the white majority. This provides a perspective of society that whites cannot have. But there is a political cost associated with majority–minority districts.

Majority–minority districts allow racial minorities to elect someone of their choosing, but minority voters sacrifice the ability to affect federal government policy. As professor David Lublin writes in *The Paradox of Representation*, "creating majority–minority districts may make individual representatives more responsive to blacks and Latinos, but reduce the aggregate responsiveness of the House of Representative to minorities."[40] The influence of racial minorities in the House will remain muted as long as minorities continue to be densely packed into majority–minority districts.

Re-Redistricting Texas

In September 2005, a grand jury in Travis County, Texas, indicted Congressman Tom DeLay (R-Texas) for committing an alleged felony that violated state laws on corporate funding of political campaigns. The indict-ment alleged DeLay's political action committee, TRMPAC (Texans for a Republican Majority Political Action Committee), had made a contribution of $190,000, which originated from corporate sources, to the Republican National State Elections Committee (RNSEC).[41] The RNSEC then funneled $190,000 to seven Republicans running for office in the Texas legislature. This transfer of funds took place in October 2002, just one month before elections. Texas forbids the use of corporate monies to finance political campaigns.

DeLay temporarily stepped aside as majority leader of the House of Representatives in Congress. The following month, a different grand jury indicted DeLay on separate charges of conspiracy and money laundering. An arrest warrant was issued for DeLay, who voluntarily turned himself in to the Harris County sheriff's office in Texas. DeLay was booked, fingerprinted, and released on $10,000 bail. DeLay claimed the charges were politically motivated and a vendetta against him. District Attorney Ronnie Earle of Travis County responded to DeLay's accusations saying, "Being called vin-dictive and partisan by Tom DeLay is like being called ugly by a frog."[42] How did Tom DeLay go from the second most powerful representative in Congress to having a mug shot? (And later appearing on the reality-TV show *Dancing with the Stars?*)

Two years earlier, the 108th Congress included 229 Republicans, 205 Democrats, and one Independent in the House.[43] Democratic representa-tives thought it possible for them to take enough House seats away from Republicans to regain control in the next round of elections in November 2004. But events in Texas had political repercussions in the House that dashed Democrats' hopes.

In 2001 Texas had a Republican governor and Republicans held a major-ity in the Texas Senate, but Democrats held the majority in the Texas House of Representatives. The Texas legislature was politically divided and unable to pass a congressional redistricting plan for its thirty-two seats. Consequently, a three-judge federal panel imposed its own redistricting plan on Texas. The federal plan minimized disruptions to existing congressional district boundar-ies, which had been established in 1991–1992. The court-mandated changes added two new districts, which Texas gained in 2000 reapportionment, and equalized population among all districts. The two new districts were drawn to favor Republicans.

In 1991–1992, Democrats controlled both chambers of the Texas legislature and enacted a partisan Democratic gerrymander. Tom Delay believed the federal judges had preserved the 1991–1992 pro-Democratic gerrymander and that Republicans had been short-changed. DeLay believed that the 2001–2002 court-imposed redistricting plan resulted in too few Republican representatives from Texas being sent to Congress.

Then in 2002, Texas Republicans gained control of the Texas House of Representatives for the first time in 130 years.[44] Not surprisingly, Republican organizations had spent over 5 million dollars to influence the outcome of the 2002 legislative elections in Texas.[45] DeLay, a federal representative for the 22nd Congressional District (Sugarland in suburban Houston), saw this as an opportunity for the Texas legislature to redraw again—re-redistricting the state's federal congressional districts now that Republicans controlled both the Texas House and Senate. This time redistricting would favor Republicans and unseat Democrats. However, Texans, both Republicans and Democrats, were against another round of redistricting.

The Waco city council and thirty mayors from West Texas opposed re-redistricting.[46] An editorial in the *Amarillo Globe-News*, located in the heavily Republican panhandle of Texas stated, "They're [state Republicans] marching in lockstep to the machinations of Washington politicians rather than heeding the advice of Texans here at home."[47] Republican Sen. Bill Ratliff was against re-redistricting because he feared it would combine sparsely populated areas of rural northeastern Texas with suburban Dallas, which would inevitably result in a Republican from the suburbs representing voters in rural east Texas.[48] The editorial board of the *Houston Chronicle* opposed re-redistricting: "At a time when Texas is grasping for pennies to immunize Texas children, legislators don't need to waste resources giving booster shots to political power plays."[49] In the same article Republican Lt. Gov. David Dewhurst said he was against re-redistricting, "Congressional redistricting is almost as attractive as contagious flu." Dewhurst would later play a pivotal role that enabled the Texas Senate to pass DeLay's redistricting plan. Texas Republicans did not view a second round of redistricting as a high priority in 2003, but DeLay was the majority leader of the House and politically powerful.

National Republican donors, and activists from outside Texas, wanted re-redistricting even if Texas Republicans were against it or ambivalent. The driving force was a desire to increase the number of Republican representatives in Congress beyond the point where Democrats could take control of the House or stop the passage of partisan legislation favorable to Republicans. Even DeLay admitted his intent to gain greater control of Congress, "I'm the majority leader and we want more seats."[50] Joel Hefley (R-Colorado), a former ethics committee chairperson, may have said it best: "[Tom] Delay, I think, is driven by power."[51]

After it became certain that re-redistricting would pass in both chambers of the Texas legislature, Lt. Gov. David Dewhurst acknowledged DeLay's participation in re-redistricting: "The majority leader [DeLay] was instrumental."[52] Several newspapers criticized DeLay's involvement, including the *Bryan-College Station Eagle*, which commented, "We didn't need redistricting in the first place, but if we are going to have it the least DeLay can do is keep his nose out of internal state politics."[53]

Both Tom DeLay and Karl Rove, top political advisor to then-president George W. Bush, played key roles in redrawing Texas's congressional district boundaries in 2003, and Texas legislators had little say in the process.[54] Law professor Steve Bickerstaff wrote in *Lines in the Sand*:

> Neither the residents of the state nor the members of the Texas House or Senate had any significant impact on the final redistricting plan. That plan was drawn in secret by a handful of persons with a common objective, working under pressure from outside partisan interests: to maximize the number of Republicans in Congress from Texas while defeating as many Anglo Democratic incumbents as legally possible.[55]

As for President George W. Bush's involvement in Texas's re-redistricting, Steve Bickerstaff writes in *Lines in the Sand*, "I believe the president bears ultimate responsibility for what happened."[56] United States Senator Joseph Lieberman (I-Connecticut) suggested President Bush's involvement: "Mr. Bush could end this in a minute . . . the buck stops in the oval office."[57]

And in Texas, the *Waco Tribune-Herald* declared, "as sure as the sun rises and sets, the White House has been pulling every string at its disposal in Texas to increase Republican representation in Congress."[58] President Bush was aware of the re-redistricting efforts by Republicans in his home state of Texas, having said, "well, good, I'd like to see that happen."[59]

Republicans also wanted to unseat all of Texas's white Democratic representatives in Congress and thereby stigmatize the Democratic Party in Texas as the party of racial minorities. Texas Republicans expected white Democratic voters would then switch to the Republican Party. Republican consultant Grover Norquist was not shy about their strategy: "No Texan need grow up thinking that being a Democrat is acceptable behavior."[60]

It had been over a century since any state had redistricted more than once in a decade. The Texas constitution does not prohibit it, nor does the U.S. Constitution or federal laws. The U.S. Constitution requires that redistricting occur after each decennial census; however, it does not limit the number of times redistricting can occur.

Opponents of mid-decade redistricting argue that redrawing district lines too often has the potential to keep voters from removing incumbents who have not served them well. Incumbents who believe they will be voted out could redraw their district boundaries to replace voters who will vote against them. As political science professor Bernard Grofman states, "no one in his right mind believes there's a good reason to do mid-decade redistricting except for political gain."[61]

Neither the Texas House nor the Texas Senate had enough Democrats to vote down a re-redistricting plan backed by Republicans. But there were enough Democrats to prevent a quorum from being established. A quorum, or minimum attendance, is necessary for a legislature to be in session. In May 2003 fifty-one Democratic lawmakers from the Texas House were absent. A quorum could not be established. Progress on DeLay's re-redistricting plan stalled. Texas state officials were unsure where the Democratic lawmakers had gone and asked state officials in New Mexico to arrest the AWOL Democrats if they turned up in New Mexico. The Democratic attorney general of New Mexico responded jokingly that New Mexico's police "were on the lookout for politicians in favor of health care for the needy and against tax cuts for the wealthy."[62] The attorney general was mocking Republicans who were against expanding health care coverage and had lowered federal taxes on the country's wealthiest households. New Mexico was not about to help find the wayward Texas legislators, and they were not in New Mexico.

Officers with the Texas Rangers located the lawmakers at a Denny's restaurant in Ardmore, Oklahoma. The Democrats were staying at the adjacent Holiday Inn. Texas officials then asked the FBI to arrest the state-hopping Democrats. The FBI refused to get involved because the whereabouts of Texas Democrats was not a federal matter. The Rangers then asked the lawmakers if they were being held against their will. Unable to either arrest the lawmakers or prove they had been kidnapped, the Rangers returned to Texas empty handed. The sheriff of Carter County, Oklahoma, said of the Texas Democrats, "we're glad to have them here," and stationed a county police officer at the Holiday Inn to deter anyone trying to force the return of the Democrats to Texas.[63] The Democrats received national and international media attention because of their exodus. They returned to Texas four days later after it had become too late in the legislative session to enact DeLay's re-redistricting plan.

Texas Gov. Rick Perry, a Republican, would have to call three special sessions of the legislature that summer before DeLay's re-redistricting plan passed. During the second special session, eleven Democrats from the Texas Senate fled the state to prevent a quorum. This time the Democrats went to New Mexico, where they stayed for forty-five days. New Mexico Gov. Bill Richardson, a Democrat, welcomed the AWOL Texas senators: "This is a wonderful time of the year to visit the Land of Enchantment. New Mexico has a long history of helping people on the run."[64] The Democratic senators ultimately returned to Texas because they expected Republican Governor Perry would continue calling special sessions until DeLay's plan was enacted. The Democrats had exhausted the available options to stop re-redistricting.

In October 2003 Texas Governor Perry signed re-redistricting into law after the third special session of the Texas legislature—but not without further political intrigue. Historically, by tradition not law, passage of a redistricting bill in the Texas Senate required two-thirds of senators to vote in favor. However, Texas Republicans did not control two-thirds of the votes in the Senate. There were twelve Democratic senators and only eleven were needed to prevent a two-thirds vote. Texas Lt. Gov. David Dewhurst, a

Republican, waved the two-thirds vote rule, which enabled Republicans to pass re-redistricting with a simple majority. Dewhurst had originally agreed to adhere to the two-thirds rule but the political pressure got to him. The *Amarillo Globe-News* wrote of Dewhurst's decision: "Standing amid all this chaos is David Dewhurst, who until the other day had sounded very much like his own man rather than a partisan hack who's willing to jump at the loudest command."[65] That same day Democrats filed a lawsuit, which was later joined by LULAC (League of United Latin American Citizens), the GI Forum, the NAACP (National Association for the Advancement of Colored People), and MALDEF (Mexican American Legal Defense and Education Fund).

DeLay's re-redistricting plan had to overcome one additional hurdle before it could be put into effect. The Voting Rights Act required that any redistricting plan in Texas must be approved by the U.S. Justice Department. Congress passed the Voting Rights Act in 1965 to reverse a century of disenfranchisement of racial minority groups. Texas is covered by the Voting Rights Act because of the state's history of disenfranchisement of African Americans and Mexican Americans. Eight members of the career legal staff at the Justice Department reviewed DeLay's re-redistricting. The eight unanimously agreed the plan violated the Voting Rights Act and should not be approved, which would have stopped re-redistricting in Texas. Historically, the attorney general, who heads the Justice Department, has followed the recommendations of the legal staff, but not this time. John Ashcroft, a political appointee of the George W. Bush administration, overruled the findings of the legal staff and approved DeLay's re-redistricting plan.

DeLay's 2003 re-redistricting took effect with the 2004 elections. De-Lay's plan shifted 9.8 million Texans among thirty-two congressional districts. Texas State Representative Phil King, a Republican, said the goal of re-redistricting was "to defeat as many Democratic incumbents as possible in order to give us five or six additional seats."[66] It shifted Texas's congressional House delegation from fifteen Republicans and seventeen Democrats to twenty-one Republicans and eleven Democrats—Texas Republicans gained six seats in Congress.

Some of the Democratic representatives who were unseated had held powerful positions on House committees, which benefited their constituents and Texas. Voters, and the state, lost this advantage when Democrats with seniority were replaced by freshman Republicans. This loss was not of concern to some Texans, as then-president Bush was from Texas. The most prominent Democratic Congressman unseated due to re-redistricting was Martin Frost, the third highest-ranking Democrat in the House. His district had encompassed the Dallas–Fort Worth area and included a significant number of African Americans.

The national consequences of Texas's re-redistricting became apparent in January 2005 when the number of Republicans in the House increased to 232.[67] This not only continued Republican control of the House but also provided an additional margin by which to pass legislation opposed by Democrats. In July the House passed CAFTA (Central American Free Trade Agreement, H.R. 3045) by a margin of 217 to 215.[68] CAFTA, sponsored by Tom DeLay, eliminated many trade barriers between the United States and Costa Rica, the Dominican Republic, El Salvador, Guatemala, Honduras, and Nicaragua. Even though Republican president George W. Bush supported the bill, twenty-seven Republicans voted against it. Only fifteen Democrats voted for it. Only one Republican from Texas—Ron Paul—voted against CAFTA.[69] The bill would have failed to pass if not for the additional Texas Republicans who were elected to the House after DeLay's re-redistricting in 2003.

DeLay's re-redistricting plan was still not out of the woods, even after elections had been held for the redrawn districts. In 2006 the U.S. Supreme Court, ruling in *LULAC v. Perry*, upheld most, but not all, of the redrawn boundaries in DeLay's plan.[70] Then Congressman Rahm Emanuel (D-Illinois), who would later become President Obama's chief of staff, said of the court's ruling, "Every redistricting is a partisan political exercise, but this is going to put it at a level we have never seen."[71] Additionally, the court ruled that the state of Texas had violated the Voting Rights Act because DeLay's plan chopped up the 23rd Congressional District in Laredo. Attorney General John Ashcroft had erred in approving DeLay's plan.

The Laredo district was a majority–minority district created for Hispanics in 1991–1992. While Hispanics were a majority of the population, they did not comprise the majority of voters. Many Hispanic residents of Laredo were either too young to vote or were foreign residents—both legal and illegal—

and ineligible to vote. This gave whites the majority vote, even though the district was created to allow Hispanics to send their preferred candidate to Congress.

Republican Henry Bonilla, who is Hispanic, had represented the 23rd District since 1993. The expectation had been that a Democratic Hispanic would be elected to represent the majority of the Democratic Hispanic community of Laredo. However, Bonilla's support came from white Republicans, not Hispanics. In 2002 Bonilla had won only 8 percent of the Hispanic vote in his district and only narrowly defeated a Hispanic Democratic challenger.

The looming demographics of Laredo would eventually unseat incumbent Bonilla. As young Hispanics reached voting age, they would inevitably outnumber white voters, and Bonilla would be unseated. To avoid this scenario, Republicans used DeLay's re-redistricting plan to remove 100,000 Hispanics from District 23, thereby ensuring that Bonilla's white constituents would remain the voting majority.

The court's ruling disallowed DeLay's changes to the 23rd District and a three-judge panel redrew the district's boundaries for the 2006 congressional elections. The judges removed Republican areas from the 23rd District and added heavily Democratic areas to provide Hispanics with a true majority–minority district. Four surrounding districts would also have to be redrawn to accommodate changes to District 23. This was the third time in five years that these districts had been redrawn. Justice Kennedy wrote the court's opinion in which he maintained that the re-redistricting plan for the 23rd District was meant to crack a "cohesive" and "politically active" community of Hispanics.[72] Furthermore, Kennedy wrote that Republican re-redistricting of the 23rd District was intended "to benefit the officeholder, not the voters."

The demographics of the newly redrawn 23rd District caught up with Republican Bonilla, who lost re-election to Democrat Ciro Rodriguez in November 2006. Rodriguez, a U.S. citizen, had been born in Mexico.

Tom DeLay was "easily the most powerful Republican on Capitol Hill," and "had been gently warned in the past by his fellow Republicans that he was repeatedly pushing the legal limits of rules applicable to members of Congress."[73] In 2004 a complaint was filed against DeLay with the House ethics committee, alleging he had accepted a bribe. The committee sent DeLay a letter of admonishment that stated his actions "at a minimum created the appearance that donors were being provided special access to Representative DeLay regarding the then-pending energy legislation."[74] On a separate issue the ethics committee warned DeLay that his efforts to involve federal agencies to return Texas Democratic representatives from Oklahoma, "went beyond the bounds of acceptable conduct."[75]

In January 2006 DeLay resigned as the Republican majority leader of the House and was replaced by John Boehner (R-Ohio). In June DeLay resigned his seat in Congress because of the two criminal indictments against him in Texas. He did not return to Texas, instead claiming Virginia as his state of residence.[76]

Texas is expected to add at least three congressional seats from 2010 reapportionment for a total of thirty-five or more. At least two of those seats correspond to the population of illegal aliens in the state.

The trial against DeLay for money laundering and conspiracy started in November 2010—five years after the initial indictments.[77] DeLay was found guilty on November 24. DeLay's defense presented five witnesses, while the prosecution had over thirty. DeLay was convicted of channeling $190,000 in corporate donations to Texas state elections in 2002. He could be sentenced to life in prison.

Maintaining the Status Quo in California

Congressional redistricting in Texas in 2003 was an unbridled political war. While in California in 2001–2002, redistricting was a love fest. Democrats and Republicans agreed to a bipartisan gerrymander—a "nonaggression pact"—from which California sent too few Democratic representatives to Congress.[78]

In California in 2001 Democrats were the majority in both the California House and Senate. The governor was Democrat Gray Davis. The Democrats could have passed a pro-Democratic gerrymander to increase the number of Democratic representatives elected to Congress. But they did not, as they feared a repeat of events from the previous round of redistricting.

In the 1991–1992 round of redistricting in California, Democrats controlled the legislature, but the governor was Republican. The governor vetoed the Democratic redistricting plan, and a federal court appointed a group of retired judges to impose their own plan. The court-appointed judges "drew a relatively large number of politically mixed districts and gave little regard to the protection or electoral safety of incumbent legislators."[79] This was good for voters but bad for incumbents. Redistricting in 1991–1992 had not favored Democrats, and they did not want a repeat. California Democrats did not want outsiders drawing their congressional district boundaries.

In the 2001–2002 round of redistricting, Republican leaders in California threatened to challenge any congressional redistricting plan that was unfavorable to incumbent Republicans.[80] Jim Brulte, then the California Senate Republican leader, afterward admitted that the threat had been a bluff.[81] But the Democrats, concerned that a Republican legal challenge would result in California again being forced to accept redistricting by a panel of judges, took the bluff seriously and compromised. The California Democrats settled on a sure thing—the status quo—instead of tempting outside interference, which could have had unknown consequences. Herb Alexander, professor emeritus of political science at the University of Southern California, explained, "if a redistricting plan goes to court, both parties lose control. And once it goes to court, you never know what the outcome will be."[82]

The job of drawing a bipartisan redistricting map went to Michael Berman, a Democratic consultant and brother of California Congressman Howard Berman. On the surface, a bipartisan solution would appear to be a positive compromise. However, law professor Samuel Issacharoff stated: "When the parties collude together in the bipartisan gerrymander, the voting public has no allies and no chance at a voice."[83] In reality, the only compromise in a bipartisan plan is that redistricting is manipulated to re-elect incumbents from both parties, which limits choices for Democratic, Republican, and Independent voters.

Michael Berman had been involved in California redistricting since the 1970s. He was an expert and aware of the history behind previous redistricting plans. Michael Berman was paid a total of $600,000—$20,000 each— from thirty incumbent congressional Democrats to redraw district lines favorable to them.[84] Democratic Congresswoman Loretta Sanchez thought it a good investment: "If my colleagues are smart, they'll pay their $20,000, and Michael will draw the district they can win in. Those who have refused to pay? God help them."[85] There is another perspective to Michael Berman's redistricting prowess. Steven Hill, author of *Fixing Elections: The Failure of America's Winner-Take-All Politics*, writes, "To hear [Loretta] Sanchez talk about it, the money was tantamount to a bribe, the type of 'protection money' one might pay to a local mafia don to protect your turf."[86] Michael Berman's consulting firm received $75,000 from his brother Howard's campaign committee (Berman for Congress) during the 2002 election cycle.[87]

Berman's redistricting map guaranteed to protect every California incumbent, with the exception of Republican Steve Horn, who represented a competitive district in southern California. Democrats would get the additional House seat from 2000 reapportionment. Berman met with Karl Rove, political advisor to President George W. Bush, to obtain assurances that the National Republican Party would not challenge Califor-nia's redistricting plan. Tony Quinn, a Republican redistricting expert, admitted, "The congressional lines . . . are part of a private deal cut by Karl Rove and the Democrats."[88]

Every congressional incumbent was re-elected in 2002 after the new congressional district boundaries had gone into effect. Even Horn was re-elected. But not everyone was satisfied with the outcome. MALDEF challenged the redistricting plan in court, claiming it did not adequately represent Hispanics in California. MALDEF President Antonia Hernandez said the 2001–2002 California congressional redistricting plan would "effectively suppress the political voice of thousands of Latinos for the next ten years."[89] Based solely on the population of Hispanics in the state, there should have been thirteen Hispanic representatives from California in the House after 2001–2002 redistricting. However, there were only seven. Hispanics in California were incensed as they expected additional Latino representatives. However, white incumbent Democrats were concerned that redrawing boundaries to provide for new Hispanic representatives might put white incumbents in danger. Berman's redistricting plan had sacrificed additional Hispanic representatives to re-elect white incumbent Democrats, some of whom supported pro-Latino policies. In *Cano v. Davis*, a federal court ruled against MALDEF's legal challenge to the bipartisan gerrymander.[90]

Michael Berman's brother Howard, a Democratic Congressman from the San Fernando Valley of Los Angeles, provides an example of how redistricting affected Hispanic voters. Howard Berman did not want too many

Hispanics in his district for fear of losing to a Hispanic challenger.[91] So his brother Michael moved Hispanics out of Howard's district into the adjacent district of fellow Democratic Congressman Brad Sherman. This was part of Michael Berman's 2001–2002 redistricting plan. But Sherman did not want more Hispanics in his district either, and for the same reason. Although both Howard Berman and Brad Sherman, who are white, promoted pro-Hispanic policies and had been supported by Hispanics, they both feared a Hispanic challenger. When Sherman complained to Democratic Party leaders, he was told "to keep quiet or the entire Valley Latino community would end-up in *his* district."[92] Sherman was re-elected because Michael Berman had not shifted enough Hispanics into Sherman's district to affect the outcome.

California will likely keep its current fifty-three congressional seats after 2010 reapportionment. At least two of those seats will be due to the population of illegal aliens in the state.

Why Is This Important? Congressional Representatives Do Not Represent Everyone

David Winston, an expert at redistricting, helped Republicans draw partisan congressional district boundaries that increased the number of Republicans in the House of Representatives in Congress. Winston is well aware of the effect congressional district boundaries have on politics: "When I, as a map-maker, have more of an impact on an election than the voters, the system is out of whack."[93] Winston has seen the consequences also. "You have a political process that disenfranchises everybody."[94] After Census 2000, the political shenanigans surrounding redistricting in Texas and California had a profound effect on all American residents.

We inherently expect our congressional representatives to act equally on the needs of all their constituents. Yet, we discount that the purpose of an election is to select the candidate who represents the views of most voters. U.S. Supreme Court Justice John Paul Stevens explains the consequences: "Elected officials in some sense serve two masters: the constituents who elected them and the political sponsors who support them. Their primary obligations are, of course, to the public in general, but it is neither realistic nor fair to expect them wholly to ignore the political consequences of their decisions."[95]

Will a candidate elected for his or her anti-abortion stance be responsive to female constituents who want federal government funding for late-term abortions? Will a candidate, elected for his or her plans to introduce stringent enforcement of immigration laws, help an illegal resident obtain legal status? Will a congressional representative from oil-rich Texas vote to fund alternative energy sources to the benefit of all Americans? The gerrymandering of congressional districts—not the voters—determines how political issues are addressed, as the winner has been selected before the election. California Republican William M. Thomas makes this clear, "you have the creation of districts that are more selected by the candidate than the constituent." [96]

In House elections following the 2001–2002 round of redistricting, fewer incumbents were defeated than had lost in decades. Only sixteen incumbents lost in 2002 as compared with an average of thirty-five from 1972, 1982, and 1992.[97] Mark Braden, an attorney for the Republican Party said, "Turnover in 2002 was way too low."[98] These remarks were in the context that Republicans controlled the House and were the winners in redistricting nationwide. Braden blamed the low turnover on the focus by both Democrats and Republicans to protect incumbents. In some states both parties compromised on redistricting to keep their incumbents in office.

Yet, gerrymandering districts does not guarantee future results. The political tide that gave Republicans control of the House in 1994 shifted in 2006 when Republicans lost thirty seats in the House. Republicans went from a majority of thirty to a minority of thirty-one.[99] Nationwide, not a single Democratic incumbent lost in the midterm elections of 2006.

Nonpartisan districting is more likely to result in more competitive elections and greater turnover in representatives. However, individual states are less likely to adopt nonpartisan districting methods unless all states adopt similar measures. A state such as New York, with a Democratic majority in the House, may not willingly adopt nonpartisan redistricting unless Texas, with a Republican majority in the House, also adopts nonpartisan redistricting. A state that unilaterally adopts nonpartisan districting will have fewer senior legislators in strong political positions to benefit their state. This would place states with "fair" districting methods at a political disadvantage compared to states that allow redistricting to secure safe seats for incumbents. Consider the following opinion in the *Los Angeles Times*: "but why should

California Democrats be fair to Republicans when they have no guarantee that Republicans in the rest of the country will behave likewise? I will support a nonpartisan redistricting of Democrat-dominated California on the same day I can be assured of similar fairness in Republican states."[100] This may be the reason that only seven states use independent nonpartisan commissions to draw congressional districts.[101]

Minorities should reconsider the broader consequences of majority—minority districts packed with minority voters. While this may give minorities "feel good" representation, it significantly limits progress on pro-minority government policies. An alternative to majority—minority districts, where minorities number at least 65 percent of the population, is to have minority "influence" districts where minorities number from 40 to 50 percent of voters—not total population. This would spread the influence of minorities to multiple districts while retaining enough numbers to have an effect on who gets elected. It would allow minorities to spread their influence to a greater number of congressional representatives, which would translate into more action on minority issues in Congress. This is true for Hispanics in particular because they are the largest growing ethnic population, but most live in geographic clusters across the country.

The 111th Congress (2009–2010) had twenty-four Hispanics in the House.[102] Before majority–minority districts went into effect in 1993 there were only eleven.[103] However, there would need to be sixty-seven Hispanics in the House to reflect the size of the Hispanic population nationwide. Professors Chris Garcia and Gabriel Sanchez write in *Hispanics and the U.S. Political System: Moving into the Mainstream*, "For the rate of Latino members of the House of Representatives to continue to rise, Latinos will need to win in electoral districts where Latinos are not the majority population."[104] This requires a re-evaluation of the utility of majority–minority districts. Have they reached the limit for expanding minority representation in the House?

Tom DeLay's re-redistricting of Texas designed minority districts so that over time Hispanic districts would become increasingly Hispanic, and African American districts increasingly African American. Re-redistricting in Texas gerrymandered minority voters into majority–minority districts to minimize their influence until the next round of redistricting, which would not take place until 2011–2012. The result is that while the population of Hispanics in Texas continues to grow, their political influence is muted. So, Latino leaders who claim Hispanics will increasingly influence American politics need only see what happened to Hispanic voting power in the Texas re-redistricting of 2003 and California in 2001–2002. When he was a U.S. Senator for Illinois, President Barack Obama expressed support for creating competitive districts that would "reduce the number of guaranteed African American districts, but might also force the kinds of dialogue and parties actively seeking support from not-so-easily-identifiable racial groups."[105]

Sam Hirsch, an attorney for Democrats, summarizes the effect of gerrymandering on Congress: "Partisan gerrymandering is also transforming Congress. With little reason to fear voters, representatives increasingly cater to party insiders and donors, rather than to the political center where most Americans reside. Bipartisan compromise around moderate policies takes a backseat to party loyalty, resulting in historic levels of polarization. And further polarization only fuels the bitterness that promotes more gerrymandering."[106] This was reflected in the virulent political discourse on health care legislation in Congress during 2009–2010. While some Democrats in the House voted against health care legislation, not a single Republican voted *for* health care legislation.[107]

Gerrymandering of congressional districts is against the best interests of Americans—regardless of political affiliation. Since the 1990s, the House has been divided into winners and losers, and driven by heightened partisan politics and a lack of compromise. Representative Bob Filner (D-California) explains the consequences: "Your own constituents don't understand at all why these common things can't get passed . . . but it's impossible when both parties are trying to game the system rather than just solving problems.'"[108] Comments from former Sen. Robert Dole (R-Kansas) illustrate the divisive political discourse dating to the early 1990s, "Hello gentlemen! What are we against today?"[109]

3

ILLEGAL WORKERS

Turning Mexican Landowners into Wage Laborers

Our Anglo-Saxon race [have] been land stealers from time im-
memorial, and why shouldn't they [be]? [1]
— Mexican American War Gen. William Worth, 1845

It's Legal to Be Illegal

My phrase "It's legal to be illegal" resulted from the Texas Proviso legislation
enacted in 1952, which provided businesses with a loophole for hiring undocumented workers without fear of penalties. Until 1987 the Texas Proviso
was the backbone of laissez-faire immigration polices in the United States. In
1987 Congress passed legislation barring undocumented workers, but these
laws have not been enforced. The undisguised use of illegal workers, begun
by Texas Proviso, remains the norm. The Texas Proviso spawned the large
population of illegal immigrants living in the United States today.

The full effect of the Texas Proviso did not appear until after 1965. In
the late 1960s, the dreadful working conditions of migrant farm workers, first
televised in 1960 in *Harvest of Shame*, still existed in Florida: "It was just ter-
ribly poor, the worst abuses that one heard of in the *Harvest of Shame* were
present there [Immokalee, Florida], but beyond what I had heard about."[2]
"The camp [migrant worker housing] consists of a dozen windowless ply-
wood shacks . . . all without toilets or running water."[3]

Illegal foreign workers, many from Mexico, provided an increasing share of farm labor. Agricultural employers preferred illegal workers because they were paid less than American farm labor and rarely complained about working conditions. During the 1970s and 1980s, the number of illegal immigrants from Mexico and other parts of Latin America began to rise alongside legal refugees. These undocumented workers spread into urban centers across the country, working jobs that required little education or skill.

In the mid-1970s politicians in the United States began showing concern over the increasing number of immigrants arriving. From 1975 to 1980 about 400,000 refugees entered the country legally from Vietnam, Cambodia, and Laos. During a six-month period in 1980 about 125,000 immigrants came from Mariel, Cuba, but not all *Marielitos* obtained refugee status. In 1980 the population of Salvadorans in the United States was about 100,000. By 1990 it had grown to over 500,000, as Salvadorans fled civil war in El Salvador. "Many people flee because they are stamped as collaborators with the guerrillas and their life is in danger; because being marked is enough to cause the worst to happen," said Salvadoran Archbishop Rivera y Dama in 1980.[4] Nicaraguans also fled civil war and came to the United States. These Central American conflicts resulted, in part, from America's foreign policy. Unlike what had occurred with Cubans in the 1960s, the American government did not grant refugee status to these Salvadorans and Nicaraguans.

By 1980 about 3 million illegal immigrants resided in the United States. Foreign workers were becoming visible on Main Street, U.S.A.[5] Since then, public opinion polls have shown that a majority of Americans want a reduction in immigration. By 1990 the number of illegal immigrants had risen to about 3.5 million. Over 60 percent came from Mexico and other parts of Latin America. Asians and Europeans also added to the population of illegal aliens. In the late 1980s about 250,000 illegal Irish immigrants made their way to metropolitan areas along the Atlantic Coast from Baltimore to Boston.

The Immigration Reform and Control Act (IRCA) of 1986 was heralded as the "fix" for illegal immigration. Competing viewpoints on immigration had clashed in Congress since the 1970s. Family farm owners wanted to maintain their status quo access to low-wage Mexican labor. Republican Sen. Orrin Hatch said in 1985: "This country cannot afford to attempt immigration reform, while ignoring the vital interests of small farmers who produce our agricultural necessities, including reasonably priced, high quality, fresh fruits and vegetables."[6]

Others, like Democratic Sen. Howard Metzenbaum, also believed illegal immigrant labor was harmful to the United States: "Massive employment of illegal aliens only keeps working conditions bad and wages low. American agricultural workers will accept the jobs that are available, provided they pay a decent wage and provided there are decent working conditions."[7] Would enough Americans move into seasonal farm work if wages increased? It is impossible to be certain, because American farmers have always had access to low-wage immigrant labor. Hispanics fought against employer sanctions in IRCA because it might lead to discrimination against those who look foreign. California Democratic Representative Esteban Torres gave this opinion in 1986: "Criminal sanctions would result in discrimination. . . . If employers know that they can be handcuffed and arrested if they make the wrong decisions, I seriously doubt that they will take a chance and hire anyone who does not look or sound like Americans."[8]

The historically strong influence of agribusiness was present during IRCA hearings. From Wyoming Republican Senator Alan Simpson: "there is no way to satisfy the perishable fruit growers. . . . They are heavy hitters; they spend big bucks, and they are quite effective."[9]

IRCA went into effect in 1987 and granted amnesty to undocumented immigrants who had lived in the United States for an uninterrupted period of at least five years. Opponents argued that amnesty gave preference to illegals over other immigrants waiting to enter the country legally. Opponents also viewed amnesty as rewarding illegal behavior. Supporters of amnesty argued that not providing amnesty raised the potential of instituting a permanent lower stratum of society. About 3 million illegal aliens became legal residents, of which 2.3 million were from Mexico.

IRCA contained provisions for employer sanctions to halt the employment of undocumented workers. However, sanctions were not enforced and IRCA only slowed illegal immigration for two years. Representative Romano L. Mazzoli and Senator Alan K. Simpson, co-authors of the Immigration Reform and Control Act of 2006, wrote: "Administrations of both stripes are loathe to disrupt economic activities—i.e. labor supply in factories, farms, and businesses. And we know that disruptions in the labor supply are the natural, unavoidable, and even desirable consequence of strong border and workplace enforcement."[10]

IRCA also created a new class of legal immigrant farm worker to meet demands from growers for seasonal labor. However, this did not stop further increases of undocumented workers in agriculture as U.S. Senator James McClure (R-Idaho) had predicted: "Five years from now, seven or eight years from now, we will have another illegal alien problem, calling for amnesty, because this does nothing to solve the basic problem . . . it does not close our borders to illegal immigration. It winks at it."[11] Similarly, U.S. Representative Henry Gonzalez (D-Texas) questioned the real-world impact of IRCA: "Let there be no mistake about it. This bill [IRCA] . . . guarantees that those who want to exploit cheap, foreign labor . . . can continue to do so with impunity."[12] Senator McClure and Representative Gonzalez were correct. IRCA was doomed to fail.

In 2009 there were nearly 11 million illegal aliens living in the United States, and over 60 percent of those were from Mexico. Nearly 800,000 illegal aliens were apprehended in 2008—88 percent were natives of Mexico. For Mexicans, low-wage jobs in the United States provide economic opportunities that do not exist in Mexico, where unskilled labor earns a pittance. The undocumented Mexican population works predominately in low-skill industrial jobs and low-wage service jobs such as construction, food preparation, landscaping, and housekeeping where "they are consistently paid less than legally authorized workers doing the same job and often lack standing to enforce fundamental workers rights."[13] In 2005 over half of farm laborers in the United States were undocumented. In particular, businesses that pay low wages for dangerous work, such as meatpacking and poultry processing, seek illegal workers. Hispanics have the highest rate of deaths from work-related injuries.[14] Poultry processing, like meatpacking, has high turnover rates and high injury rates. Turnover at Tyson Foods can be as high as 200 percent annually.[15]

Undocumented workers are unlikely to report dangerous working conditions as it could result in the loss of their job. They are also unlikely to claim benefits for work-related injuries. Undocumented Mexican workers in the poultry industry increased significantly in the late 1980s. In 2000 Mexican immigrants accounted for more than one in four workers in meatpacking.[16]

Mexican immigrants comprise the largest population of working poor in the United States. The Mexican government has no incentive to reduce out-migration to the United States. Mexican workers in the United States send a significant portion of their earnings, or remittances, to their families in Mexico. Remittances are the second largest source of foreign exchange for Mexico, totaling $23 billion in 2006. Oil exports rank first. Remittances from the United States exceed foreign investment in Mexico and account for about 3 percent of Mexico's gross domestic product (GDP).

Remittances raise the standard of living in the poorest regions of Mexico and act as an efficient form of foreign aid that bypasses inefficient and corrupt government bureaucracies. Between 1995 and 2006 about 5 percent of Mexican households received remittances from family members working in the United States. These are the poorest households in rural Mexico, which use the money for basic living expenses such as food, housing, and education.

Ten percent of Mexico's native-born population lives in the United States. This exodus of poor Mexicans to the United States relieves social and political pressures in Mexico, which reinforces nonaction by Mexico's politicians. Before 2006 Mexico's politicians prohibited emigrant Mexicans from voting. However, the growing importance of remittances has increased the political power that Mexicans living in the United States now exert on Mexico's politics.

There exists a calliope of American organizations with a public policy position on immigration. Agribusiness has been the biggest proponent for open immigration. Their focus has been to obtain low wage, unskilled, or low skilled, laborers to pick fruits and vegetables. Recently, high-tech companies such as Microsoft, Intel, Sun, and Texas Instruments have lobbied for increased immigration, claiming a shortage of talented high-tech workers in the United States. Computer geeks are not the typical undocumented worker.

Immigration lawyers lobby for laws that favor their clients, who include immigrants and their families. Numerous Hispanic and Asian groups lobby for immigration policies that benefit their ethnic base. Hispanics, however, are not a uniform constituency. Immigration issues of importance to Cubans, who came to the United States as political refugees, differ from immigration issues of importance to Mexicans who came to the United States to escape poverty.

Groups concerned with population growth or environmental issues want to reduce immigration. However, these groups overlook that immigrants keep the United States from falling into negative population growth, as is happening in parts of Europe. Negative population growth brings with it the potential for a declining economy. Nativist, anti-immigration, and racist groups hope to stop all immigration. In contrast, the moral codes of many religious organizations dictate a pro-immigration stance.

Think tanks exist that are both pro- and anti-immigration. Historically worker unions have been anti-immigrant, but their position has begun to moderate. Unions increasingly view immigrants as an untapped source of new membership because union membership is declining.

The most influence on immigration policy has come from American businesses, which lobby for low-wage immigrant workers and against sanctions on employers. Businesses do not want to enforce immigration laws, and they do not want to be agents of the police. Conversely, supporters of employer sanctions want better methods for verifying a worker's legal status and an emphasis on enforcement against businesses that knowingly hire large numbers of illegal workers. Hispanic representatives in Congress vote against employer sanctions fearing businesses would respond by not hiring anyone who looks foreign. The flipside is that a lack of employer sanctions results in the exploitation of undocumented workers.

Since 1993, American immigration policy has focused on reducing the number of undocumented immigrants through enhanced border enforcement. The result has been counterproductive. Increased border control has lead to seasonal workers living permanently in the United States. Historically, illegal Mexican workers would remain in the United States for short periods and then return to Mexico. In the early 1990s about 20 percent of unauthorized Mexican migrants had returned to Mexico after six months.[17] By 2002 only about 7 percent had returned. Undocumented workers now fear they will not be able to get back into the U.S. if they cross the border into Mexico.

The availability of jobs may be the main cause of illegal immigration into the United States. Rahm Emanuel, a Democrat and former chief of staff for President Obama, supports employer sanctions to reduce illegal immigration: "There are over 20 million businesses in the U.S.; the main attraction for people coming to this country is work and there has been almost zero enforcement. . . . You have got to have a real consequence to hiring illegal immigrants if you want to fight it."[18] Former Republican Congressman Tom Tancredo also links the prevalence of illegal immigration to the availability of jobs: "take away the jobs and, I think, you can stop much of the illegal immigration. . . . Second, you go after employers who hire illegals."[19]

In 1997 Fresno County, California, had agricultural sales of $3.3 billion —over half of California's agricultural revenue. Meanwhile, four in ten of the county's 800,000 residents lived in poverty and unemployment measured 12 percent. Farmers in Fresno County still claimed a labor shortage existed and wanted to increase the availability of low-wage Mexican workers.[20]

In 1998 the Immigration and Naturalization Service (INS) raided Georgia onion fields during the harvest. About half of the laborers were undocumented. Farmers mounted political pressure on the INS and the raids stopped.

DeCoster Farms in Iowa has been violating labor laws for decades and has paid millions of dollars in fines for employing illegal workers.[21] In 2002 five undocumented women workers claimed they had been raped by supervisors, who threatened to either kill the women or have them deported if they went to the police. DeCoster Farms paid $1.53 million to the women. In 2003 the owner pleaded guilty to hiring undocumented workers. He was fined and put on probation. Again in 2007, fifty-one illegal immigrants, including children, were discovered working at a DeCoster plant. Apparently, penalties for employing illegal workers are not severe enough to deter DeCoster from continuing the practice.

In 2001 a federal grand jury indicted six managers at Tyson Foods for smuggling illegal workers from the Southwest to various Tyson plants.[22] Undercover agents from the INS had been investigating Tyson for over two years. Managers at Tyson arranged for false papers and paid smugglers as much as $200 for each of the 136 illegal workers. One of the indicted managers later committed suicide. The government's indictment alleged that Tyson Foods preferred illegal workers:

> Due to their illegal status and vulnerability as a result of their fear of being arrested and deported . . . [they] were: (a) frequently forced to be more productive than legal workers . . . (b) frequently subjected to

less humane working conditions than legal workers . . . and (c) less likely than legal workers to complain to Tyson management, to file a grievance with governmental agencies, to seek workers' compensation benefits, and to be absent from work.[23]

At the trial, two of the indicted Tyson managers directly involved in the smuggling testified against the company. The government presented numerous witnesses and collaborating evidence. However, the jury acquitted Tyson Foods of most charges. Jurors believed local managers were responsible for the human smuggling and upper management had been unaware.

In May 2008 federal officials raided the Agriprocessors kosher meatpacking plant in Postville, Iowa. Officials detained nearly 400 undocumented workers—about half of the company's workforce including children.[24] The chief executive of Agriprocessors, Sholom M. Rubashkin, was convicted of numerous business fraud charges in November 2009 and sentenced to twenty-seven years in prison.[25]

Agribusinesses, from states such as Arizona, have historically formed an effective lobby against federal efforts to control immigration. Businesses in these states have profited greatly from low-wage illegal labor. However, communities with large concentrations of undocumented residents experience increasing costs in social services and more crime. While businesses have benefited, taxpayers, the social safety net, and communities have suffered.

Voters are becoming aware that businesses drive illegal immigration and more states are legislating employer sanctions. As of April 2007, forty-one states had pending legislation to curtail the employment of illegal workers. In Oklahoma, Mississippi, and Utah, legal residents who have lost their job can sue a former employer if the business knowingly employed illegal workers.

States blame the federal government for the high numbers of illegal immigrants, as stated by former Arizona Gov. Janet Napolitano, "because Congress has failed miserably."[26] Federal government auditing of employers to ensure they were checking employee citizenship status fell by more than 70 percent between 1993 and 2003.[27] In 2001 there were 9,500 border agents and only 124 federal agents enforcing immigration laws among employers.[28] In 2003 only four employers nationwide faced prosecution for hiring illegal workers. In 2005 the federal government fined only three employers for hiring illegal workers.[29]

More aliens cross the border illegally into the United States through Arizona than through any other border state.[30] Arizona responded with the Legal Arizona Workers Act (LAWA), which is the toughest employer sanctions legislation targeted at illegal workers in the United States. The law enables the state of Arizona to suspend the business license of employers who hire undocumented workers. LAWA states that "an employer shall not intentionally employ an unauthorized alien."[31] The employer is held accountable even if he or she did not know the employee, or contractor, was an illegal alien. Employers that repeatedly violate LAWA can have their business license permanently revoked. LAWA went into effect on January 1, 2008, and applies to businesses of all sizes.

LAWA has been upheld by the U.S. Court of Appeals for the Ninth Circuit. The U.S. Supreme Court will review the law with a ruling expected in 2011. Other states have passed laws to penalize employers who hire illegal workers only to have the legislation overturned by a federal court. LAWA has so far passed federal scrutiny, in part, because of how the law deals with two issues. First, federal law bars states from imposing penalties, such as fines or jail time, on business owners who employ illegal workers. However, federal law does not restrict states from revoking business licenses. LAWA puts an employer out of business by revoking his or license to operate. Second, states do not have the authority to determine citizenship status because immigration is within the purview of the federal government. LAWA relies on the federal government's E-Verify system to determine citizenship.

E-Verify is a free Internet-based system operated by the U.S. Department of Homeland Security. E-Verify is a voluntary program that allows employers to verify a U.S. Social Security Number (SSN). In January 2010 the program had over 180,000 participating businesses and had responded to over 3 million queries in the last three months of 2009.[32] E-Verify provides the name and birth date associated with a SSN. This capability eliminates the use of forged nonexistent SSNs and allows a business to link a SSN to another form of identification such as a driver's license, birth certificate, or passport. E-Verify responds to 92 percent of inquiries within seconds.[33] Employees have a grace period and an alternative route to prove they are legal residents when E-Verify cannot confirm their SSN. A business must keep the employee during the grace period.

Arizona businesses and immigrant groups oppose LAWA. A main concern is that the state of Arizona relies on the public to identify businesses hiring illegal workers. Anyone can file a complaint via the Internet against a business suspected of hiring illegal aliens.[34] Opponents claim this has the effect of discouraging businesses from hiring anyone who looks or sounds foreign, which can result in discrimination against legal foreign residents and minorities. A person filing a knowingly false complaint can be charged with a misdemeanor. Opponents of LAWA do not believe this is enough to deter frivolous complaints in Arizona where anti-immigrant sentiment is high. There have also been incidents in which businesses fired employees who did not pass E-Verify without allowing them the mandated alternative methods for proving they were legal residents.

LAWA reversed the flow of illegal immigrants into Arizona before prosecutors filed any cases. Tens of thousands of illegal aliens left Arizona voluntarily. The number of tenants in apartments in Phoenix and Tucson began to drop. The Arizona public school system had a budget surplus in 2008, in part, because of a drop in enrollment of nearly 70,000.[35] Officials from the Mexican state of Sonora, which borders Arizona, complained that there were not enough jobs in Sonora, and that "Mexico is not prepared for this, for the tremendous problems" that would result from the large numbers of Mexicans leaving Arizona.[36] The first employer sanctions case was not filed until November 2009, which was nearly two years after the law had gone into effect. The first case was against Scottsdale Art Factory for knowingly hiring illegal workers through a subcontractor.[37]

In April 2010 the state of Arizona took a highly controversial step in further efforts to rid the state of an estimated 450,000 illegal residents.[38] Gov. Jan Brewer signed into law Arizona Senate Bill 1070, considered the most stringent anti-immigration law in the country.[39] The law makes it a crime in Arizona to be in the state illegally and requires Arizona police to question anyone suspected of being an illegal alien. Some Arizona police consider the law to be a misuse of limited police resources: "We don't have enough officers on the street to look for other stuff [immigration status] like that. If they're not doing anything, they're just being normal people."[40]

Hispanics fear the law will lead to racial profiling and President Obama expressed opposition to the law. The Arizona law exacerbates the divide on immigration reform within the Republican Party.[41] Ironically, some conservative Republicans oppose Arizona's controversial law while some moderate Republicans support it. For Republicans, the number of Hispanic votes they need to get elected likely influences each elected official's stance. The U.S. Justice Department is challenging the bill in court because it argues that the Constitution grants immigration enforcement to the federal government, not states.

If Arizona had implemented Senate Bill 1070 earlier, there may have been sufficient population loss to cost the state a congressional seat. However, because Arizona implemented the law after the Census 2010 population count, the number of congressional seats apportioned to Arizona will remain unchanged for another decade regardless of how many illegal aliens leave the state.

Illegal immigration has grown, in part, because states that benefit most have historically obstructed attempts by the federal government to manage immigration. Since the late 1960s, the main immigrant destination states have been Arizona, California, Florida, Illinois, New Jersey, New York, and Texas. After congressional reapportionment in 2000, California (three), Florida (one), and North Carolina (one) received five additional representatives because of their population of undocumented residents. Otherwise, one additional seat would have gone to each of the following states: Indiana, Michigan, Mississippi, Montana, and New York. After reapportionment in 2010, California (two) and Texas (two) will likely get added congressional representation because of their population of illegal residents. These four seats would otherwise have gone to Louisiana, Minnesota, Montana, and Ohio.

Illegal immigration from Mexico to the United States has its origins at the Alamo in the former northern Mexican province of Tejas—now the Lone Star State of Texas.

The Alamo: Tejas Becomes Texas

"Remember the Alamo," is part of the American vocabulary, but what are we remembering exactly? Any given American might describe it as a battle between Texans and Mexicans that the Texans lost. Events surrounding the

Alamo provide an explanation for America's historical mistreatment of people of Mexican heritage. Today's prevalence of illegal Mexican immigrants in the Southwest has its roots at the battle at the Alamo mission in 1836.

Spanish Franciscans founded the Alamo mission around 1722 in the northern Mexican (New Spain) region of Tejas, which meant *friends* or *allies* to the Spanish explorers who named the region. Tejas was sparsely populated and had few Mexican citizens. In 1820 Mexican residents living in Tejas—Tejanos—numbered about 4,000. They were outnumbered ten to one by the native Indian population of about 40,000.

In 1803 the United States purchased the Louisiana Territory from France and inherited the Tejas border with Mexico. Mexican politicians believed the United States would try to take Tejas as America expanded westward to the Pacific Ocean. The Mexicans were right.

The Mexican government instituted generous land grant policies to encourage settlement of Tejas, thereby deterring invasion by the United States military. Americans left the United States and settled in Tejas where each family was given over 4,400 acres. Mexico expected these expatriate Americans to become loyal Mexican citizens.

The first colonists from the United States arrived in Tejas in 1823. By 1830 more than 20,000 foreigners lived in Tejas —compared to about 3,000 Mexicans. Mexican citizens showed no desire to settle the barren lands of Tejas, which were difficult to reach from the populated central region of Mexico. It was easier to get to Tejas from the United States than from other Mexican provinces. On April 6, 1830, the Mexican government stopped issuing land grants in Tejas to settlers from the United States. Mexico then tried to convince Cherokee Indians to settle in Tejas as a counterweight to the population of American settlers. These were the same Cherokees who had been forcibly relocated from Georgia and Tennessee to the Louisiana Territory after the United States Congress enacted the Indian Removal Act of 1830. The Cherokees declined Mexico's offer to settle in Tejas.

Maintaining sovereignty over Tejas became increasingly difficult for Mexico. The economy of Tejas was more closely linked to the United States than to Mexico, which undermined allegiance to Mexico. Ships routinely sailed between Tejas and the American ports of New Orleans, Philadelphia, and New York, creating a prosperous trade. By the mid 1830s, the population of Tejas was about 50,000—mostly American settlers. Mexico had lost both its population and economic links to Tejas.

Except for the Mexican upper class, most Mexicans in Tejas did not want independence from Mexico. Foreign settlers that wanted an independent Texas were typically young, unmarried men who were recent arrivals from the United States. They were American southerners who either owned slaves or supported slavery, which was illegal in Mexico. Most of these men were illiterate. In contrast, older, married foreign settlers opposed independence. They had lived in Tejas since the first American settlers arrived and preferred the status quo in which the Mexican government had little participation in their affairs. These were mostly American northerners who did not own slaves.

On March 2, 1836, rebel Tejanos—Texans—seceded from Mexico and declared Tejas to be the newly independent Republic of Texas. A few days later, on March 6, a small group of Tejano rebels was defeated at the Alamo in San Antonio by a larger force of Mexican federal troops under the command of Gen. Antonio López de Santa Anna. In the famous battle at the Alamo, a group of foreign settlers, along with members of the Mexican upper class, fought Mexican federal soldiers. The Alamo conjures images of American frontiersmen such as Jim Bowie and Davy Crockett. American history depicts Bowie and Crockett as independently minded Americans fighting for an independent Texas. However, both Bowie and Crockett had severed their ties to the United States. Jim Bowie settled in Tejas in 1828 and became a Mexican citizen and married a Mexican woman. Davy Crockett left Tennessee in 1834 after losing re-election to Congress.

> And I concluded my speech by telling them that I was done
> with politics for the present, and that they might all go to hell,
> and I would go to Texas.[42]
>
> —Davy Crockett, 1834

Bowie and Crockett fought, and died, for their newly adopted country—the Republic of Texas—which would allow slavery. The following month, on April 21, Texan soldiers got revenge when they defeated Mexican federal forces at San Jacinto. The famous battle cry "Remember the Alamo!" originates from the Battle of San Jacinto. After losing at San Jacinto, Mexican General Santa Anna withdrew Mexican federal troops from Texas. The Republic of Texas had won independence from Mexico.

Alongside Bowie and Crockett, Mexicans also died defending the Alamo. Their names are recorded as Juan Abamillo, Juan Antonio Badillo, Carlos Espalier, Gregorio Esparza, Antonio Fuentes, Jose Toribio Losoya, and Andres Nava. Contributions by Mexicans to Texan independence are omitted from Texas's populist history, which fosters the misconception that all Mexicans opposed independence.

> Like most passionate nations, Texas has its own private history
> based on, but not limited by, facts.[43]
>
> —John Steinbeck, 1932

The Alamo marked a defining event in the history of the Republic of Texas and its myths. After the Texan defeat at the Alamo, Americans who had settled in Tejas started treating all Mexicans as unwanted. Mary J. Jaques said in 1894: "It is difficult to convince these people that a Mexican is a human being. He seems to be the Texan's natural enemy; he is treated like a dog, or, perhaps not so well."[44]

The Alamo was followed twelve years later by the Mexican-American War, which reinforced the forged stereotype that all Mexicans were anti-Texas and subsequently anti-American. After the Mexican-American War, many American settlers throughout the Southwest would look down on people of Mexican heritage—including those born in the United States, despite the fact that Americans were the aggressors at both the Alamo and in the Mexican-American War.

The Mexican-American War? Or Mexico's War of Defense?

Manifest Destiny and Expansionism became one and the same with United States policies in the mid to late 1800s. The generation of Washington, Jefferson, and Madison had passed, and their political offspring felt compelled to outdo the founding fathers. Elected officials, the media, and business titans proclaimed that the United States had a divine right—a destiny and a duty— to encompass all lands from the Atlantic to the Pacific.

> The bountiful continent is ours, state on state, and territory on
> territory, to the waves of the Pacific sea.
>
> —Ralph Waldo Emerson, 1844

The Union had nearly doubled from fourteen states in 1790 to twenty-six in 1840. The country's population had more than quadrupled from nearly 4 million to over 17 million during that time. In 1790 the geographic area of the United States was slightly less than 900,000 square miles. By 1840 the country had doubled in area to nearly 1.8 million square miles.

In 1845 America entered the industrial age with about 1 million residents working in manufacturing. Railroads and steamships were hastening travel and trade. Telegraph lines were spreading and facilitating communication between major cities. Baltimore and Washington, D.C., were connected by telegraph in 1844. The population and economy were growing and Americans were proud of their country's accomplishments.

Then Texas happened.

The Republic of Texas first requested annexation into the United States in August 1837. It was unsuccessful. Several subsequent attempts to annex Texas were defeated because Congress feared it would fuel antagonism over slavery between the North and South. Would Texas be a pro-slavery or anti-slavery state? Abolitionists in the northern United States viewed the annexation of Texas as an attempt by southern states to add another slave state and thereby increase pro-slavery representation in Congress.

By the mid-1840s, the population of Texas had grown to about 125,000, due mostly to continued immigration from the United States. The American public became increasingly supportive of expatriates in Texas. In 1844 James Polk of Tennessee was selected as the Democratic Party presidential nominee after he proclaimed the annexation of Texas as the primary goal of his presidency: "I am in favor of the immediate re-annexation of Texas to the territory and Government of the United States." The Whig Party selected Henry Clay from Kentucky as their presidential candidate. In contrast to Polk, Clay opposed annexing Texas, as he feared it would lead to war with Mexico: "So far from Mexico being silent, she repeatedly and solemnly declared that she would consider annexation [of Texas] as war with her [Mexico]."[45] The

Mexican government had lost two separate wars with Texas but refused to acknowledge its rebellious region as a separate country.

Polk defeated Clay in the presidential election of November 1844 by a slim margin of popular votes. New York was the pivotal state for Polk, where he won by just over 5 thousand votes. New York's thirty-six Electoral College votes gave Polk a majority in the Electoral College. Being a slave owner, Polk should not have won anti-slavery New York. However Clay, like Polk, was also a slave owner and a southerner. In retrospect, in 1844 Americans were more concerned about Texas than the ever-present issue of slavery. In his inauguration speech on March 4, 1845, President Polk made clear his intention to annex Texas: "I regard the question of annexation as belonging exclusively to the United States and Texas . . . To enlarge its [United States] limits is to extend the dominions of peace over additional territories and increasing millions . . . by adding another member to our confederation [United States] . . . and opening to them [foreign countries] new and ever-increasing markets for their products." Polk, Texas, and Manifest Destiny were inseparable, and the annexation of Texas was a foregone conclusion. Congress annexed Texas into the Union as the twenty-eighth state in December 1845. It was the fifteenth slave state.

Texas would secede again in 1861 as part of the southern Confederacy. In a bit of historical irony, during the American Civil War the Texas-Mexico border was not blocked by Union forces, making Mexico the only foreign market open to the Confederacy. Texas—the rebellious region of Tejas— had only its former ruler, Mexico, for foreign trade.

While the public supported the annexation of Texas, they were not fully aware of Polk's intentions. In addition to Texas, Polk wanted to obtain all of Mexico's northern states. This would give the United States sovereign rule of territory from the Atlantic to the Pacific. In a letter to John Slidell in November 1845, Polk wrote, "I am exceedingly desirous to acquire California." This was one month *before* the United States annexed Texas.

At first, Polk tried to purchase the northern Mexican states, but the Mexican government refused to sell. Polk was adamant that the United States needed to obtain these lands as part of America's geographic expansion to the Pacific Ocean. It was America's "Manifest Destiny." Polk believed a war with Mexico the only alternative, but he had no good reason to declare war on Mexico.

Polk intentionally provoked an incident along the Mexican border that would justify a military invasion of Mexico. On April 25, 1846, sixteen American soldiers were killed, wounded, or taken prisoners by the Mexican cavalry in Mexico along the Rio Grande. It was irrelevant to Polk that the incident had occurred in Mexican territory. Polk spoke to Congress in 1846: "But now, after reiterated menaces, Mexico has passed the boundary of the United States, has invaded our territory and shed blood on American soil. She has proclaimed that hostilities have commenced, and that the two nations are now at war."

Today, this would be considered the grandest of political spin because the Americans had trespassed and crossed into Mexico. The Mexican cavalry had not crossed into the United States nor had Mexico declared war against the United States. The Mexicans had defended Mexican territory from invading American troops. Lt. Col. Ethan Allen Hitchcock, grandson of Revolutionary War hero Ethan Allen, said of the incident: "It looks as if the government sent a small force on purpose to bring on a war, so as to have a pretext for taking California and as much of this country [northern Mexico] as it chooses."[46]

Mocking the president, a Whig Congressman stated that what Polk wanted was not, "peace with Mexico, but a piece of Mexico."[47] Nonetheless, once American blood was shed it became political suicide for any member of the House of Representatives to oppose the war. On May 13, 1846, Congress declared war on Mexico. On May 30, Polk wrote in his diary, "I declared my purpose to be to acquire for the U.S. California, New Mexico, and perhaps some others of the northern provinces of Mexico whenever a peace was made." Polk got his contrived war with Mexico—Mr. Polk's War—which became known in American history as the Mexican-American War.

Mexico did not declare war until two months later in July. Mexican history books would later call the war Guerra de la Defensa—the War of Defense. President Ulysses S. Grant served in the Mexican-American War. In his memoir he wrote: "Only I had not moral courage enough to resign . . . one of the most unjust [wars] ever waged by a stronger against a weaker nation."[48]

The Mexican-American War lasted two years—from 1846 to 1848. The United States was the undisputed victor. On February 2, 1848 Mexico and the United States signed the Treaty of Guadalupe Hidalgo, which ceded 525,000 square miles of northern Mexico—over half of Mexico—to the United States in return for $15 million. Mexico also relinquished its claim to Texas. The ceded lands in northern Mexico—the Mexican Cession— would eventually encompass all, or part, of the American states of Arizona, California, Colorado, New Mexico, Nevada, Texas, Utah, and Wyoming.

In 1865 the American Civil War ended when Robert E. Lee of the southern Confederacy surrendered to Ulysses S. Grant at Appomattox Court House in Virginia. The two men did not speak of the war they were ending in which over 600,000 had died. Instead, they reminisced about the Mexican-American War in which both had served, along with Jefferson Davis and Thomas "Stonewall" Jackson.

After the Mexican-American War, about 100,000 Mexican citizens became foreigners in the United States without having moved. Hence the Mexican saying, "We didn't cross the border, the border crossed us."[49] Most former Mexican citizens initially stayed on their lands. Americans began moving in large numbers into lands of the Mexican Cession. Americans migrated to Texas for land and to California for gold.

The Treaty of Guadalupe Hidalgo had promised that Mexican citizens would retain ownership of their property and would be offered United States citizenship at a future unspecified date. However, after the treaty was signed, the U.S. Senate rejected article ten, which had guaranteed Mexicans continued ownership of their lands.

The Mexican-American War created suspicion of the United States among Latin American countries that continues even today.

Mexicans Lose Their Land

Americans began to appropriate land from Mexicans soon after Texas declared independence from Mexico in 1836. Within six years, Americans had obtained nearly 1.5 million acres of land previously owned by Mexicans. Mexicans with rancheros lost their land through intimidation, vigilantism, death threats, fraud, or confiscation by state or federal government. Sam Houston, president of Texas, remarked in 1848: "Mexicans are no better than Indians . . . I see no reason why we should not go on the same course, now, and take their land."[50]

American soldiers who had fought for Texan independence received land as payment.[51] These soldiers often took whatever lands they wanted from Mexicans, regardless of existing land grants:

> This family like other loyal [to Texas] Mexican families were driven from their homes, their treasures, their cattle and horses and their lands, by an army of reckless, war-crazy people. . . . These new people distrusted and hated the Mexicans, simply because they were Mexican, regardless of the fact they were both on the same side [against Mexico] of the fighting during the war [for Texan independence].
>
> The Americans of the Texian [sic] frontiers are, for the most part, the very scum of society—bankrupts, escaped criminals, old volunteers, who after the Treaty of Guadalupe Hidalgo, came into a country protected by nothing that could be called a judicial authority, to seek adventure and illicit gains.[52]
>
> —Abbé Emanuel Domenech, 1858

Mexican landowners left Texas in fear of losing their lives even though they had supported Texan independence. When Mexican landowners returned to Texas they found that local sheriffs had assessed exorbitant taxes on their lands. Fraudulent land claims were common against the few Mexicans who had been able to keep their ranches. Mexicans feared that land grants from the Mexican government would not be honored or that it would be too costly to defend their claims in court. Texas judges often made rulings on land ownership to their own benefit. Mexicans had no recourse but to sell their lands to Americans at a fraction of their value. Antonio Córdova was living in Arizona at the time: "All that land, the house, the well and the equipment, for $3,000! A lot of people [Mexican or Mexican American] sold their land that way. . . . Then we would end up with nothing—no land, no cattle, no money."[53]

By 1900 in Texas, most upper class Mexican families with large landholdings had been displaced. Over time, these upper-class families subdivided their land into smaller and smaller parcels through inheritance. American men married the daughters of upper-class Mexican families, thereby gaining ownership of lands previously owned by Mexicans. Hidalgo County, Texas, provides a good example. Between 1848 and 1900, all recorded land transfers in Hidalgo County were from persons with Spanish surnames to persons with non-Spanish surnames.

Some upper-class Mexican ranchers held on to their land but lacked steady income. American banks refused to provide Mexicans with credit. Mexicans could not obtain loans to pay taxes, buy additional land, build water wells, add livestock, or fence their property. The Mexican elite would sell lands and livestock when they needed income. A common saying among American ranchers at that time was "If the owner [Mexican] won't sell, his widow will."

In New Mexico, Mexicans began to lose their lands after the Mexican-American War. Mexican families in New Mexico held "community" land grants awarded to them by the Spanish monarchy before Mexico had gained independence from Spain. Each household had a small private plot with the remaining lands belonging to all the households in the grant. The common lands provided farming, hunting, grazing, and timber.

The Spanish monarchy had issued about 150 of these community land grants in New Mexico. Under Mexican law, the lands had been collectively owned and worked, but their legal status was challenged after New Mexico became American territory. The United States did not recognize "community" property. The history of the San Miguel del Vado land grant illustrates what happened to Mexican landowners in New Mexico after the Mexican-American War.

In 1794 Spain controlled New Mexico. The Spanish gave 315,000 acres in northeastern New Mexico—the San Miguel del Vado grant—to fifty-two families in "common" ownership. In 1897 the U.S. Supreme Court ruled that the vast majority of these lands, with the exception of 5,000 acres, belonged to the U.S. government.[54] This caused a domino effect throughout the Southwest as millions of acres of communal Spanish lands were transferred in ownership from former Mexican citizens to the U.S. federal government. These new federal lands were then either sold to Americans, American businesses, or kept by the government. In New Mexico alone, 13.6 million acres went from communal lands to the U.S. Forest Service. The Carson and Santa Fe National Forests in New Mexico today consist of lands obtained mostly from community land grants dating to the Spanish.

In California, anti-Mexican vigilantes forced Mexicans from their claims on gold mines soon after the end of the Mexican-American War. In 1850 the California legislature enacted the Foreign Miners License Tax, which levied a tax of $20 per month on immigrant miners. The tax was motivated by resentment from American miners against Mexicans and Chinese who were having more success mining gold. Many of the Mexican miners had been in California before American miners had arrived. The Foreign Miners License Tax had the desired effect—most Mexicans and Chinese miners had left the mines one year after the tax was imposed.

In short, Texan independence and the Mexican-American War resulted in a deliberate transfer of land ownership from Mexicans to Americans throughout the Southwest. Although it is not discussed here, similar events took place in California and Arizona. Mexicans lost their land holdings due to a combination of fraud, intimidation, coercion, taxes, a lack of access to capital, and laws intent on transferring ownership to the U.S. government. A few upper-class Mexican families, with large land holdings and political connections, kept their lands through a handful of generations.

Most Mexicans who owned land before the Mexican-American War ultimately became landless and poor. Former Mexican landowners often had no alternative but to work as a ranch hand for the person who bought their land. Later, commercial farms would replace ranching and Mexicans, both American-born citizens and immigrants, would turn to farm labor for employment.

These events replayed throughout the Southwest from the 1830s to the early 1900s. By the 1920s, families of Mexican heritage had become landless and limited to low-wage labor for employment. American settlers and businesses prospered from this forced transfer of wealth. American agribusiness has benefited the most, and has institutionalized low-wage farm labor—both legal and illegal—in the Southwest since the 1880s.

Historically, southwestern agribusiness has successfully lobbied the U.S. Congress *for* an open border policy with Mexico and *against* penalties on employers that hire illegal workers.

Addicted to Low-Wage Labor

"Addict" best describes the relationship between farmers in the Southwest and farm labor. Southwestern farmers—corporate agribusiness—have been addicted to cheap labor since the 1880s.

From 1876 to 1886, an economic boon in cattle ranching took place in Texas. Railroads had linked Texas to cities in the North and Midwest, facilitating the transportation of cattle to northern markets. The cattle baron emerged, but Mexican ranchers were excluded. Mexicans were denied credit to expand their herds. Then in the late 1880s, the boon in cattle ranching receded and the demand for cowboys to work herds began to decline. Wire fencing and railroads put an end to the need for cowboys to herd cattle from Texas to Chicago. Ranchers adjusted to decreasing profits by employing Mexican cowboys in preference to whites, as Mexicans would work for less. From the Coleman-Fulton Pasture Company in Texas: "Replacing white cowboys with Mexicans, who would undoubtedly work for less, and for reducing the work year to nine months."[55] Farming soon replaced ranching in Texas, and the desire for cheap labor shifted from year-round ranch hands working cattle to seasonal wage labor to pick crops.

The early history of farm labor in California differs from events in Texas. California's Chinese laborers, who had built the transcontinental railroad, became unemployed after completing the railroad in 1869. These Chinese laborers then moved into agriculture as the demand increased for agricultural products from California. Chinese immigrants remained the main source of farm labor in California until the 1880s.

Anti-Chinese sentiment among whites in California led to the Chinese Exclusion Act of 1882. This federal legislation halted nearly all immigration from China and denied citizenship to Chinese immigrants living in the United States. Romualdo Pacheco, a representative from California, sponsored the Chinese Exclusion Act. Pacheco had been born in Santa Barbara when California was still part of Mexico. He was a Republican and the first Hispanic to serve as a regular member of the House of Representatives. Ironically, today's anti-immigrant sentiment against Hispanics echoes the anti-Chinese sentiment in Pacheco's Chinese Exclusion Act.

The Chinese Exclusion Act drove the Chinese out of agriculture in California. Growers in California wanted Chinese labor but were unable to counter the massive anti-Chinese views prevalent in California at that time. This caused a labor shortage that growers filled with Japanese immigrants. Then in the early 1920s, anti-Japanese sentiment led to enactment of the Immigration Act of 1924 (also know as the Johnson-Reed Act), which barred all immigration from Asia. Social Darwinism, with its preference for northern Europeans, was at the core of anti-Asian sentiment. Growers shifted their main source of low-wage labor to Mexico.

The population of Mexican farm laborers had begun to increase in California during World War I. During the war, the Immigration Act of 1917 was meant to reduce immigration into the United States and required each immigrant to pay an $8 head tax and pass a literacy test. This law threatened to end the supply of low-wage Mexican labor to southwestern agribusiness. In response, southwestern growers obtained a "temporary" suspension specifically for Mexican labor. "The small farmer and laboring man wishes the Mexicans were out of the country. The big grafting man fancies them; they work cheap."[56] "It is to the interest of the wealthy to have them here, and they [the wealthy] run the government."[57] Mexicans were also recruited to work in war-related industries in the Midwest.

American businesses justified paying Mexican workers low wages by arguing that Mexican workers were mostly single men without a family to support. This was a convenient lie. Unattached Mexican men sent significant amounts of their earnings to their families in Mexico. Growers also preferred Mexican laborers because they would fade away when they were not needed, "When we want you, we'll call you; when we don't—git."[58] In the 1920s, Congress exempted Mexican laborers from immigration quotas because of the ability to deport them when they were no longer needed: "You reserve the right to deport them when you get too many? . . . Were you able to deport them when the need had passed? . . . Are you having any trouble in getting them out of the country since bringing them in?"[59]

During the Mexican Revolution (1910–1920), about 219,000 Mexicans immigrated legally to the United States. Political instability continued in Mexico throughout the 1920s, resulting in over 450,000 Mexicans entering the United States legally between 1921 and 1930.

In the 1920s Mexicans became the largest ethnic group of farm laborers in California. Mexicans, legal and illegal, found jobs in agriculture in California,

Texas, and the Midwest; mining in Arizona and New Mexico; as well on the railroads throughout the Southwest. Towards the late 1920s, Mexican laborers migrated as far as Alaska to work in fish canneries and Pennsylvania to work in steel mills. Acclaimed Hollywood actor Anthony Quinn was born in Mexico to parents who were migrant workers in the United States. Starting at age four, Quinn worked alongside his parents in the farm fields. His father fought with Pancho Villa in the Mexican Revolution. Quinn describes his family's struggle as immigrant farm workers in his autobiography *The Original Sin*.

During the 1920s, sugar beet growers in Michigan and Ohio were hiring about 10,000 Mexican laborers each year. This threatened to create a wage war for Mexican labor among American agribusiness. Growers in Texas took steps to reduce the loss of Mexican labor to the Midwest. Texas enacted the Emigrant Labor Agency Laws, which charged out-of-state labor recruiters $7,500. The law was ineffective and Texas growers adopted other countermeasures to stop the loss of Mexican labor to Midwestern states.

Men holding shotguns "supervised" Mexicans as they picked crops. During the harvesting season, Mexican laborers who refused to work would be found guilty of vagrancy and fined. They would be given the option of going to jail or paying the fine by picking crops for a local grower. Texas highway patrol officers charged Mexican car owners with bogus motor vehicle violations to keep them from leaving Texas. Trucks carrying Mexican workers to jobs outside of Texas drove at night on less-traveled roads.

Everything changed when the Great Depression struck in 1929. Unemployed whites would take any work—even as farm laborers. Mexican labor was demonized for taking jobs from Americans. Many Mexican Americans, who were American citizens, were forcibly deported. Over 450,000 Mexicans were either deported or voluntary left the United States.

"The attitude toward Mexicans changed very decidedly after 1929, and repeatedly one hears politicians, miners, and farmers who previously justified the contracting of Mexican labor at starvation wages denouncing the children or grandchildren of those immigrants and demanding that they be sent back to Mexico 'where they belong.'"[60]

In 1930 congressional reapportionment awarded three congressional representatives to Texas based on the size of the state's Mexican population.

California received one congressional representative because of the Mexican population in that state. Yet, both Texas and California kept these representatives throughout the 1930s as the Mexican population was being deported. Otherwise, the seats would have gone to Alabama, New Jersey, Rhode Island, and Wisconsin.

By 1934 approximately half of agriculture laborers in California were white, which contrasted with decades of dominance by Chinese, Japanese, and Mexicans. Many white farm laborers—known often as Okies—came from impoverished families from the dust bowl states of Oklahoma, Texas, and Arkansas. In Arizona, by 1937 whites were the largest farm labor force for the first time in the state's history.

From the earliest days, the staunchest supporter of imported Mexican labor has been agribusiness in the Southwest, which benefits economically from an open border with Mexico:

> The large growers' groups have found the law inadequate to their uses; and they have become so powerful that such charges as felonious assault, mayhem and inciting to riot, kidnapping and flogging cannot be brought against them in the controlled courts. They practice a system of terrorism that would be unusual in the Fascist nations of the world. A continuation of this approach constitutes a criminal endangering of the peace of the State.[61]
>
> —John Steinbeck

> If Mexican immigration were barred, it would mean that industry and agriculture would compete for labor, and the price of farm labor would mount. But, if agriculture is permitted to exploit its own exclusive labor sources, then no competition exists and agriculture wages can be kept at a subsistence level.[62]
>
> —Pacific Rural Press, 1927

With the onset of World War II in 1941, the decade-long hiatus on imported Mexican labor ended. In 1940 there had been over 1 million white Americans working as migrant farm workers. In 1942 the number dropped to about 60,000. Whites left the farm fields to fight in World War II or work in war-related industries. Mexican immigrants were again welcomed as farm laborers.

Los Braceros

Rosie the Riveter is an icon of American industrial might during World War II. She represents the millions of women who entered the workforce during the war years. However, the contribution to the war by "Luis the Laborer" has been forgotten. Note the highly anticipated 2007 television documentary about World War II by Ken Burns, which omitted the contributions made by Mexicans and Mexican Americans to the war.

Whites stopped working as farm laborers in the early 1940s. They enlisted in the military to fight in World War II or took jobs in war industries. Once again, Mexican immigrants were needed for farm labor. In the 1940s several million Mexicans came to the United States to work in agriculture to feed America, its troops, allies, and European civilians.

In 1942 the United States began the Bracero (Spanish for "arm") Program in a negotiated agreement with the Mexican government. It was a voluntary immigration program that supplied businesses in the United States with low-wage Mexican labor. The program established a minimum wage and set standards for housing and working conditions to protect Mexican workers, who had suffered previous exploitation from American agribusiness. The majority of braceros worked as farm laborers, but the program was not exclusive to agriculture. Braceros also maintained the railroad system in the United States during the war.

The typical bracero was male, age seventeen to twenty-two, and from a small Mexican town. He worked low-skill, entry-level jobs. The majority of braceros worked in the Southwest, but the initial agreement excluded Texas, which had a prolific history of exploiting Mexicans and Mexican Americans. Texas would later have the largest population of braceros. In 1959 about 50,000 farms nationwide relied on bracero labor.

The Bracero Program was in effect from 1942 to 1964. During this period, about 4.7 million Mexicans obtained temporary legal entry into the United States as part of the program. In contrast, during this same time period only 560,000 Mexicans were given permanent residency in the United States. This equates to eight temporary bracero workers for one permanent non-bracero Mexican immigrant. The peak year for bracero workers was 1959 when about 450,000 Mexican farm workers obtained temporary legal entry through the Bracero Program. Between 2000 and 2009, about 220,000 illegal Mexican immigrants entered the United States annually.[63]

The demand for Mexican labor was so great that illegal Mexican immigrants in the United States were given immediate legal status if they went to work in agriculture. Illegal immigration soared as undocumented Mexicans entered the United States looking to be caught and made legal braceros. In Texas in 1947, 55,000 Mexican workers became instantly legal when their undocumented status became known. Events became more surreal in the early 1950s. When discovered, illegal Mexicans were told to step across the border into Mexico and return directly to be hired as a legal bracero.

The Bracero Program was intended to overcome a temporary labor shortage during World War II, but the program continued until 1964. American agribusiness repeatedly lobbied Congress to continue the program after the war ended. Southwestern agribusiness claimed a permanent labor shortage existed, even though farm mechanization after World War II decreased the demand for seasonal farm labor. Manuel Peña Jr., a migrant worker, testified before Congress in 1962, saying, "there has never been a genuine shortage of U.S.-born farm workers, except during World War II."[64]

Opponents of the Bracero Program argued that white Americans would work as farm laborers with a higher minimum wage and better working conditions. However, growers set the hourly wage at a level so low that white Americans would not take farm jobs. Growers then argued that low wage braceros were the only alternative because Americans were not willing to work as farm laborers.

Braceros generated an economic windfall for states where they worked. Businesses reaped profits from low-wage Mexican laborers, both legal and illegal. Through the Bracero Program, the U.S. government supplied American businesses with nonunion workers earning low wages.

> Because of the economic interests that are involved in the wet-
> back [illegal Mexican worker] problem, no real, sincere effort

> has been made to solve it. . . . As long as it is possible to hire
> the wetbacks at ten cents an hour, they will be coming across
> the border until kingdom come. . . . Somebody is making a
> filthy dollar out of it.[65]
>
> —Democratic Sen. Hubert Humphrey, 1952

Financial investors like banks, which provided capital to these businesses, also profited.

The Mexican government supported the Bracero Program to ensure reasonable pay and adequate working conditions for Mexican citizens employed on American farms. However, many American growers disliked the Bracero Program and sidestepped the program. Growers hired undocumented Mexicans, paying them below the bracero minimum wage of thirty cents per hour, and did not provide basic housing facilities such as potable water or bathrooms. These illegal Mexican laborers worked in deplorable conditions, earned less than braceros, and thus undermined the Bracero Program. In 1952 the Mexican government threatened to end the program if Congress did not make it illegal to hire undocumented Mexicans. Congress responded by enacting the Texas Proviso.

The Texas Proviso stipulated that employers would be penalized for hiring undocumented workers— but only if the employer knew the person was an illegal immigrant. The law did not require workers—immigrants— to provide documentation of their residency status. Congress made it legal to hire illegals. Thereafter, undocumented laborers started moving from agriculture into industrial jobs in greater numbers. In 1954, two years after passage of the Texas Proviso, the INS apprehended over four thousand undocumented workers in Los Angeles, California. Over 60 percent were employed in industrial jobs, and only 24 percent were in agriculture. The Texas Proviso remained the status quo legislation until the Immigration Reform and Control Act was passed in 1986.

Illegal immigration increased as American employers routinely hired undocumented Mexicans, bypassing the minimum standards established by the Bracero Program. Undocumented workers were soon hired by electric utility companies, railroads, meatpackers, and canneries.

The Bracero Program ended for various reasons on both sides of the border. American unions and Mexican Americans came to see the program as suppressing American wages. Civic and church groups witnessed mistreatment of braceros and called for the program to end. Americans turned against the program in the early 1960s after CBS aired the television documentary *Harvest of Shame*, which exposed the poverty of migrant farm workers.

The Mexican government withdrew support because American businesses were exploiting bracero workers by ignoring contracted agreements on working conditions and minimum wage. An informational bulletin produced by the INS in 1955 read: "A practice exists in the Rio Grande Valley whereby employers require workers to accept less pay than the minimum wage [thirty cents per hour] in their contracts in order to retain their jobs."[66] In 1962 the federal Department of Labor raised the minimum wage for braceros to seventy cents per hour. To maintain low wages, growers shifted to Mexican laborers not participating in the Bracero Program.

Through congressional apportionment, the population of Mexican workers, both legal and illegal, generated extra congressional representation for the Southwest during the bracero years. Southwestern states used this added representation to hamper efforts by the federal government to control illegal immigration. Note the parallel to congressional politics during America's years of slavery. Southern plantation owners used the slave population to increase their representation in Congress via the Three-Fifths clause. The South used this added representation to forestall the abolition of slavery.

During the years of the Bracero Program, Congress cut funding to the Border Patrol and took a laissez-faire approach towards illegal immigration from Mexico. Such lax immigration enforcement was encouraged by southwestern agribusiness. Unlike prior decades, the decennial census in 1950 and 1960 did not include a separate subtotal of Mexican residents. Was this done intentionally to mask the impact of braceros on congressional apportionment?

After 1964, the Texas Proviso enabled American businesses to expand their use of low-wage Mexican labor without being penalized. Between 1965 and 1970 after the Bracero Program ended, the INS reported an increase of 600 percent in the number of of illegal Mexican males apprehended while working in agriculture. In the early 1960s the INS reported yearly apprehensions of illegal immigrants at fewer than 100,000. In 1966, the first year without braceros, annual apprehensions increased to nearly 140,000. By 1972 it was about a half-million per year, and by 1985 it had risen to about 1.5 million annually.[67]

The Bracero Program officially ended in 1964, and the last braceros worked into 1965. The program was intended to stem the flow of undocumented workers from Mexico, but when it ended it had the opposite effect. "The Bracero Program appears to have been simultaneously a major cause of as well as a significant cure for the illegal alien problem."[68]

The Bracero Program reestablished and deepened the economic ties between American businesses and Mexican labor that began during World War I. When the program ended the hiring networks that linked American employers to Mexican labor remained. A lack of enforcement by the Border Patrol and the INS allowed immigration of undocumented Mexicans to continue in large numbers after the Bracero Program ended. Because of the Texas Proviso, former braceros were rehired to do the same work as before without regard for their legal status, and for less pay. Wages and working conditions for Mexican workers deteriorated because the minimum standards established by the Bracero Program no longer existed.

Why Is This Important? Business Profits Drive Illegal Immigration
Until the 1940s Mexicans and Americans crossed the U.S.-Mexico border without fanfare or official documents. The border is roughly two thousand miles long and includes four American states and six Mexican states. Over 80 million people live in these ten states. Fourteen cities straddle both sides of the border including El Paso, in Texas, and Ciudad Juárez, in the Mexican state of Chihuahua. The border is a political boundary that has arbitrarily split extended families of aunts, cousins, and grandparents since the Mexican-American War. The regions on either side of the border have a common culture superimposed on two distinct nations.

The prevalence of undocumented Mexican workers in the United States is mistakenly attributed to the Bracero Program, which ended in 1964. In hindsight, the relationship between Mexican immigrants and American businesses originated much earlier—in the 1870s. Then in the early 1900s, southwestern agribusiness started to lobby Congress for unrestricted immigration with Mexico and minimal government oversight of their employment practices. The underlying causes of illegal immigration from Mexico remain unchanged and the prevalence of illegal workers has expanded beyond agriculture and beyond the Southwest.

As the number of acres of farmland and the prevalence of agribusiness increased in the Southwest, so too did the demand for low-wage labor from Mexico. Specifics varied between and within states, but the common denominator was the increasing dominance of corporate farms. Often, investors from other parts of the country owned the corporate farms. Except during the decade of the Great Depression, whites would not work for the low wages set by growers, and the availability of labor from Mexico kept wages low. Mexican immigrants crossed the border in increasing numbers as labor demands increased.

The tenor of American laws on immigrant labor has not changed over the past one hundred years. In 1911 the Dillingham Immigration Commission reported that Mexican labor was disposable: "While they [Mexican laborers] are not easily assimilated, this is of no very great importance as long as most of them return to their native land. In the case of the Mexican, he is less desirable as a citizen than as a laborer."[69] A 1952 editorial in the *New York Times* pointed to Texas and the Southwest for encouraging the flow of undocumented Mexican labor into the United States: "It is remarkable how some of the same Senators and Representatives who are all for enacting the most rigid barriers against immigration from Southern Europe suffer from a sudden blindness when it comes to protecting the southern border of the United States. This peculiar weakness is most noticeable among members from Texas and the Southwest, where the wetbacks happen to be primarily employed."[70]

America has thrived from succeeding waves of displaced immigrants coming to the United States with hopes of working their way to success. More immigrants live in the United States now than at any other time in the country's history. However, immigrants comprised a larger percentage of the American population in the early 1900s due to the fact that the population of native-born Americans is also larger now.

America built its economic might with generations of low-wage immigrant labor. The immigrant has enabled American businesses to reduce costs. In return, immigrants had the opportunity to better their lives through hard work. Citizenship also gave them a stake in the country's future. Today it is different. As before, American businesses continue to benefit from low-wage immigrant labor, but many of today's immigrants are illegally employed and stuck in low-wage jobs. Have business interests manipulated Congress in order to have a permanent pool of disposable low-wage labor? Political science professor Wayne Cornelius writes, "Much of the illegality in low-skilled employment today is 'manufactured' illegality: a direct function of unrealistically low quotas for low-skilled foreign workers, quotas that are set so low for political rather than market-based reasons."[71] Do employers prefer the status quo in which they can hire illegal workers at wages lower than allowed by law and have them work longer hours?

If low-cost, unskilled immigrant labor has been good for American businesses, it does not mean that a permanent underclass of illegal workers is good for the society. The typical story of most American families, excluding African Americans and Native Americans, has been of increasing upward mobility with each succeeding generation. However, the typical immigrant story is changing. Undocumented immigrants are unable to improve their status merely by hard work because their illegal status keeps them underpaid and limits the types of jobs available to them. While business profits may thrive in these circumstances, the cost of state and federal programs for low-income households goes up.

Undocumented workers are "frequently victimized by employers who know of their vulnerability" and force them to work long hours, deny them rest and meal breaks, and constantly threaten them with deportation. Businesses argue that they are not forcing unauthorized immigrants to take jobs and that illegal workers know the risks.[72] Such attitudes can broaden into employers denying basic worker rights to legal residents. When illegal workers are abused, does it encourage disdain for all workers among business owners and managers? Seeing that they can exploit vulnerable undocumented workers, will business owners seek to exploit the poor, the elderly, the sick, or the young? Will persons who become accustomed to taking advantage of illegal workers develop a feeling of entitlement?

Consider the mindset of businesses witnessed by "food libel laws." These state laws limit public dissent on practices by agribusiness, meatpackers, and other producers of perishable foods. Thirteen states have food libel laws, and Colorado considers it a criminal offense.[73] In 1996, cattle ranchers in

Texas sued Oprah Winfrey over comments made on her television show. The Texas Beef Group believed Oprah unfairly portrayed American beef as unsafe. Winfrey was exonerated after two lawsuits by the Texas Beef Group. Opponents of these laws argue that they infringe on the first amendment, which guarantees free speech.

What type of politician will such business owners support using the excess profits derived from underpaid illegal workers? Tom Tancredo, former congressional representative from Colorado, makes clear how the political parties benefit from illegal immigration: "The Democratic Party looks at massive immigration, legal and illegal, as a source of voters. The Republican Party looks at massive immigration, legal and illegal, as a source of cheap labor, satisfying a very important constituency."[74]

For Republicans, the benefit of illegal immigration is tangible and immediate because Republicans follow the money. The Republican Party has no incentive to halt illegal immigration because its contributors profit from it. President George W. Bush proposed a guest worker program in May 2006, which was vague and not supported by Congress or the public.[75] Mark Krikorian, executive director of the Center for Immigration Studies, stated that Bush had no real intent to address immigration reform: "The administration hasn't given any detail. . . . They're not interested in passing it. . . . They're just interested in talking about it. . . . They don't want to offend this side or the other side, so they punt."[76]

In contrast, the benefit to Democrats in the form of additional voters is delayed because illegal immigrants cannot vote. Before Democrats can reap additional votes, the party has to wait either for undocumented aliens to obtain citizenship, which is unlikely, or for their American-born children to reach voting age. In April 2010 President Obama and Senate Majority Leader Harry Reid, a Democrat from Nevada, sought to undertake comprehensive immigration reform. However, Republicans objected as Senate Minority Leader Mitch McConnell explained, "I just don't think this is the right time to take up this issue . . . our time would be better spent at the federal level on other issues."[77] Sen. Lindsey Graham, a Republican from South Carolina, also opposed undertaking immigration reform. Graham withdrew from climate change legislation he had been collaborating on with Democrats in protest of Democrats' efforts to address immigration reform.

Building fences and increased policing along the Mexican border have not eliminated illegal immigration, and it will not end as long as Mexico has an ample supply of unemployed citizens and the United States has businesses willing, and allowed, to employ them. "[I]t is rarely doubted that 'illegal aliens,' . . . are an economic boon to those businesses that employ them directly or subcontract with other firms that do."[78]

Between 1993 and 2004, the federal government increased spending on border control five-fold, and tripled the number of border agents.[79] It did not stop the flow of illegal aliens from Mexico.

In 2006 the federal government fined Golden State Fence Company $5 million for hiring illegal workers, which numbered as many as 250. Some of the company's projects included the border fence in San Diego, California, separating the United States and Mexico. Apparently, illegal workers working for Golden State Fence Company built portions of the border fence meant to deter illegal immigration.[80]

Employing illegal workers has corrosive consequences on American society. It creates a permanent underclass that generates excess business profits. Businesses funnel these profits to politicians to maintain the status quo. To end this parasitic relationship requires that businesses stop employing illegal workers. Employers will not voluntarily stop hiring illegal workers because there is too much profit in underpaying workers. The alternative is to have an ample foreign worker program that extends worker protection and minimum wage standards to all workers. In 2006 when he was a senator in Illinois, President Barack Obama expressed support for a guest worker program: "We must . . . replace the flow of undocumented immigrants coming to work here with a new flow of guest workers."[81]

In the wake of the Legal Arizona Workers Act, lawmakers in Arizona began working towards a state-run Arizona Temporary Worker Program to allow employers to hire immigrants legally as temporary workers. Similarly, the federal government should legitimize the economic ties that have existed between American businesses and Mexican labor for over one hundred years. Michael Earls and Jim Kessler said it well: "A person was more likely to be eaten by an alligator than to be prosecuted for hiring an illegal alien."[82]

4

HOW THE UNITED STATES
DISENFRANCHISES
ITS CITIZENS

The U.S. Department of Justice should immediately initiate the litigation process against Florida state officials whose list maintenance activities during the 2000 presidential election discriminated against people of color in violation of federal law or resulted in the denial of people of color to have equal access to the political process.[1]

—Recommendation 1.8 from *Voting Irregularities in Florida During the 2000 Presidential Election,* United States Commission on Civil Rights

Disenfranchisement Dejá Vu in Florida

Most Americans believe that George W. Bush won the presidential election in 2000 because Bush received 537 more popular votes than Al Gore in Florida. In 2001 the U.S. Commission on Civil Rights debunked this commonly held belief during an investigation on voting irregularities in Florida. The Commission reported, "despite the closeness of the election, it was widespread voter disenfranchisement, not the dead-heat contest, that was the extraordinary feature in the Florida election. The disenfranchisement was not isolated or episodic. And state officials failed to fulfill their duties in a manner that would prevent this disenfranchisement.[2]

African Americans were the most affected and the most likely to be denied their voting rights. In Miami-Dade County, over 65 percent of names purged from voter lists were African Americans, although African Americans accounted for only 20 percent of the county's population.[3] Nationwide, African Americans overwhelmingly voted for Al Gore in the 2000 presidential election. Al Gore would likely have won Florida, and become president, if not for widespread voter disenfranchisement in Florida.

The Commission could not determine the exact number of disenfranchised persons. After the election, the attorney general of Florida received 3,600 allegations of voting irregularities. These came from both Democrats and Republicans, and various minority groups including African Americans, Asians, and Hispanics.

Minority and low-income areas had higher rates of spoiled ballots. These are unclear or disqualified votes, which are not counted. Spoilage rates in areas with large percentages of African American voters were above the statewide average. However, spoilage rates were below the statewide average where voters were predominately white. On Election Day in Gadsden County, which is a rural, low-income, and predominately African American county, twelve of every one hundred votes (12 percent) were disqualified. In contrast, in Leon County, which is adjacent to Gadsden County and is affluent, less than two votes for every one thousand ballots cast were disqualified. At precinct 255 in Miami-Dade County, which is over 50 percent Hispanic, punch card machines failed and thirteen of every one hundred votes (13 percent) were missed.[4] Statewide, about 90,000 votes from punch card machines were disqualified. Bush won in Florida by 537 votes—less than 1 percent of the disqualified punch card ballots.

Throughout Florida, polling locations closed at 7:00 p.m. even though people were still in line to vote. Voting at the water works department in Boynton Beach stopped early, at 6:15 p.m., when the gates to the facility closed. The gates were on an automatic timer that had not been reset for Election Day. Precincts that were required to have bilingual ballots and language assistance failed to comply as mandated by the Voting Rights Act. A Florida elections official testified that some polling locations were physically inaccessible to voters with disabilities, which violated the Voter Accessibility for the Elderly and Handicapped Act. There were instances in which the location of precincts changed without proper public notification.

The Commission reported that Floridians were not on voter lists on Election Day after having completed voter registration forms at the Department of Highway Safety and Motor Vehicles or through a social service agency. Their voter registration had not been transmitted to the corresponding supervisor of elections office. Poll workers corroborated accounts of disenfranchisement of voters who were properly registered. Marilyn Nelson, a poll worker in Miami-Dade County for fifteen years, told the Commission: "By far this was the worst election I have ever experienced. After that election I decided I didn't want to work as a clerk anymore."[5]

African Americans were more likely to have their names wrongly purged from voter lists. Barbara Phoele, a poll worker in Broward County, testified to the Commission that she observed mostly African Americans and Hispanics not allowed to vote, and that officials at her precinct did little to correct the situation.[6] Donnise DeSouza, who is African American, had been a registered voter in Miami-Dade County since 1982.[7] On Election Day she was not allowed to vote because the poll worker said her name was not on the list of registered voters. After the election, the elections office discovered that her name had been on the list of registered voters. Donnise DeSouza did not vote on Election Day because a poll worker made a mistake that should have been resolved at the precinct.

Heavily Democratic Palm Beach County cast an inexplicably high number of votes for presidential candidate Patrick J. Buchanan—a conservative. This resulted from a poorly designed "butterfly" ballot that confused voters. Rabbi Richard Yellin stated, "Arrows did not line up with the holes."[8] Poll workers gave Harold Cousminer, who is visually impaired, a magnifying glass to use with the butterfly ballot, but it was of little use.[9] His wife had to vote for him because the magnifying glass did not work with the butterfly ballot. In addition to mistaken entries, over 19,000 butterfly ballots were disqualified because confused voters had punched the ballot for two presidential candidates. In Duval County, another poorly designed ballot resulted in the disqualification of 21,796 votes. Bush won by 537 votes, which equals 1 percent of the poorly designed ballots that were disqualified.

Florida is one of eight states that bars former felons from voting. Some states allow disenfranchised former felons to regain their voting rights after completing their sentences, but not Florida. Statistics show that African American males are particularly affected. In Florida, about one in three disenfranchised former felons are African American men.[10] Furthermore, one-third of disenfranchised former felons in the United States live in Florida. This is not necessarily because Florida has a high crime rate, but because Florida leads the nation in pursuing the disenfranchisement of former felons. Florida began disenfranchising felons in 1868.[11] The states of Florida, Kentucky, Virginia, and the country of Armenia are the only democratic governments that ban former felons from voting for life.[12] Nationwide, about one in ten African American males are disenfranchised former felons. This mutes the effectiveness of the African American vote.

What happened to Wallace McDonald illustrates the adverse consequences resulting from Florida's single-mindedness in identifying former felons. Wallace McDonald was convicted of a misdemeanor for falling asleep on a public bench in Tampa in 1959. Misdemeanors, such as DUI or underage drinking, usually incur a fine and do not result in a loss of voting rights. McDonald had been voting regularly since the 1950s but was mistakenly included in the felon exclusion list because of the misdemeanor in 1959. McDonald was denied the right to vote in the presidential election of 2000 because he had fallen asleep on a public bench in Tampa forty-one years earlier.

Willie D. Whiting Jr. was on the felon exclusion list and was told by a poll worker on Election Day that he could not vote. Whiting insisted this was a mistake and contacted the supervisor of elections of Leon County. He voted after election officials determined he had been mistaken for Willie J. Whiting.

Disenfranchising former felons mutes minority voting because minorities are over represented in America's prisons. This practice exacerbates the disenfranchisement of minorities who have not committed felonies because minorities are more likely to be included on felon exclusion lists by mistake. David Leahy, Miami-Dade County supervisor of elections told the Commission, "we're removing a lot of people from the rolls when I know for a fact based on the appeal forms that I get back that this is not a truly accurate list. It's drawn off the Florida Department of Law's database and that database was never intended for this purpose, but it's being used for this purpose."[13]

The felon exclusion list also included Florida residents who had felony convictions outside Florida but had their voting rights restored. For the November 2000 election, Florida had a felon exclusion list that made 57,746 Floridians ineligible to vote. About half the names on Florida's felon exclusion list mistakenly identified persons who did *not* have a Florida felony conviction. The Commission reported: "The Florida legislature's decision to privatize its list maintenance procedures without establishing effective clear guidance for these private efforts from the highest levels, coupled with the absence of uniform and reliable verification procedures, resulted in countless eligible voters being deprived of their right to vote."[14] Bush's 537 votes represent about 2 percent of the number of Floridians mistakenly included on the felon exclusion list.

In 2000 George W. Bush won the presidential election after beating Al Gore in Florida by 537 votes. Yet, over one hundred thousand Floridians—mostly minorities and African Americans—were denied their right to vote on Election Day. African Americans nicknamed Florida's then-governor Jeb Bush as "Jeb Crow," an allusion to Jim Crow laws that disenfranchised African Americans in the South for nearly a century after the Civil War.[15] Former president Jimmy Carter wrote of Jeb Bush in a *Washington Post* Op-Ed in 2004, "Florida's governor, Jeb Bush, naturally a strong supporter of his brother [President George W. Bush], has taken no steps to correct these departures from principles of fair and equal treatment or to prevent them in the future."[16]

The presidential election of 2000 was not typical, but it does reflect America's history of using extralegal practices to hinder voter participation. A faction among the framers of the Constitution feared the public, and wanted to minimize the political power of everyday Americans. This is reflected in the Constitution, which lacks an inherent incentive to encourage voter participation.

Renewal of the Voting Rights Act
In 2006 Congress renewed the Voting Rights Act for another twenty-five years. Before the Voting Rights Act of 1965, most states in the South and

Southwest used restrictive criteria to minimize voter participation among African Americans, Hispanics, and poor whites. Collectively, these hindrances to voting are known as Jim Crow laws. They included literacy tests, poll taxes, restrictive residency standards, inconvenient access to voter registration, and extralegal practices. African Americans were further intimidated into not voting by threats to employment, physical intimidation, cross burnings, and lynching. At the signing of the Voting Rights Act, President Lyndon B. Johnson called the act "one of the most monumental laws in the entire history of American freedom."[17] The Voting Rights Act returned voting rights to poor whites, African Americans, Hispanics, Asian Americans, Native Americans, and Native Alaskans.

Elections officials interpreted Jim Crow laws subjectively. In Louisiana, an African American was denied the right to vote when he wrote the following interpretation of the Constitution: "One may assemble or belong to any group, club or organization he chooses as long as it is within the law."[18] Yet the written entry "FRDUM FOOF SPETGH" from a white person was accepted. Poll taxes kept the poor, both whites and minorities, from voting. A $2 poll tax in 1880 would cost $296 today.[19] In Mississippi, the poll tax could be paid only during the Christmas season, forcing the poor to pick between voting or buying Christmas gifts.[20]

The Voting Rights Act enabled the federal Justice Department to eliminate Jim Crow laws and other barriers to voting in federal, state, and local elections. Initially in 1965, the Voting Rights Act covered all, or portions of, Alabama, Alaska, Arizona, Georgia, Hawaii, Idaho, Louisiana, Mississippi, North Carolina, South Carolina, and Virginia. The federal government focused on these states as the most egregious at disenfranchising minorities. Voter suppression was not limited to blacks and Hispanics in the South and Southwest. Hispanics were also disenfranchised in the northern states of Connecticut and Massachusetts where older immigrant citizens, with limited English skills, were denied help with voting instructions. The Voting Rights Act eliminated an English language competency test that the state of New York had required of Spanish-speaking Puerto Ricans, who are considered American citizens.[21] In 1970 Congress expanded the Voting Rights Act to include all, or portions of, California, Connecticut, Maine, Massachusetts, New Hampshire, New York, and Wyoming. Then in 1975, Florida, Michigan,

South Dakota, and Texas were added to counter vote suppression among Hispanics and Native Americans. The Voting Rights Act broadened in scope to require municipalities, with a significant population of non-English speakers, to provide foreign language help during the voting process.

The Voting Rights Act has been extremely effective at enfranchising minorities. Before 1965 less than one in ten African Americans in Mississippi registered to vote.[22] By 1968 the number had grown to six in ten. In Alabama, voter registration among African Americans grew from 20 percent to 50 percent between 1965 and 1968.[23] Nationwide, more African Americans registered to vote in the two years following enactment of the Voting Rights Act than had been registered in the prior one hundred years.[24] In 1965 there were only seventy-two African American elected officials in the South. By 1993 the number had grown to nearly 5,000. The number of Hispanic elected officials nearly tripled between 1973 and 1991.[25]

The Obama campaign in 2008 raised voter registration among minorities.[26] In Georgia voter registration among eligible African Americans rose from 68 percent in 2000 to 73 percent in 2008.[27] In comparison, a lower 71 percent of eligible white Georgians were registered in 2008. In Mississippi in 2008, 82 percent of eligible African Americans registered to vote, which was higher than the rate of 75 percent for eligible whites. Nationwide, voter registration among Hispanics rose from 57 percent in 2000 to 59 percent in 2008. Among Asians, voter registration rose from 52 percent in 2000 to 55 percent in 2008.

Even though the Obama campaign increased participation among minorities, disparities remain in the number of minorities elected to state and local positions. Twelve of the top fifteen states with the largest gap in minority elected officials, in statewide offices, are currently covered under the Voting Rights Act.[28] Elected officials in parts of the United States continue efforts to undo the enfranchisement successes of the Voting Rights Act.

In 1998 the federal Department of Justice sued the City of Lawrence, Massachusetts, for violating the Voting Rights Act. The majority of residents in Lawrence were Hispanic, however, there was only one Hispanic on the nine-member city council. The seven-member school board, comprised of at-large members, had only one Hispanic.[29] In at-large elections, several representatives are elected for a single geographic area, and voters cast ballots for multiple candidates. Typically, in at-large elections the majority voting-bloc controls who gets elected to all positions. At-large voting districts are a means of nullifying groups of voters with disparate interests. The City of Lawrence addressed the claims of the lawsuit from the Department of Justice. Voter registration among Hispanics increased and the number of Hispanics on the city council quadrupled to four.[30] The community elected a second Hispanic to the school board.

Voting provides citizens with ownership of their political system and a sense of responsibility for their society. Among Hispanics, language assistance has increased both political participation and the sense of ownership in the future of their communities. In 1992 Republican Congressman Hamilton Fish Jr. made clear the importance of involving naturalized immigrants in the country's political process: "It seems evident to me that by enabling language minority citizens to vote in an effective and informed manner, we are giving them a stake in our society, and this assistance provides true access to government that I trust will lead to more, not less integration and inclusion of these citizens in our mainstream."[31]

In the short term, foreign language assistance helps mostly older immigrants; however, their American-born children and grandchildren will exhibit the long-term effects. When naturalized immigrants participate in the political system by voting, they pass on to their offspring the importance of civic involvement. Isabel Melendez, a Hispanic grandmother in Lawrence, sees the effect on Hispanic children: "This week, I saw two young people talking, and I heard one say, 'One day, I'm going to be mayor.'"[32] Most American-born Hispanics speak English fluently, and one in three will marry a non-Hispanic. The civic impact of providing foreign language help to older immigrant voters will be felt by future generations of Americans from every ethnic group.

In 1999 the Board of Supervisors of Dinwiddie County, Virginia, wanted to move a polling precinct from a predominately African American area to an area of predominately white residents. Dinwiddie County is covered under the Voting Rights Act and requires approval from the federal Justice Department before changing the location of a voting precinct. The Justice Department denied the request, which Dinwiddie County did not challenge.

In Waller County, Texas, in 2003, the district attorney threatened to charge students at Prairie View A&M University with a felony if they voted.

This violated a 1978 federal court ruling, which mandated registering Prairie View students as county residents. Prairie View A&M is a historically black college. The Texas attorney general ruled in favor of the students saying, "It [the right to vote] is the bedrock of democracy and a right that preserves all other basic civil and political rights, and it must be and will be vigorously defended."[33]

The Waller County Board of Commissioners also tried to reduce the number of hours available for early voting at the precinct closest to Prairie View. This was an attempt to suppress voting in a March 9 primary election, which had two Prairie View students on the ballot. Prairie View would be closed on March 9 for spring break. Waller County is covered under the Voting Rights Act and failed to seek approval for the change in voting hours. The Lawyers' Committee for Civil Rights, NAACP, and American Civil Liberties Union joined in lawsuits against the Waller County district attorney and Board of Commissioners. The Prairie View students prevailed. The district attorney apologized for his threat to arrest students who voted, and the Board of Commissioners restored the original voting hours at the Prairie View precinct. The district attorney later resigned, and one Prairie View student won in the primary election.

In Baltimore in 2003 anonymous flyers appeared in African American neighborhoods. They stated—incorrectly—that anyone with unpaid parking tickets or unpaid rent would not be able to vote.[34] Similarly, in an African American neighborhood in Milwaukee in 2004, anonymous flyers wrongly warned felons and their relatives that they could not vote.[35] In Cuyahoga County, Ohio, in 2004, 31 percent of African Americans were asked for identification before being allowed to vote. In contrast only 18 percent of non-blacks were required to present identification before voting.

Vote suppression also affects whites. In predominately white New Hampshire on Election Day in 2002, consultants hired by the Republican Party jammed the phone lines of the Democratic Party office.[36] The intent was to disrupt the Democrats' efforts to get out the vote. Four participants in the scheme were sentenced to jail time. Republican John E. Sununu won election to the federal Senate by a margin of only 19,751 votes, which was less than 5 percent of votes cast. Sununu served only one term in the Senate. In 2008, Democrat Jeanne Shaheen, who had lost to Sununu in 2002, defeated him.

The Voting Rights Act also protects white voters (*United States v. Ike Brown and Noxubee County*).[37] When the Voting Rights Act was enacted in 1965, all elected officials in Noxubee County, Mississippi, were white—even though 70 percent of the population was African American. Today, African Americans are still 70 percent of the population but hold 93 percent of elected offices. In 2007 the U.S. federal court ruled in favor of the white population, which claimed discrimination by African American elected officials. The court imposed remedial actions on Noxubee County to increase the number of elected white officials. This is the first case in which the Voting Rights Act was used to protect a minority white population.

In Atkinson County, Georgia, in 2004 the Board of Registrars sent letters to about 80 percent of the county's Hispanic residents challenging their right to vote. [38] The challenge was illegal and targeted solely residents with a Hispanic surname. Also in 2004, a similar event occurred in Long County, Georgia, when election officials challenged the citizenship of Hispanic residents. Election officials had no evidence that Hispanic residents were not citizens before challenging their right to vote (*United States v. Long County, Georgia*).[39]

In 2009 a federal court ruled against at-large elections for commissioners in Lake Park, Florida (*United States v. Town of Lake Park, Florida*).[40] African Americans account for about 40 percent of the town's voting age population; however, no African American had been elected as a town commissioner since Lake Park was founded in 1923. In 2008 Salem County and the Borough of Penns Grove, New Jersey, settled a complaint by the Justice Department, which claimed violations of the Voting Rights Act targeted at Hispanics (*United States v. Salem County and the Borough of Penns Grove, New Jersey, et al*).[41] In 2007 a federal court ruled that the City of Walnut, California, did not provide enough language assistance to Chinese and Korean voters with limited English proficiency (*United States v. City of Walnut, California*).[42] Between 2001 and 2007 the U.S. Justice Department filed fifty-six lawsuits to protect the right to vote of minorities, the disabled, illiterate persons, and whites.

In Texas in 2003 Republicans manipulated redistricting to increase their control of congressional seats from fifteen to twenty-one. The Voting Rights Act limited their ability to manipulate district lines to minimize the influence of minority voters. If not for the Voting Rights Act, Texas Republicans would have further increased their congressional representation artificially.[43]

The United States has the lowest voter participation rate of any industrialized country. About 70 percent of eligible Americans register to vote; however, in Mexico over 90 percent of eligible Mexicans register.[44] Low voter participation in the United States has its basis in the cultural origins of the country, including slavery. The framers of the Constitution left it to the states to determine who could or could not vote. Before the Civil War, voter eligibility was limited mostly to white male property owners who were at least twenty-one.[45] John Adams, the second U.S. president, believed voting should be limited to property owning males: "very few Men, who have no Property, have any Judgment of their own. They talk and vote as they are directed by Some Man of Property, who has attached their Minds to his Interest."[46] Nearly one-third of constitutional amendments added after the Bill of Rights in 1791 focus on granting voting rights.[47] Even today, the Constitution still lacks a discrete right to vote.

Renewal of the Voting Rights Act in 2006 extends to all Americans a fundamental right that had been excluded by the framers of the Constitution.

The Electoral College Fosters Fraud

"We the People" do not really elect the president—the Electoral College does. Who are they? They are 538 select persons—electors—collectively referred to as the Electoral College. Why did the framers create the Electoral College? If you ask three people, you are likely to get at least three different answers, and possibly blank stares.

Political parties, usually either Democratic or Republican, select their electors before a presidential election. On Election Day, citizens cast their vote for the elector who represents their preferred presidential candidate. Typically, the presidential candidate who wins the most popular votes also wins the most votes from electors, and becomes president—but not always.

In 1991 David Abbott and James Levine predicted in *Wrong Winner: The Coming Debacle in the Electoral College* that the winner of the 1996 presidential election would lose the popular vote but win the most votes in the Electoral College: "In the not very distant future the candidate who loses at the polls will become president of the United States. He or she will be a 'wrong winner,' the choice of the official electoral college but the runner-up in the popular vote."[48] Amazingly, Abbott and Levine were off by only one presidential election. In 2000 George W. Bush lost the popular vote to Al Gore. However, Bush became president because he won the most votes in the Electoral College. Bush was a wrong winner.

When the Constitution was written in 1787, it was widely accepted that George Washington would be the first president of the United States. However, the process for electing a president was undecided, and there were practical issues that needed consideration. We need to appreciate the day-to-day realities of life when the Constitution was written and the Electoral College established. The largest American cities were on the Atlantic coast. These port cities stretched from Charleston, South Carolina, to Boston, Massachusetts. Inland was wilderness and farms, and inland travel was along rivers and lakes. Overland travel was slow and tedious, and limited to a few sluggish dirt roads. Few bridges had been built.

Consider that George Washington and his troops crossed the Delaware River in boats on Christmas Day, 1776, to attack the Hessian garrison at Trenton, New Jersey. There was not a bridge. The crossing was dangerous, as the river was choked with ice, and floating ice could damage the boats. Washington and his troops would make this crossing several times that winter in rain, sleet, and snow.

In 1787 communication was difficult and hampered by a population with a high rate of illiteracy. Political parties did not exist and candidates did not campaign for themselves. In New England, many white males could read and write. In contrast, education was uncommon in other states stretching from New York to Georgia. High illiteracy made newspapers—broadsides—of little use outside New England and the major port cities. A faction of the framers feared there were not enough educated Americans to seat a well-informed Congress.

The Constitutional Convention split into two factions on the method of electing a president. A faction of the framers wanted the president elected by Congress because they feared giving too much political power to the public. In 1787 only two of the thirteen states provided for the election of governors by popular vote. In most states, the legislature picked the governor. In contrast, others among the framers thought election by Congress would result in the executive branch of government—the presidency—being controlled by Congress.

Alexander Hamilton sided with those who distrusted the public, and questioned the ability of voters to discern between candidates. Hamilton argued against electing the president by popular vote: "Your people, sir, are a great beast!"[49] Elbridge Gerry, a delegate from Massachusetts, expressed a similar view: "In Massachusetts it had been fully confirmed by experience that they [the people] are daily misled into the most baneful measures and opinions by the false reports circulated by designing men, and which no one on the spot can refute."[50]

Delegates from small population states, such as Charles Pinckney of South Carolina and Roger Sherman of Connecticut, also preferred that Congress elect the president. Otherwise, small population states feared presidential candidates from the most populous states would have an advantage: "The latter [people] will never be sufficiently informed of characters. . . . They will generally vote for some man in their own State, and the largest State will have the best chance for the appointment [presidency]."[51]

Before the Civil War, eligible voters included mostly white male property owners who were at least twenty-one years old.[52] Such restrictive voting rights reduced the size of the voting population. In 1790 Virginia was the most populated state, but nearly 40 percent of its population was made up of slaves who could not vote.[53] In a nationwide popular vote, Virginia would have a voting population comparable to Pennsylvania, which had few slaves. This was characteristic of the population differences between northern and southern states. Sixty percent of the country's nonslave population lived in northern states. If the president were elected by popular vote, southern states would have needed to broaden their voting rights to include slaves to offset the larger voting population in northern states. However, this was anathema to the southern aristocratic society. The country was also a male-dominated society that showed little desire for women's suffrage. An alliance formed between delegates who did not trust the public and those from small population states.

Gouverneur Morris of Pennsylvania sided with delegates who wanted election by popular vote: "He [the president] ought to be elected by the people at large, by the freeholders of the Country. . . . If the Legislature elect, it will be the work of intrigue, of cabal, and of faction."[54] Electing the president directly by popular vote was viewed as ensuring the presidency would be politically independent from Congress. George Mason of Virginia presented a pragmatic view. He thought it impractical for the public to make an informed decision: "The extent of the Country renders it impossible that the people can have the requisite capacity to judge of the respective pretensions of the Candidates."[55]

The framers discussed the method for selecting a president on twenty-one different days and generated over thirty votes on the issue. It may have been the most pondered part of the Constitution. At one point Elbridge Gerry of Massachusetts said, "We seem to be at a loss on this head."[56] Gerry was referring to the revolving-door discussions on a method for electing a president. The framers often undid changes they had previously adopted.

Eventually, the framers crafted a compromise mechanism for electing George Washington to the presidency. The lack of roads, limited communication, and a large illiterate population argued against the direct election of a president by popular vote. Instead, each state would appoint delegates—electors—who would vote for a presidential candidate. This group of presidential electors became known as the Electoral College. Electors were free to select the candidate they thought would most help their state. Electors were expected to focus on the needs of their state. Political parties did not exist at that time. Each state legislature would decide how to pick its electors. It wasn't until after the Civil War that all states selected their electors by popular vote.

The Electoral College awards electors to states based on their representation in Congress. As historian Shlomo Slonim states, "the Electoral College was simply a special congress elected to choose a president, without the shortcomings of the real Congress."[57] The number of electors for each state equals its number of congressional representatives plus senators. After reapportionment in 2000, California, the most populated state, had fifty-three representatives and two senators, resulting in fifty-five electors in the Electoral College. Wyoming, with the smallest population, had one representative and two senators, resulting in three electors in the Electoral College. Today, the Electoral College consists of 538 electors, including three for the

District of Columbia. A candidate must win at least 270 electoral votes to become president.

Congressional apportionment determines the number of representatives for each state, and thus influences the Electoral College. During the Constitutional Convention, Hugh Williamson of North Carolina unmasked an insidious feature of the Electoral College. The selection of a president by electors would favor southern slave states, which were over-represented in the House of Representatives, as slaves were counted in apportionment but were not allowed to vote. James Madison also viewed the slave population as disproportionately helping slave states if electors chose the president.

In 1790 Virginia was the most populated state and, therefore, had the largest congressional delegation, with nineteen representatives in the House. About five of Virginia's representatives were due to the slave population of nearly 300,000. More slaves lived in Virginia than the entire population in eight other states. If the president were elected by a direct popular vote, less than half of Virginia's population would have been eligible to vote. This would have eliminated the larger population advantage Virginia had over northern states, where there were fewer slaves. After the census of 1800, Pennsylvania had 10 percent more free residents than Virginia, but 20 percent fewer electoral votes.[58] Thus, slave states gained additional political power if electors selected the president.

Massachusetts Representative Samuel Thatcher stated in 1803: "The representation of slaves adds thirteen members to the House in the present Congress, and eighteen Electors of President and Vice-President at the next election."[59] In hindsight, the slave population had a momentous effect on the Electoral College. Six of the first ten presidents were slave-owners from Virginia, which was the most populous state and had the largest slave population.

As they had with slaves, the Electoral College also failed to encourage voting rights for women. The Electoral College fosters an incentive to disenfranchisement as only a simple majority—one vote—can award all the state's electoral votes. Law professors Akhil Amar and Vikram Amar state: "Under the Electoral College . . . a state had no special incentive to expand suffrage—each state got a fixed number of electoral votes based on [total] population, regardless of how many or how few citizens were allowed to vote or actually voted. As with slaves, what mattered was simply how many women resided in a state, not how many could vote there."[60] Women did not gain the right to vote until 1920. The League of Women Voters of the United States recommends that Congress abolish the Electoral College.[61]

The Electoral College would meet once every four years to select a president and then disband. Each subsequent presidential election would be decided by a new set of electors chosen from each state. In 1787 this was a practical solution.

The Electoral College was a means to an end, and not much thought was given to drawbacks in the compromise. After all, everyone expected that George Washington would be the first president. Problems with the Electoral College process became evident with the election of John Adams in 1796. Political parties evolved during Washington's presidency (1789–1797). In the 1796 presidential election, Washington was not a candidate and electors voted for a presidential candidate based on their political party's interests. The Electoral College shifted from representing states to electing a president to benefit a single political party. The framers did not foresee the rise of political parties and the effect they would have on the Electoral College and America's political system.

The Electoral College is certainly the most challenged part of the original Constitution. There have been over one thousand attempts to either change or abolish the Electoral College.[62] About one of every ten constitutional amendments that have been proposed has focused on the Electoral College. The first attempt to abolish the Electoral College was in 1816, less than thirty years after the first presidential election in 1789. Only one change— the twelfth amendment in 1804—has passed. Originally, electors voted for their two preferred presidential candidates without specifying a choice for president or vice-president. This caused a tie in the Electoral College vote in the presidential election of 1800. Both Thomas Jefferson and his running mate, Aaron Burr, received seventy-three electoral votes. The tie threw election of the president into the House of Representatives. After much political intrigue, Jefferson was elected president and Burr vice president. After the twelfth amendment was enacted, electors had to specify separate votes for the presidential and vice-presidential candidate.

A bill to abolish the Electoral College passed in the House of Representatives in 1968, but was filibustered in the Senate. In 1979 President Jimmy Carter supported a bill to abolish the Electoral College, but it again failed to pass in the Senate. A recent drive to abolish the Electoral College came in the wake of Al Gore's loss to George W. Bush in the 2000 presidential election. Hillary Rodham Clinton, then senator-elect of New York, raised the issue saying, "I believe strongly that in a democracy, we should respect the will of the people, and to me, that means it's time to do away with the Electoral College and move to the popular election of our president."[63] In 2005 Representative Raymond "Gene" Green (D-Texas) introduced House Joint Resolution 8, which would abolish the Electoral College. Sen. Dianne Feinstein of California introduced a similar bill in the Senate—Senate Joint Resolution 11. Committees are currently reviewing both bills.

Some argue that the Electoral College enhances the power of small population states, while others think the most populous states benefit. A review of presidential elections debunks both views. Only the elections of 1876, 1888, and 2000 have resulted in wrong winners—presidents who lost the nationwide popular vote but won in the Electoral College. In each case, extralegal activities manipulated the Electoral College such that the loser of the popular vote became president. In all other presidential elections for which there are reliable historical data, the winner of the popular vote became president.[64]

The wrong winner in 1876 was Rutherford B. Hayes, a Harvard-educated lawyer and a Republican. Democrat Samuel Tilden won the most popular votes in the presidential election, but there was disputed voting in South Carolina, Florida, and Louisiana where whites suppressed voting among African Americans. Republicans and Democrats at the Capitol forged a closed-door agreement. Hayes became president, but in return he promised Democrats he would remove the remaining federal troops in the South and appoint at least one southerner to a Cabinet post.

Supporters of the Electoral College point to the 1876 presidential election as proof that the Electoral College serves a needed role. Supporters argue that Hayes would have been the Electoral College winner had southern whites not suppressed voting among southern blacks who voted overwhelmingly for Hayes. Supporters view the Electoral College as having justly countered the disenfranchisement of southern blacks in 1876. However, this overlooks the brokered deal between Republicans and Democrats, which put Hayes in office. What is certain is that Hayes was forced to negotiate with Democrats to become president. The underlying cause was disenfranchisement of African Americans in the South, which Hayes did not rectify. Republican Hayes would later be known as "Rutherfraud" Hayes and "His Fraudulency." Bush became known as "His Fraudulency the Second."[65]

Federal troops had been present in the South since the end of the Civil War to ensure the emancipation of blacks. Hayes prematurely ended the post–Civil War period of Reconstruction in the South when he removed federal troops. Segregation, voter disenfranchisement, and racial intimidation became the norm for southern blacks. The Ku Klux Klan grew in scope and influence. Not until the Civil Rights Movement of the 1960s did African Americans began to regain the rights they lost when Hayes became president in 1877.

There was another wrong winner in 1888. Republican Benjamin Harrison, grandson of ninth president William Harrison, became the twenty-third president, even though he had lost the national popular vote to Democratic candidate Grover Cleveland. Harrison won New York because of vote buying by the Republican Party. New York was the most populated state, with thirty-six electoral votes, which gave Harrison the necessary majority of electoral votes to become president. Republican political boss Matt Quay of Pennsylvania said of Harrison's victory: "A number of men were compelled to approach . . . the penitentiary to make him President."[66]

The most recent wrong winner was Republican George W. Bush in 2000. Democrat Al Gore won the nationwide popular vote, however, Bush narrowly beat Gore in Florida by 537 votes. Consequently, Florida's twenty-five electoral votes won the presidency for Bush—the forty-third president. Gore appealed the Florida vote count to the U.S. Supreme Court, which ruled in favor of Bush by a margin of five to four. The slim majority of judges were concerned about a lack of uniform standards for judging hanging/bulging chads in the manual recount in Florida.[67] (A chad is a fragment of paper produced by a hole punch in a paper ballot. A hanging, or bulging, chad occurs when a hole punch fails to complete detach.)

What then has been the utility of the Electoral College? Reliable data on popular vote counts for presidential elections are available as early as the election of 1828. Between 1828 and 2008, in only three of forty-six elections (7 percent) have the Electoral College elected a victor—a wrong winner—other than the popular vote winner. In 93 percent of presidential elections, the Electoral College mirrored the national popular vote. History shows that the Electoral College has provided a mechanism for each of the wrong winners to circumvent the popular vote. Law professor Bradley A. Smith makes the link between the Electoral College and voter fraud: "Under the Electoral College system, fraud will tend to be localized in close states, where it can make a difference between winning or losing the state. Relatively small totals might alter the election results, making fraud an enticing prospect."[68]

The Electoral College provides a strong incentive to disenfranchise or buy votes, which some politicians may have trouble resisting. Even the revered George Washington bought votes in a practice called "swilling the planters with bumbo."[69] Washington supplied voters with over 160 gallons of various alcoholic beverages when he ran for election in the Virginia House of Burgesses in 1758. Over 1 million votes were cast in the presidential election of 2000, but the 537 votes in Florida decided the election in favor of Republican candidate George Bush. Interestingly, the three wrong winners in the tarnished presidential elections of 1876, 1888, and 2000 were Republicans.

The Electoral College also enhances the role of third-party spoilers. These presidential candidates are unlikely to win but take votes away from the favorite. In Florida in 2000, liberal Ralph Nader ran as the Green Party candidate. Nader was not expected to win but received 97,488 votes in Florida. Many of these votes would otherwise have gone to Al Gore—a Democrat. To win Florida, Gore needed only 538 votes from those 97,488 who voted for Nader. If Nader had not run in Florida, Gore would likely have been elected president in 2000. Katherine Harris, the Florida secretary of state and co-chair of George Bush's Florida campaign committee, had added Nader's name to absentee ballots before having approval from the Florida Supreme Court.[70]

The Electoral College engenders inequality among voters, which violates the Supreme Court's ruling that one person's vote be equal to that of another's.

Because electoral votes are awarded on a statewide winner-take-all basis, a lone voter in a large population state has more influence in selecting the president than a lone voter in a small population state. (Maine and Nebraska are exceptions, because their state legislatures have adopted district-level electoral voting. Both states split their electoral votes among candidates based on the popular vote percentages.)

In the 2008 presidential election, California (the most populated state) had fifty-five electoral votes. If only one person had voted in California, all fifty-five of California's electoral votes would still have gone to the winner of the lone popular vote. Wyoming (the least populated state) had three electoral votes in the 2008 election in which over 250,000 Wyoming residents voted. If only 249,999 had voted in California in 2008, all fifty-five electoral votes would still have gone to the statewide winner. Regardless of the number of voters in either state, California would have awarded fifty-five electoral votes and Wyoming three electoral votes. In short, the vote of one lone voter in California has over eighteen times the clout of a lone voter in Wyoming, violating the idea of "one person, one vote."

In Florida in 2000 Bush defeated Gore by a mere 537 popular votes; however, all twenty-five of Florida's electoral votes went to Bush. The ballots of the 2,912,253 Floridians who voted for Gore were ultimately of no value in the nationwide election. The result would have been the same if only one popular vote had been cast in the entire state of Florida. The candidate receiving that lone popular vote would have gained all of Florida's electoral votes. The most important vote is the single popular vote that gives a presidential candidate a simple majority in a state. Votes cast for the loser are of no value beyond the state border.

This winner-take-all system discourages candidates from campaigning in states where they either stand little chance of winning a majority of votes or where they are ensured victory. The Electoral College compels candidates to spend most of their time and political capital in states with uncertain outcomes. This gives disproportionate influence to large population states where the election is a toss up. In the 2004 presidential election, two-thirds of presidential campaign visits went to just five states, and over 99 percent of campaign monies were spent in only sixteen states.[71] The largest amount of campaign spending in 2004 was in Florida. In the 2008 presidential election, over 98 percent of campaign events and monies were spent in just fifteen states.[72] Again, Florida was the destination of most campaign spending. In contrast, an election by nationwide popular vote would treat voters equally regardless of their state of residence. This would create an incentive for presidential candidates to campaign actively in every state and appeal to a broader political spectrum.

The story of the hypothetical state of "New Ycxas" is telling.[73] Former senator Charles Schumer of New York proposed in the 1990s that New York and Texas pool their electoral votes into a single bloc to gain more attention from presidential candidates. In recent history, New York typically votes for Democratic presidential candidates and Texas goes Republican. Neither state is politically competitive. By combining their electoral votes, Texas and New York would become the single largest electoral prize and a diverse political battleground. The idea never made it beyond speculation.

We continue to use the Electoral College for presidential elections because it is part of the Constitution, even though it violates the equal protection clause of the fourteenth amendment. In presidential elections, the value of a lone vote varies among states because of the Electoral College and its winner-take-all feature. This violates the constitutional guarantee that states treat all persons similarly when applying the law. The Supreme Court case *Gray v. Sanders* in 1963 ruled that the use of the Electoral College for gubernatorial elections was unconstitutional.[74]

Ironically, it would be unconstitutional to create the Electoral College if it did not already exist. The Electoral College is unconstitutional except for the fact that the framers included it in the Constitution.

Leap-Frogging the Electoral College

The National Popular Vote (NPV) movement is the result of political fallout from the 2000 presidential election. NPV began in 2006 and has the endorsement of nearly two thousand legislators and numerous newspapers. Followers of NPV want to circumvent the Electoral College in electing the president by enacting a compact among state legislatures.[75]

A major motivation for the NPV movement is the massive voter disenfranchisement in the 2000 presidential election in Florida, which resulted in a wrong winner—George W. Bush. The disenfranchisement of minorities

in Florida also had a ripple effect on women voters as most women nationwide—54 percent—voted for Al Gore.[76] Had NPV been enacted in 2000,
Florida's twenty-five electoral votes would have gone to the winner of the
nationwide popular vote—Al Gore. NPV would have resulted in Al Gore
winning the 2000 presidential election.

The intent of the NPV is to "guarantee the Presidency to the presidential candidate who receives the most popular votes in all fifty states (and
the District of Columbia)."[77] The NPV aims to transform the presidential
election from fifty-one (fifty states plus the District of Columbia) separate
elections into a single national election where states are irrelevant. States that
enact the NPV bill agree to award all their Electoral College votes to the winner of the nationwide popular vote, regardless of who wins in their state. The
NPV plan would bypass the winner-take-all feature of the Electoral College.
Votes would have equal value beyond individual state borders. Under the
NPV plan a popular vote in California would be worth the same as a popular vote in Wyoming. Every single vote would help a presidential candidate
regardless of the state from which it came. NPV claims its plan will make the
presidential election into a true one person, one vote contest. It would also
encourage states and political parties to increase the number of voters, which
would court the attention of presidential candidates.

More than two of three Americans live in "safe" states that are either re-
liably "red" (Republican) or "blue" (Democratic).[78] Presidential campaigns
pay little attention to voters in these states. During the Bush versus Kerry
election of 2004, no money was spent campaigning in twenty-three states.
Consider that ten of the twelve least populated states are considered safe.
This includes both red and blue states.

How then do small population states benefit from the Electoral College?
Today they do not. The supposed benefit to small states harkens back to
when there were only thirteen states and slaves were counted in apportionment. In the presidential election of 1792, the six least-populated states
needed to unite under a single candidate in order to counter the twenty-one
electoral votes of Virginia, the most-populated state. After reapportionment
in 2010, it will be necessary to combine the electoral votes from the fifteen
least-populated states to exceed California's expected fifty-five electoral votes.
Two of California's electoral votes will likely be due to the state's population

of illegal immigrants. In the 2012 presidential election, Florida's Electoral College clout will likely have grown from twenty-seven to twenty eight electoral votes because of growth in the state's population. The electoral gap between the least and most populated state has expanded dramatically from eighteen votes in 1792 to fifty-two votes in 2010.

The Electoral College also discourages voter participation in much of the country where statewide results are a foregone conclusion. Why should supporters of the projected statewide loser bother to vote when all the state's electoral votes will go to the winner?

The NPV plan has its origin in a series of separate articles in 2001 by law professors Robert W. Bennett and Akhil Reed Amar and Vikram David Amar.[79] The Amars are brothers who argue that the Electoral College is an anachronism founded in 1787 for a fledgling country and a society that is much different from today's United States.[80] The Amar brothers posit that slavery and poor mass communication were the basis for the Electoral College. The patriarchal society of early America also differed greatly from today. Note John Adam's view on why women should be excluded from voting: "But why exclude Women? You will Say, because their Delicacy renders them unfit for Practice and Experience, in the great Business of Life, and the hardy Enterprises of War, as well as the arduous Cares of State. Besides, their attention is So much engaged with the necessary Nurture of their Children, that Nature has made them fittest for domestic Cares."[81]

The public appears to be of two, or three, minds on the legitimacy of the Electoral College. A *New York Times/CBS News* poll taken during the Florida recount in 2000 showed that the majority of the public thought— Gore was more "legitimate" than the Electoral College winner.[82] This suggests a Gore presidency would have garnered more support from the public. However, the same poll showed the majority of the public thought—that Bush should be president. At the same time, most Americans want to abolish the Electoral College. The three viewpoints are irreconcilable.

The NPV bill would put into practice the compact's terms only once there are enough participating states to have an Electoral College majority —270 electoral votes. Otherwise, the NPV would serve no purpose, as participating states would not have enough electoral votes to elect the president. After reapportionment following Census 2010, it will likely require membership from as few as the eleven most populated states to garner the minimum 270 electoral votes necessary to trigger NPV among enacting states. By November 2010, the NPV bill had been introduced in every state.[83] The District of Columbia along with six states including Hawaii, Illinois, Maryland, Massachusetts, New Jersey, and Washington had enacted the NPV bill. This will likely total about 74 electoral votes following reapportionment in 2010. NPV had passed in both the House and Senate of four other states including California, Colorado, Rhode Island, and Vermont, for another potential 131 electoral votes. These ten states (and the District of Columbia) account for over half of the minimum 270 electoral votes needed to elect a president. NPV had passed in either the House or Senate of ten additional states. The NPV movement is nonpartisan. In Democratic New York State, Republicans sponsored the NPV bill. In Republican Utah, a Democrat sponsored the NPV bill.

NPV will have to pass a constitutional challenge even if adopted by enough states to muster the minimum 270 electoral votes. The Constitution allows states to choose electors as they wish. Electors do not have to be chosen by popular vote, and initially were selected by state legislatures. State legislatures that adopt the NPV bill can award their electoral votes to the national vote winner without interference from Congress. However, Article I, Section 10 of the Constitution prohibits treaties, alliances, or confederations among states. The U.S. Supreme Court has ruled that congressional approval is necessary if agreements among states, "may encroach upon or interfere with the just supremacy of United States."[84]

Opponents of NPV argue that the plan would invalidate votes from states not participating in the compact. NPV counters that its plan does not infringe on the authority of the federal government, and that nonadopting states would not be negatively affected, as all votes would be counted towards the national totals regardless of the state in which the vote is cast. The NPV organization claims it will introduce a bill in Congress to address these issues once their plan is adopted by enough states to make it a realistic alternative to the Electoral College.

Over one thousand attempts have been made to either change or abolish the Electoral College since George Washington became the first American president. Only one amendment to change the Electoral College—the twelfth amendment—has passed. NPV promotes its plan as a viable alternative to yet another attempt to eliminate the Electoral College via a constitutional amendment, which history has shown to be futile. A constitutional amendment requires passage by two-thirds in the House and Senate, as well as ratification by at least thirty-eight states.

Rob Richie, executive director of FairVote, states, "[b]y 2012, we anticipate that the presidential election will be governed by the National Popular Vote plan for president where every vote is of equal weight."[85]

Why Is This Important? The Constitution's Missing Link: The Right to Vote

The U.S. Constitution lacks a right to vote. The Bill of Rights does not specify a right to vote. It was not until the 1940s that the U.S. Supreme Court ruled that there exists a fundamental right to vote (*States v. Classic*), but the court's rulings remain open to interpretation and challenge. The Constitution still lacks an inherent incentive to broaden and permanently secure voting rights for Americans. Law professor David Schultz states: "Nowhere in the United States Constitution is there an explicit declaration of the right to vote."[86] Congressional Representative Jackson of Illinois sponsored House Joint Resolution 28, which calls for a constitutional amendment to grant Americans aged eighteen years and over the right to vote.[87] Representative Jackson was motivated to introduce this legislation because of the disenfranchisement that occurred in Florida during the 2000 presidential election.[88]

When the Constitution was written, each American state considered itself the equal of a European nation. Was this the reason the framers allowed voting rights to be determined separately by each state, laying a foundation for a history of voter exclusion in the United States? American citizens have struggled to obtain voting rights since then. African American males obtained voting rights in 1870, only after the Civil War in which over 600,000 people died. Women did not obtain voting rights until the nineteenth amendment in 1920. The Voting Rights Act of 1965 was necessary to restore enfranchisement to minorities and poor whites.

The struggle to maintain the right to vote continues, even though much progress has been made to ensure voting rights for all males (regardless of religion or wealth), women, minorities, and the poor. Today, over one million African Americans are barred from voting because of prior criminal records, even after having completed their sentences.[89] A broader concern is the potential to disenfranchise citizens that are mistakenly placed on felon exclusion lists. In the presidential election of 2000, about 25,000 Floridians were mistakenly placed on the state's felon exclusion list and not allowed to vote. The specter of disenfranchisement from erroneous felon lists is real.

Voter suppression targeted at Hispanics and Asians shows a lack of appreciation for the economic wealth these minorities have generated for the United States. Americans of Hispanic and Asian ancestry have been part of the country's population since the late 1800s. Their low wage manual labor led to America becoming an economic giant in agriculture and manufacturing. Discouraging foreign in-migration by targeting immigrants for vote suppression works counter to the economic self-interest of the United States. Without foreign in-migration, the United States will likely enter into a period of population loss and a potential economic contraction worse than the economic meltdown that began in 2008.

Hispanics are the only major ethnic group in the United States with a fertility rate above replacement level. According to Census 2000, Garcia is the eighth most common surname in the United States with Rodriguez at ninth and Martinez at eleventh.[90] One of every three American-born Hispanics will marry a non-Hispanic. Continued attempts to suppress Hispanic voting will eventually have a spillover effect on middle-class Americans of Italian, German, English, and numerous other ancestries.

The predominately white baby boomer generation is going to depend increasingly on young Hispanic and Asian immigrant workers to provide the tax base for their retirement. To deny these immigrants a stake in the future of the United States puts the government's social safety net for the elderly at risk. Foreign language help at the polls is an important symbolic gesture that the United States welcomes political participation from all its citizens—regardless of cultural background or political affiliation.

Al Gore won the 2000 presidential election by over half a million popular votes, but the votes of 537 Floridians won the Electoral College for Bush. A surplus of explanations, whether historical, manufactured, or philosophical, exists to support, or demonize, the Electoral College. Yet Alexander

Hamilton wrote a simple and practical justification in 1788: "A small number of persons, selected by their fellow citizens from the general mass, will be most likely to possess the information and discernment requisite to such complicated investigations."[91]

The framers did not think the public was sufficiently informed to be worthwhile voters, and limited direct election to only members of the House of Representatives. Since adopting the Constitution, the country has abolished slavery, granted women voting rights, and made education mandatory. Today, computers and the Internet provide access to vast sources of information. The framers could not have imagined the United States of the early twenty-first century. Would the framers enact the Electoral College given today's reality? Would the Electoral College be created today if it did not already exist?

Over a century of political progress separates the wrong winners of presidential elections in 1876 (Rutherford B. Hayes) and 2000 (George W. Bush). Yet, the presidential election of 2000 saw political manipulation reminiscent of 1876 and 1888, which illustrates that the Electoral College does not help minorities or small population states. The Electoral College helps political interests that are best able to manipulate it.

Would voting rights have been granted to women and slaves sooner if the framers had chosen to elect the president by popular vote? Yale law professor Akhil Reed Amar suggests a tangible incentive: "In a direct presidential election, any state that chose to enfranchise its women would have automatically doubled its clout."[92] This might have created an incentive for states to increase their population of voters, resulting in a race to enfranchise residents. However, the opposite happened.

The majority of the public wants to do away with the Electoral College. As stated by the foresighted authors of *Wrong Winner*: "It is time for the founder's folly [the Electoral College] to be undone."[93] Yet, attempts to abolish it have failed. The staying power of the Electoral College may lie in the proverb, "Better the devil you know than the devil you don't."

The driving force behind the NPV movement has grown beyond events in Florida in 2000. The tribulations of the Bush presidency (2001–2009), including the second Iraq war; the war in Afghanistan; the deaths of about one thousand in Hurricane Katrina in New Orleans; the mounting national debt;

and the economic meltdown in the fall of 2008, have refocused attention on George W. Bush as a wrong winner.[94] Had the Electoral College been abolished, events in America at the beginning of the twenty-first century could have been dramatically different. Al Gore would have been elected president in 2000.

If adopted, the promoters of NPV believe their plan would reduce the temptation to commit vote fraud (vote buying) and disenfranchisement (vote suppression). They argue that to manipulate a nationwide popular vote, disenfranchisement, or vote fraud, would have to be far-reaching and occur in multiple states, which would not go unnoticed.

Either NPV or abolition of the Electoral College could dramatically increase voter participation in presidential elections. Every vote would count towards the national total, with presidential candidates paying more attention to states with higher voter turnouts. The election of the president by popular vote would establish a disincentive to disenfranchisement. For the first time since the Constitution was adopted, states would have an inherent incentive to increase their number of voters.

5

VOTER-COUNT
APPORTIONMENT

Making Congress Respond to Voters

Then there was the educated Texan from Texas who looked
like someone in Technicolor and felt, patriotically, that people of means—decent folk—should be given more votes than
drifters, whores, criminals, degenerates, atheists and indecent
folk—people without means.

—from *Catch-22* by Joseph Heller, 1961

The Unrepresentative and Uncompetitive House of Representatives
Have you seen the bumper sticker "Politicians and diapers should both be
changed regularly, and for the same reason"? The framers may have had
similar beliefs when they created the House of Representatives. The framers wanted the House to reflect the will of voters. Originally, the House was
the only federal office with membership by direct election by the public.
Framer George Mason, during the Constitutional Convention in 1787, said
the House "was to be the grand depository of the democratic principles of
the government."[1]

Members of the House were limited to a two-year term to make them
responsive to the short-term interests of voters. James Madison wrote in
Federalist #52 that the House should have "an immediate dependence on,
and an intimate sympathy with, the people."[2] The framers did not intend
career politicians to populate the House. The framers expected a short two-

year term for representatives would create enough turnover to quell incumbency. In the early years of the House, representatives typically served only one two-year term either by personal choice or by voter mandate. Today, incumbency and career politicians are the norm.

Monopolies are companies that dominate the marketplace by eliminating their competition or obstructing competitors. Monopolies intentionally thwart competition through extralegal activities. Business monopolies and incumbency in the House are similar. In the House, political parties manipulate districting, voter turnout, and election and funding laws to lessen the viability of political challengers.

Consider electoral fusion, which is the nomination of a single candidate by multiple political parties.[3] Electoral fusion allows several minor parties to pool their voters against the dominant political parties—Republican and Democratic. Electoral fusion was once popular in the United States but today only ten states allow the practice. The two major political parties promoted anti-fusion laws in the 1800s to hinder the rise of new parties.[4] Banning electoral fusion ensures that either the Republican Party or Democratic Party will govern. This results in one slight difference between the House and monopolies. The House is a duopoly— Republicans and Democrats— that work to eliminate challengers to incumbents. This is most obvious when congressional redistricting takes place following a decennial census. Gerrymandering is used to draw district boundaries to ensure the re-election of incumbents. The redistricting of congressional districts in California in 2001–2002 is a prime example. Democrats and Republicans connived to redraw congressional district boundaries such that all incumbents, regardless of party affiliation, would be re-elected.

A functioning representative democracy requires a lively and ongoing competition for both representation and political ideas. Representation without competition reinforces the existing socioeconomic conditions in a country, as shown by the former Soviet Union. True representative democracy requires a political "open market" where voters can choose between the status quo or change, and the type of change. A 2005 study by economists at the nonpartisan National Bureau of Economic Research found that "political competition . . . can have a profound impact on economic life."[5] The framers of the Constitution knew about the importance of political competition, but the political parties, via redistricting, continue to lessen competition.

Renowned political science professor Robert A. Dahl says representative democracy is "a system of control by competition."[6] Competition ensures existing office holders are held accountable to voters—or else they are replaced. In contrast, incumbents strive to minimize competition to ensure re-election. Thus, an inherent conflict exists between the best interest of voters, and job security for elected officials.

In 2002 elections were held for all congressional districts nationwide, however, at the most forty-four (10 percent) were considered competitive contests.[7] In the 2002 and 2004 congressional elections, 98 percent of incumbents won re-election. Conservative columnist George Will further suggests "incumbents are working to eliminate that awful [remaining] 2 percent."[8] Since 1985, only about 13 percent of congressional seats were won in competitive elections. In 2002 only 10 percent of districts were competitive, and in 2004 the number dropped to twenty-seven districts of 435—just 6 percent. In the 2006 House elections, fifty-five incumbents went unchallenged, and voters in those House districts had no choice. In 2008, 95 percent of incumbents won re-election and 25 percent of races went unchallenged.[9] Mark Gersh, a Democratic campaign strategist, analyzed data on incumbent re-election, which led him to the conclusion, "We've reached the point where incumbents just can't lose. Never before has there been such a preponderance of safe seats."[10] Gersh made the comment in 2003, when the Democrats were the minority party in the House. Another perspective is that high rates of incumbency reflect a House full of savvy politicians who are better than their challengers at convincing voters.

The 2010 midterm elections saw a historic number of incumbents— mostly Democrats—replaced in the House. This was viewed in part as a unique voter response to the worst economic conditions since The Great Depression.[11]

Congressional districts tend to be either predominately "red" (Republican) or "blue" (Democratic), which drives highly partisan, and polarized, representation in Congress. Few Democrats represent Republican leaning voters and vice versa, which reduces the need for bipartisan cooperation. Representatives from polarized districts are more likely dogmatic and less likely to support compromise legislation. As districts become less competitive, the need to get independent, or moderate, voters decreases. In short, noncompetitive districts breed political polarization, which becomes self-reinforcing. Political polarization may reflect increasing economic polarization in the United States where communities are increasingly either upper income (Republican) or lower income (Democrat). The decline in the number of moderate—competitive— districts could be a result of a decline in the number of middle-income Americans. Noncompetitive districts could also be the result of Americans being selective about their neighbors: Republicans preferring to live next door to Republicans just as Democrats may prefer other Democrats for neighbors.[12]

The middle-of-the-road "purple" voter typically has only an extreme choice—either scarlet red or indigo blue. In *Culture War? The Myth of a Polarized America*, professor Morris P. Fiorina writes that Americans nationwide share many similar political beliefs; however, voters are limited in their choices as the Republican and Democratic parties move farther apart and become more extreme. "Given a choice between two extremes, they can only elect an extremist."[13] Are far-left and far-right politics the reason the United States has the lowest voter participation rate among industrialized countries? Voter participation is higher in Mexico than in the United States. Does the United States have low voter participation because moderate voters have removed themselves from active participation in elections? Yes, in part. A lack of purple districts discourages moderate voters from participating in elections, which increases the influence of highly partisan voters in both parties. Robert D. Putnam, Harvard professor of public policy, states in his best-selling book *Bowling Alone*, "people who characterize themselves as being 'middle of the road' ideologically have disproportionately disappeared from public meetings, local organizations, political parties, rallies, and the like."[14]

Neither political party has an incentive to increase voter turnout by appealing to the large number of moderate voters because it would make it necessary to obtain—convince—more voters in order to win elections. Winning an election is easier when there are fewer voters and most of them are the candidate's strongest supporters.

Data suggests that elections without incumbents are more competitive than elections with incumbents.[15] Districts created to re-elect incumbents by design pose an overwhelming obstacle to challengers. Incumbency has the effect of reducing competition, which may be attributed to the ability of the incumbent to raise vastly more campaign monies than challengers can. Incumbents also receive free media coverage because they are elected officials. In 1974 median spending of winners in House elections was $41,885. By 2002 median spending for a House seat had risen to $657,359, an increase of over double the rate of inflation.[16] In the 2008 House elections, median spending by incumbents was over 1 million.[17] Combined, House incumbents raised over $200 million as compared to $34 million for challengers in the 2008 House elections.[18] That corresponds to $6 raised by incumbents for every one dollar raised by challengers. A prudent challenger would take the long odds of unseating an entrenched incumbent seriously before investing time and money.

Supporters of noncompetitive districts argue that they are good for Americans because they generate "happy" voters. Highly partisan districts reward highly partisan voters for their loyalty. This perspective overlooks the "unhappy" voters who are in effect disenfranchised by partisan districting, and the unhappy and disillusioned moderate voters who do not vote. Historical Gallup polls for 2000 through 2009 show that Independents, who are typically moderates, give Congress lower approval ratings than Republicans or Democrats.[19] Republicans are happiest with Congress when they are in the majority. Not surprisingly, Democrats are happiest when they control the House. However, Independents are never happy with Congress. In 2009 Independents comprised 36 percent of voters—the highest level in seventy years.[20] More voters identified themselves as Independents than either Democrats or Republicans.

Arguments against competitive districts follow bizarre reasoning and run counter to the intentions of the framers. Another argument against competitive districts is that they would create a House dominated by candidates who represent the moderate middle, and this is undesirable. Alternatively, we know what happens with a highly partisan House—we have that now. Political parties focus on harming the opposing party instead of addressing the interests of Americans. Note the ultra-partisan debate on health care reform in Congress in 2009. The debate followed party lines. Few representatives dared to cross the no-mans-land between the parties for fear of being blackballed by their comrades. In February 2010, Sen. Evan Bayh (D-Indiana) added his name to the list of moderate congressional representatives and senators from both parties who decided not to run for re-election. Bayh said he decided to leave the Senate because "'there's just too much brain-dead partisanship' in Washington."[21]

It should come as no surprise that competitive House districts would generate representatives more accountable to voters than representatives elected from noncompetitive districts. Michael McDonald, a professor of government and politics, likens elections in noncompetitive districts to one-party dictatorships such as in Cuba, Libya, and the former Soviet Union.[22] Larry J. Sabato, director of the Center for Politics at the University of Virginia, blames the design of district boundaries for noncompetitive elections: "Yet the real culprit . . . was the corrupt system of redistricting, the redrawing of district boundaries that occurs after each decennial census."[23] A preponderance of noncompetitive districts has lead to political polarization in the House, which does not foster good public policy. As Congressman Jim Costa (D-California) states, "I believe competitive seats make for balanced public policy."[24]

Former Representative Rahm Emanuel (D-Illinois), who was chief of staff for President Obama, suggests uncompetitive elections may foster corruption among members of the House: "One of the common threads running through the scandals involving members of Congress from both parties—such as former Representatives Duke Cunningham (R-California) and Tom DeLay (R-Texas) and current Representatives Bob Ney (R-Ohio) and William Jefferson (D-Louisiana)—is that they each came from gerrymandered districts where they never have faced an opponent who can effectively challenge their actions."[25] Candidates in uncompetitive elections do not receive the scrutiny that comes when strong challengers raise thorny questions.

In the 1990s, reformers heralded term limits as the Holy Grail for eradicating incumbency in the House. Term limits impose a maximum number of terms an elected official can serve, with a three-term (six years) maximum being typical for representatives. Term limits force a minimum turnover among elected officials and prevents long-term incumbency. Republicans featured term limits prominently in their "Contract With America" campaign during 1994 congressional elections. The Republicans were coy in their pledge for term limits. The "Contract With America" promised a House vote on term limits—not to enact term limits. In 1995 Republicans in the House voted on several bills for term limits, but none passed. Republicans did impose an eight-year limit on the speakership, but repealed it eight years later in 2003 in order to allow Republican J. Dennis Hastert (Illinois) to remain Speaker of the House indefinitely.[26]

The framers rejected term limits as stated by Alexander Hamilton. "Nothing appears more plausible at first sight, nor more ill-founded upon closer inspection."[27] The U.S. Supreme Court has ruled it unconstitutional for states to impose term limits on their federal representatives. The court ruled that states could not dictate qualifications for federal offices. In short, only the federal government can decide who can or cannot run for Congress.[28] The court worried that term limits might enable incumbents to manipulate state laws to tailor qualifications to benefit themselves. Ironically, the Court's ruling against term limits was due, in part, to a fear that state-mandated term limits would foster incumbency. To impose term limits on Congress, the House would have to pass legislation enacting term limits on its own members. It is not likely that term limits will be enacted because incumbents are accustomed to getting re-elected. In 2010 the longest serving member of the House was John Dingell (D-Michigan), age eighty-four, who had served in the House since 1955—over twenty-five terms.[29]

Several states have tried setting term limit laws for state legislators with mixed results.[30] While term limits force a turnover in state-elected officials, it has not resulted in an increased turnover of seats between political parities. Seats held by a Democrat incumbent usually go to another Democrat, once the incumbent has reached his or her maximum number of elected terms. The same is true for Republican districts. Term limits have not increased political competition except for possibly the "open" year in which the incumbent cannot be re-elected. Viable challengers and the opposing political party wait for the incumbent to be forced out by the term limit before mounting a competitive race. The forced turnover of legislators has made state legislatures, the Senate, and the House of Representatives less powerful and less able to control state budgets. The executive branch has gained more control of government in states with term limit laws. In state legislatures, term limits failed to increase political competition and voter participation. Term limits have reduced incumbency, but have not changed political party control of districts. Redistricting creates districts that are either predominately Republican, or predominately Democratic, and polarized. Even if adopted at the federal level, the impact of term limits on state legislatures suggests that term limits might not reduce political partisanship in Congress.

We do not have a true nationwide two-party system in Congress. Political columnist David S. Broder likened the United States House of Representatives to the British House of Lords, where membership was traditionally limited to the aristocracy. Broder states, "Now they [U.S. Congressional Representatives] have more job security than the queen of England—and as little need to seek their subjects' assent."[31]

Every ten years, following a nationwide census, state legislatures redraw congressional district boundaries. Another round of redistricting will follow the decennial census of 2010. Ultimately, creating competitive districts must be the cornerstone of congressional redistricting if political competition is to increase and moderation return to the House.

The Myth of One Person, One Vote

The United States was founded on colonists' grievance of "no taxation without representation" toward the British Parliament. The British taxed their American colonies but did not allow them representation in Parliament. The British government countered that colonists were represented by "virtue of their relation to English voters."[32] Colonists showed their disregard for such virtual representation through the Declaration of Independence and the Revolutionary War.

Certainly, lessons from America's founding and subsequent history contradicts the legitimacy of virtual representation, which assumes that voters will act in the best interest of nonvoters. Any modicum of representation that nonvoters may obtain via virtual representation is offset by the exploitation that voters inflict on nonvoters. American history clearly shows that counting nonvoters in apportionment only worsens the plight of nonvoters.

Slaves were counted in apportionment, but it worked against them. Counting slaves gave added representation to the slave owner. Women were counted in apportionment but they did not receive the right to vote until 1920. Who represented women before 1920? Congressional historian Robert

Remini states that women felt betrayed when the fourteenth amendment excluded them from voting. "They could no longer trust men in seeking their own rights."[33] Between 1877 and 1965 African Americans in the South were counted in apportionment but were denied the right to vote through Jim Crow laws and intimidation. Who represented African Americans during this period? Mexican Americans in the Southwest were similarly disenfranchised. Who represented them?

Consider Tom Tancredo, a former Republican Congressman from Colorado. Tancredo's home state of Colorado had about one-quarter of a million unauthorized residents in 2008 and he wants to deport them:[34] "Then the ones [illegal immigrants] who remain, we could begin deporting—and, yes, I mean deporting, the word nobody wants to use, but you see if you are here illegally, that's the punishment, deportation."[35]

The illegal Colorado residents that Tancredo wants to deport were counted in apportionment. Counting them helped the voters who elected Tancredo and hurt the illegals. It also increased the representation of voters in other states with large populations of unauthorized residents. In particular, California and Texas have a history of counting immigrants in apportionment and then expelling them but keeping the added representation.

In 1880 California was apportioned an additional congressional seat because of its population of 75,000 Chinese. Then in 1882 Congress passed the Chinese Exclusion Act, which barred, and reversed, Chinese immigration to the United States. Chinese residents in the United States were also denied citizenship. Who represented the interests of the Chinese in the 1880s? California kept the additional congressional seat throughout the decade as Chinese immigrants returned to China. Otherwise, it would have gone to Mississippi.

In 1930 reapportionment, Mexicans, both U.S. citizens and noncitizens, provided Texas with three additional congressional seats, and California one. The 1930s was the decade of the Great Depression and large numbers of Mexicans, including U.S. citizens, were deported to Mexico. American whites viewed Mexicans, including those who were American citizens, as taking American jobs away from whites. The deported Mexicans had been counted in apportionment in 1930. Who represented them? Both Texas and California kept the congressional representatives derived from the deported

Mexicans. Otherwise, the seats would have gone to Alabama, New Jersey, Rhode Island, and Wisconsin.

In 2009 the Reverend Miguel Rivera, and the National Coalition of Latino Clergy and Christian Leaders, called for a boycott of Census 2010 by Hispanics. Rivera's group claims a membership of over 20,000 evangelical churches in thirty-four states. His organization claims 3.4 million undocumented members.[36] Rivera reasons that a boycott by Latinos will motivate Congress to pass immigration reform and improve the lives of the nearly 12 million undocumented residents in the United States. He believes Congress has been deaf to the plight of illegal immigrants because they cannot vote. As Kevin R. Johnson, professor of law and Chicana/Chicano studies states, "undocumented persons may live in the country for many years without any direct political voice."[37]

Rivera's leverage is that a boycott would result in an undercount of illegal immigrants in the 2010 census, which would cause some states to lose representatives. This could happen if the undercount were large enough. Rivera argues that a looming loss of seats will motivate Congress to pass legislation favorable to illegal immigrants, but he is mistaken. The undocumented population does not have a broad enough effect on apportionment nationwide to motivate enough House members. Only California and Texas have a large enough concentration of illegal immigrants to affect apportionment. After 2010 reapportionment California and Texas will likely gain two additional seats each, due to their population of illegal immigrants. These four seats will be taken from Louisiana, Minnesota, Montana, and Ohio. The congressional delegations of the other forty-four states remain unaffected by illegal residents. Most of the country has no stake in Rivera's boycott and it is in the interest of the four states losing seats to California and Texas to support the Latino boycott.

The Reverend Luis Cortes headed the opposition to Rivera's Latino boycott. Cortes argues that opponents of immigration reform will benefit from an undercount: "Ultimately, it means more political power for the people who don't like immigrants."[38] Cortes, like most, assumes that the extra House seats derived from the undocumented population would inherently benefit the undocumented. However, Cortes forgets to take redistricting into account. California is a prime example of the disconnect between apportionment and representation. After reapportionment in 2000, California obtained thirteen seats because of the Hispanic population. However, in 2009, California had only seven Hispanic congressional representatives. Who got the other six seats? Did they go to supporters or opponents of Hispanic priorities? An anonymous website comment to a news article posted at *California Political News & Views* suggests what may have happened to the six seats: "That's sure true here in the Central Valley [California]. There's a large illegal immigrant population in the census counts used to draw district lines, but since the illegal immigrants cannot vote, the Congressional seats most often go Republican. No coincidence most of these Republican Representatives are in agriculture and have no qualms with illegal immigration. Gee! I wonder why?"[39]

What combination of states lost the six Hispanic seats to California? If those six seats had not gone to California, would they belong to supporters of Hispanics in some other state? Texas and New Mexico also had one seat each that should have gone to a Hispanic, but did not because of redistricting. When Cortes argues that the undocumented should be counted in apportionment, he fails to consider the unpredictability of redistricting. Most people make the same mistake.

Both Rivera and Cortes are partly right and partly wrong. Neither fully appreciates the entire scope of apportionment. Both Rivera and Cortes understand that illegal immigrants have no political power because they cannot vote. What about the majority—Hispanic congressional districts created as "safe" seats for Hispanics? Apparently, it has not improved the plight of undocumented Hispanics. Creating safe districts for minority populations does not ensure that a minority candidate will win an election. Consider the 29th Congressional District in Houston, Texas. After reapportionment in 1990, the 29th District was created with a majority 60 percent Hispanic population.[40] A Hispanic was expected to represent the district in Congress. In 1992 Gene Green, who is white, beat Hispanic Ben Reyes by 180 votes in the Democratic Party runoff.[41] Green defeated Reyes again in the 1994 Democratic primary. In 1996 Green defeated two Hispanic challengers— Democrat Felix Fraga and Republican Jack Rodriguez. Green is the only representative elected by voters of the 29th District since the district was created in 1992. Why has a Hispanic-majority district routinely elected a non-

Hispanic? While Hispanics are a majority of the population in the 29th District, they are not a majority of voters.

In the landmark legal rulings *Wesberry v. Sanders* and *Reynolds v. Sims* in 1964, the U.S. Supreme Court mandated that congressional districts had to be equal in population within each state.[42] This ruling intended to correct the historical practice by states of creating districts with different population sizes. Elected officials would bunch groups such as minorities and urbanites into as few districts as possible to reduce their political influence. This practice continues today, but the ruling requires that districts be of equal population, which imposes some limitations on redistricting. In the early 1900s European immigrants—mostly Catholics—and African Americans flocked to America's cities. Migration from rural areas to the cities also increased. Protestants, in rural areas, were becoming a minority and manipulated redistricting to remain in power. The practice is known as malapportionment and it was the status quo before the 1964 court rulings. This practice reached an extreme in 1920 when Congress failed to reapportion—a violation of the Constitution. From the early 1910s until the 1930s, congressional district boundaries remained unchanged even though the country underwent significant demographic and migration shifts. The Court's mandate in 1964 for equal population districts within each state was intended to obtain voter equality—one person, one vote.

However, the Court's rulings do not guarantee one person, one vote as explained by law professor Sanford Levinson, "our system is better described as . . . equal constituents per voting representative."[43] The Court did not specify that districts had to have equal populations of voters. Hypothetically speaking, the Court's rulings would allow for a district composed of only voters and another of only nonvoters, as long as the populations remain equal. Furthermore, the Court did not specify what population. Total population? Citizens? Registered voters? Only voters? This raises an important issue for congressional representation. The Court suggested in *Gaffney v. Cummings* that total population might not reflect the preferred basis for apportionment: "If it is the weight of a person's vote that matters, total population . . . may not actually reflect that body of voters whose votes must be counted and weighed for the purposes of reapportionment, because 'census persons' are not voters."[44] Using total population for apportionment is based on a hodgepodge of federal cases, which can be contradictory and often are a response to local circumstances that differ from the national norm.

The Court ruled in *Burns v. Richardson* that aliens and temporary residents do not need to be counted in apportionment. The case addressed redistricting for the state legislature of Hawaii, which has a sizable population of temporary residents because of military bases on the island of Oahu. The circumstances on Oahu are not typical of most communities in the country. In contrast, the federal court ruled in *Garza v. County of Los Angeles* that districts should be apportioned based on the entire population. The Garza ruling addressed the large concentration of noncitizen immigrants in Los Angeles County. Such a high concentration of noncitizens is not typical of most communities. The findings in *Burns v. Richardson* are contradictory to Garza, and each is unique to local circumstances. *Burns v. Richardson* also gives state legislatures the leeway to either include or exclude children for the purposes of state districting, which makes it inconsistent if applied to congressional apportionment.[45]

Mandating equal population districts within each state does not result in one person, one vote. Disparity in population exists between congressional districts in different states. Such disparity is unavoidable. To have equal population districts nationwide, it is necessary for district boundaries to cross state lines. However, Congress apportions representatives to states and therefore districts cannot cross state lines. Consequently, residents of different states are unequally represented. In 2008 Arizona's 2nd Congressional District had a population of nearly 1 million, compared to Rhode Island's 1st Congressional District with a population of about 525,000.[46] The difference in total population is a disparity of nearly two to one. Consequently, one person, one vote does not exist across state lines.

The effectiveness of a single vote also varies among states. In the 2008 congressional elections, 480,900 Montanans voted for one congressional representative. In contrast, in the 29th Congressional District in Texas (metropolitan Houston) only 106,794 votes were cast for a single House seat.[47] Districts created to advance Hispanic representation, such as the 29th in Texas, may include fewer voters than other districts in the same state. This happens because Hispanic populations contain a disproportionate number of nonvoters such as children and noncitizen immigrants. In the *Yale Law*

Journal, attorney Carl E. Goldfarb states, "Many of those noncitizens have clustered in a few areas, especially South Florida and Southern California."[48] Such a high concentration of noncitizens is not typical of the majority of congressional districts. If apportionment changed to include only voters, one scenario would have about 175,000 voters in the smallest district and about 300,000 voters in the largest district. This range is roughly one-third of the current disparity in voter population between the smallest and largest districts.

In 1990 Los Angeles County, California, had the second highest concentration of noncitizen adults (27 percent), and therefore the highest concentration of nonvoters in the country.[49] In comparison, nationwide, about 6 percent of the country's population comprised noncitizen adults. Los Angeles in 1990 was the setting for the landmark legal ruling in *Garza*.[50] Hispanic voters in Los Angeles used the Voting Rights Act to sue the Los Angeles County Board of Supervisors, claiming that redistricting had diluted the Hispanic vote. Hispanics, citizens and noncitizens alike, outnumbered the population of non-Hispanics in the county. However, there was not a single Hispanic on the five-member County Board of Supervisors.

While Hispanics were the majority of the population in Los Angeles County, they were not a majority of citizens/voters. Only about half of the adult Hispanics were citizens. The County Board of Supervisors had opposed creating a majority Hispanic district because it "unconstitutionally weights the votes of citizens in that district [Hispanic majority] more heavily than those of citizens in other districts."[51] The Board of Supervisors argued that a majority Hispanic district would have significantly fewer voters than other districts, causing unequal representation among the five districts—a violation of one person, one vote. The alternative was to draw districts based on the number of citizens, or total population, which splinters the Hispanic vote and was the current predicament.

The federal court sided with Hispanic voters and imposed a redistricting plan that ensured one "safe" Hispanic seat on the board. As expected, the plan resulted in an uneven distribution of voters among the five districts. In District 1, only four in ten residents were eligible voters, while in District 3 more than six in ten were eligible voters. Consequently, fewer voters were needed to elect a board member in District 1 than in District 3.

The *Garza* ruling violates the principle of electoral equality of one person, one vote. Ideally, the voting power of eligible voters would be kept equal by creating districts with an equal numbers of voters. However, doing so in Los Angeles County would have denied Hispanics representation on the County Board of Supervisors. Representation is gauged by the ability of a group to elect one of their own to office. *Garza* pitted one person, one vote against the desire for a minimum level of representation by a minority group. In Los Angeles County in 1990, providing minimum representation for Hispanics appeared to be irreconcilable with one person, one vote.

Judge Alex Kozinski, a member of the Ninth Circuit Court that ruled on *Garza*, dissented from the court's majority ruling. The panel of three judges that ruled on Garza agreed that Los Angeles County had discriminated against Hispanics. However, Kozinski disagreed with the other two judges on the remedy. Kozinski argued that apportionment could be based on eligible voters, and that *Garza* violated the U.S. Supreme Court's ruling that stressed the idea of one person, one vote as dictated by *Reynolds v. Sims*.[52] Furthermore, Kozinski argued that one person, one vote was of greater importance than having districts with equal populations. For Kozinski, keeping the voting power of citizens equal was paramount. Law professor Grant Hayden writes, "the notion that people exercising equally weighted votes should elect representative bodies had been central to our notion of government from the country's inception."[53] The two judges who formed the majority in *Garza* believed otherwise.

The majority ruling in *Garza* found it more important that districts be equal in total population—not voters. Two districts could have the same number of voters, but different total populations. The two judges argued that residents in more populous districts would have less access to government services, and that this was unfair. Such reasoning rings hollow given that large population differences will always exist between congressional districts in different states. The argument also fails to consider intangibles such as varying levels of responsiveness among elected officials. A large population district with a responsive representative might be better served than a small population district with a representative who is indifferent to his or her constituents. Is it preferable to have a large population district that is politically competitive or a small population district that is uncompetitive?

Supporters of *Garza* argue further that all residents, regardless of age or citizenship status, should be included in the apportionment base. They trust that inclusion in apportionment will inherently provide a "modicum" of representation—even for nonvoters such as illegal immigrants. This is an example of virtual representation in which nonvoters hope that voters convey their interests. American history provides ample evidence that voters do more harm than good to nonvoters.

In 1991 the Texas state legislature supposedly created the 29th Congressional District as a majority Hispanic district to advance Hispanic representation similar in intent to *Garza* in Los Angeles County. However, the 29th District has never had a Hispanic representative. The majority of the population is Hispanic, but the majority of voters are not. This demographic is contrary to the intent of *Garza*, which ruled in favor of population-based apportionment without regard to the number of voters. The 29th District illustrates the disconnect between being counted and being represented.

Children are counted in apportionment. Should they be? Who represents children? Who votes for children? Do all parents vote for policies that benefit all children? Do all parents vote? Professor Elizabeth Cohen suggests parents do not necessarily vote in the best interest of their children: "Parents are expected to represent children at the ballot box when, in fact, it is likely that the interests of those children may run contrary to the interests of their parents. School improvements mean higher taxes for parents, not all of whom are willing to sacrifice for their children. Or parents may not vote at all (many don't)."[54]

Do parents use their added voting power to increase public spending on education while cutting spending on health care for the elderly? Will parents sacrifice the needs of grandparents? Parents can deceive themselves into thinking that what is in their own best interest is also in their child's best interest: "While raising children may involve a degree of selflessness unimaginable to the childless, it is also true that few parents can see the degree to which they impose conceptions of 'best interests' on their children because those conceptions suit their own (adult) interests."[55] Do parents in wealthy communities vote to fund health care and daycare programs for children in low-income communities? Will fixed-income retirees vote to fund schools adequately?

Some argue that parents should be given extra votes because they have children.[56] This is already taking place through apportionment and redistricting. What would be done with the extra votes for children who live in juvenile detention centers, orphanages, or psychiatric care facilities? Should adults who work in orphanages and psychiatric wards to be given extra votes? Should guards in juvenile detention centers be given extra votes? Should single parents have double the vote of married couples with children?

Counting children in apportionment can be used against their best interest when their parents are illegal residents. Consider the congressional district of former Colorado Congressman Tom Tancredo, who has expressed his desire to deport illegal residents. Counting the children of illegal immigrants in Tancredo's district adds weight to the voters who elected Tancredo. Ironically, counting children of illegal immigrants in Tancredo's district harms the children's parents, which cannot be good for the kids.

Nationwide in 2008, about one in four (24 percent) of U.S. residents were minors who could not vote, but the prevalence of children varies among the fifty states.[57] Utah has the highest percentage of children with nearly one in three (31 percent) residents under the age of eighteen. Texas is second highest at 28 percent. Maine, Vermont, and West Virginia have the lowest percentage of children with about one in five (21 percent) residents under the age of eighteen. After reapportionment in 2000, California gained two additional seats because of its population of children, and Texas gained one. States with higher percentages of children have an advantage in apportionment. The solution is to exclude children from apportionment and thereby limit the advantage they give to parents and certain states. Such exclusion would further limit the effect of adult voters, either good or bad, to "one person, one vote," which would result in true electoral equality.

This begs the question of prisons in sparsely populated rural areas. Prisoners are also counted in apportionment. Should rural areas have increased representation because of prison populations who cannot vote? Hartley County, Texas, had a population of about 5,500 in 2000. Half of the county's population were residents of a prison. The town of Somers, Connecticut, had a population of about 10,400 in 2000; however, about 2,300 (22 percent) were residents of two state prisons and could not vote. In February 2010 legislators in New York State introduced bills to end prison-based gerrymandering in New York.[58] The bill would require prisoners to be counted in their home communities instead of where they are incarcerated. Prison-based gerrymandering provides a perverse incentive for local elected officials to promote longer prison sentences with the intent to maintain or increase the prison population in their districts, thereby reducing the number of votes needed for election.

Ultimately, counting the nonvoting population in apportionment enhances the ability of voters to either help, or hinder, nonvoters. It is a roll of the dice to count someone in apportionment without giving him or her the right to vote, unless one believes that elected officials are more likely to be influenced by the demands of nonvoting constituents than what voters want.

Voter-Count Apportionment: An Incentive to Enfranchisement

The concerns of Americans in 2011 are similar to their concerns in 1940. From 2008 through 2010, the United States suffered the worst economic downturn—The Great Recession—since The Great Depression in the 1930s. In 2011 like 1940, there is much anti-immigrant sentiment and foreigners are viewed as taking American jobs.

In January 1941 the Brookings Institute released a book titled *Congressional Apportionment* written by Laurence Frederick Schmeckebier. Schmeckebier proposed that apportionment should be based on the number of voters, "It is therefore recommended that there be adopted a constitutional amendment providing that apportionment be based on votes cast. . . . The direct effect of such an amendment would be to reduce the representation of states where a large proportion of the electorate is deprived of the suffrage by either legal or extra-legal means. An indirect effect would be that persons who are entitled to vote would find an incentive to exercise the suffrage if they could thereby contribute to preventing a decrease in the representation of the state."[59]

Widespread disenfranchisement of African Americans and Mexican Americans had reduced voter participation in southern and southwestern states. Schmeckebier argued that voter-based apportionment would create a disincentive to disenfranchisement and increase voter participation. Some Republicans in the House had argued similarly after the Civil War. They wanted the fourteenth amendment to base apportionment on voters, but the idea was rejected. The House was all male and they feared voter-count apportionment would create an incentive to extend voting rights to women. Furthermore, southern states did not want legislation that would create an incentive to allow African American males to vote. Would over 100,000 Floridians have been disenfranchised on Election Day 2000 if voter-count apportionment had been adopted? Schmeckebier wanted to eradicate the disenfranchisement of African Americans and Mexican Americans that Republicans in the House had wanted to prevent decades earlier. Law professor Grant Hayden states, "there is evidence that the framers intended members of the House of Representatives . . . to be elected by people with equally weighted votes."[60]

On January 20, 1941, the *Chicago Daily Tribune* printed the article "Propose House Apportionment on Voting Basis" regarding Schmeckebier's book. (Mass communication in 1941 depended on newspapers and radio. Televisions were too expensive for most homes, computers did not exist, and no one could have imagined the Internet at that time.) On December 7, 1941, the Japanese bombed Pearl Harbor and the United States plunged into World War II, and the country forgot Schmeckebier's call to change congressional apportionment to a basis of voters.

After reapportionment in 2000, California obtained three seats because of their undocumented population, and North Carolina gained one seat. Otherwise, the four seats would have gone to Indiana, Michigan, Mississippi, and Montana. Following reapportionment in 2010, undocumented residents will likely account for two seats in both California and Texas.[61] Otherwise, the seats might have gone to Louisiana, Minnesota, Montana, and Ohio. The winners are voters in California and Texas, who will benefit from the additional representation in the House from January 2013 to January 2023. All other voters nationwide lose because the four extra seats enhance even further the dominance of California and Texas in the House. After 2010 reapportionment, California will have the largest delegation and Texas the second largest. Combined, they will control about eighty-nine seats, or one in five (20 percent) representatives nationwide. The three most populous states will account for about 27 percent of representatives, and the five most populous states will control about 37 percent of seats. The tangible harm that comes from including nonvoters in congressional apportionment is that it greatly distorts congressional representation among the states. Starting in January 2013, the House will have the most imbalanced distribution of representatives since 1870.

If undocumented residents are excluded from apportionment, then who should be included? Only citizens? Only registered voters? Only voters? Practical considerations should be considered when deciding among these options. Obtaining an accurate population count of citizens is impossible. That leaves registered voters and actual voters as the remaining options. The widespread disenfranchisement in Florida in the 2000 presidential election shows that even registered voters are at risk of being denied the right to vote. In 2004 former president Jimmy Carter wrote of continued voter disenfranchisement in Florida: "The disturbing fact is that a repetition of the problems of 2000 now seems likely."[62] African Americans may have also been disenfranchised in Cleveland, Ohio, in the 2004 presidential election.[63] Ultimately, apportionment based on the number of votes cast—voters—remains the only practical and effective option to both deter disenfranchisement and equalize the power of a single vote across the country. Voter-based apportionment is the best option to ensure the right to vote and promote voter participation for every American citizen.

With voter-count apportionment, the allocation of representation in the House would be based on the number of voters participating in House elections (or some combination of House and presidential elections). Voter-count apportionment should be used only with the federal House of Representatives, and not for state or local governments. There is competition for congressional seats among the fifty states such that states can add, or lose, representatives every ten years during reapportionment. Voter-count apportionment will create an incentive for states to increase voter participation with the goal of increasing the state's representation in Congress. Such competition does not exist for state and local governments. State legislatures have a fixed number of districts and local boards have a fixed number of elected members. Consequently, there is no means of increasing representation and therefore no incentive to increase voter participation. Voter-count apportionment is not meant to affect the court's ruling in *Garza* since it applies to the local Los Angeles County Board of Supervisors, with its set five members. Nor would voter-count apportionment apply to state legisla tures such as California, which has forty senate districts and eighty assembly districts. Voter-count apportionment would apply to California's fifty-three federal House districts and the remaining 382 federal House districts apportioned among the remaining forty-nine states.

Table 1 (pages 137–38) lists the apportionment of congressional seats if voter-count apportionment were based on the five consecutive House elections from 2000 to 2008. The average number of voters from these five congressional elections was entered into the existing apportionment formula known as the "method of equal proportions."[64] Undocumented residents and children are excluded because they do not vote. Adult citizens who choose not to vote are excluded. A total of thirty-two seats would shift among twenty-seven states. Seventeen states would gain seats while ten states would lose seats. Twenty-three states would remain unaffected.

The biggest loser would be Texas, which would lose eleven seats when compared to the likely outcome from reapportionment after Census 2010. California would lose nine seats—the second largest loss. Florida would lose three seats. The biggest winners would be Michigan, Minnesota, and Ohio, all of which would each gain four seats compared to Census 2010 apportionment. Massachusetts would gain three seats. This redistribution of representation in the House reflects a shift from states with low voter participation such as Arizona (60 percent), Texas (56 percent), and Utah (53 percent), to states with high voter participation such as Minnesota (75 percent, the highest), Maine (71 percent), and Wisconsin (71 percent). Voter-count apportionment would also result in a South-to-North redistribution of representation. States losing representation are all in the South or Southwest, and states gaining seats are all in the northern half of the lower forty-eight states.

Voter-count apportionment would reverse decades of losses among northern states and result in a more balanced distribution of representatives among the fifty states. Voter-count apportionment would create an incentive for states to draw congressional district boundaries to increase voter participation, and encourage more moderate disaffected citizens to vote. However, voter-count apportionment will be unpopular with incumbents as it would foster more competitive elections. As political science Professor Bernard Grofman says, "No politician likes competitive seats."[65]

State	Voter Participation in 2008 (Eligible Voters)	Census 2000 Apportionment	Likely Census 2010 Apportionment	Average Number of Voters in Congressional Elections 2000–2008
Alabama	62%	7	7	1,499,195
Alaska	65%	1	1	270,747
Arizona	60%	8	9	1,636,069
Arkansas	54%	4	4	732,497
California	63%	53	53	9,987,328
Colorado	68%	7	7	1,776,547
Connecticut	67%	5	5	1,266,735
Delaware	67%	1	1	306,945
Florida	64%	25	26	5,135,677
Georgia	64%	13	14	2,604,288
Hawaii	52%	2	2	382,197
Idaho	61%	2	2	510,688
Illinois	63%	19	18	4,302,373
Indiana	61%	9	9	2,087,624
Iowa	70%	5	4	1,252,301
Kansas	63%	4	4	1,015,133
Kentucky	63%	6	6	1,433,652
Louisiana	70%	7	6	1,112,628
Maine	71%	2	2	617,977
Maryland	68%	8	8	2,007,710
Massachusetts	67%	10	9	2,645,717
Michigan	68%	15	14	4,042,800
Minnesota	75%	8	7	2,453,729
Mississippi	70%	4	4	929,084
Missouri	66%	9	9	2,353,036
Montana	65%	1	1	414,619
Nebraska	67%	3	3	658,668
Nevada	60%	3	4	672,604
New Hampshire	71%	2	2	545,655
New Jersey	64%	13	12	2,770,741
New Mexico	63%	3	3	628,712
New York	59%	29	28	6,301,238
North Carolina	68%	13	13	2,918,584
North Dakota	68%	1	1	271,818
Ohio	66%	18	16	4,452,420
Oklahoma	59%	5	5	1,141,220
Oregon	68%	5	5	1,498,513
Pennsylvania	62%	19	18	4,562,940
Rhode Island	67%	2	2	385,314
South Carolina	66%	6	7	1,340,988
South Dakota	68%	1	1	350,698
Tennessee	56%	9	9	1,923,963
Texas	56%	32	36	5,777,038
Utah	53%	3	4	746,259
Vermont	65%	1	1	274,901
Virginia	69%	11	11	2,546,962
Washington	67%	9	10	2,364,008
West Virginia	53%	3	3	560,370
Wisconsin	71%	8	8	2,360,812
Wyoming	64%	1	1	215,883

Apportionment Based on the Average Number of Voters 2000 to 2008	Difference From Actual Census 2000 Apportionment	Difference From Likely Census 2010 Apportionment
7		
1		
7	-1	-2
3	-1	-1
44	-9	-9
8	1	1
6	1	1
1		
23	2	-3
12	-1	-2
2		
2		
19		1
9		
6	1	2
5	1	1
6		
5	-2	-1
3	1	1
9	1	1
12	2	3
18	3	4
11	3	4
4		
10	1	1
2	1	1
3		
3		-1
2		
12	-1	
3		
28	-1	
13		
1		
20	2	4
5		
7	2	2
20	1	2
2		
6		-1
2	1	1
9		
25	-7	-11
3		-1
1		
11		
10	1	
3		
10	2	2
1		

Table 1: *Effect of Voter-Count Apportionment*

Source:

Column 2: U.S. Census Bureau, 2008 Voting and Registration (http://www.census.gov/hhes/www/socdemo/voting/index.html)

Column 3: U.S. Census Bureau, Census 2000 Congressional Apportionment (http://www.census.gov/population/www/censusdata/apportionment/index.html)

Columns 4 and 6: Based on author's calculations using the "Equal Proportions Method" from the U.S. Census Bureau (http://www.census.gov/population/www/censusdata/apportionment/computing.html)

Column 5: Office of the Clerk of the U.S. House of Representatives (http://clerk.house.gov/member_info/electionInfo/index.html)

(Calculations in Table 1 were done before Census 2010 population counts were released and do not reflect official 2010 reapportionment results.)

Why Is This Important? Removing Vestiges of Slavery

In October 2009 Sen. David Vitter, a Republican from Louisiana, introduced legislation (S.AMDT.2644) in the 111th Congress (2009–2010), that required the U.S. Census Bureau to include a question on citizenship on the Census 2010 questionnaire. Vitter wanted to use the count of noncitizens to exclude them from apportionment. The proposed legislation to modify the census questionnaire was flawed because the data collected on citizenship would have been circumspect. Foreign residents, both legal and unauthorized, may have responded that they were citizens fearing they would otherwise be deported. The bill died when ruled non-germane because questionnaires for Census 2010 had already been printed after a long period of review by Congress and the public. Vitter's bill was political theater, which has come to typify Congress.

Also during the 111th Congress, Candice Miller, a Republican from Michigan, introduced House Joint Resolution 11 with twenty-seven co-sponsors, six of which were Democrats. Miller's bill is the most far-reaching to date in favor of limiting the apportionment population to only citizens. The bill includes this sentence: "Representatives shall be apportioned among the several states according to their respective numbers, which shall be determined by counting the number of persons in each State who are citizens of the United States."[66]

Representative Miller introduced similar legislation in 2005 and 2007. It has never made it past committee review. Using 2008 population counts and 2000 reapportionment, Miller's proposal would shift eleven seats among seventeen states. California would lose five representatives and Texas would lose two. Illinois, Massachusetts, New Jersey, and Ohio would each lose one seat. Eleven states would gain one seat each. Ironically, Miller's co-sponsors from Illinois, New Jersey, and Ohio were supporting a bill that would reduce their state's representation in Congress.

Excluding noncitizens from apportionment is a recurring issue. In the 2008 presidential platform, the Republican Party called for including only citizens in congressional apportionment.[67] The 101st Congress (1989–1991) introduced two bills with the intent of excluding illegal populations from apportionment. House Joint Resolution 199 would have amended the Constitution to include only citizens and legal foreign residents in the apportionment count: "Representatives shall be apportioned among the several states according to their respective numbers, counting the whole number of persons in each State who are citizens of the United States or lawfully admitted for permanent residence in the United States." This same session of Congress considered House Resolution 1468 with forty-eight representatives co-sponsoring the bill. The legislation would have excluded illegal aliens from the decennial census count but included Americans living abroad. Both bills were referred in committee and no further action was taken.

The current method of congressional apportionment is based on Section 2 of the fourteenth amendment (ratified 1868), which states that "representatives shall be apportioned among the several States according to their respective numbers, counting the whole number of persons in each State, excluding Indians not taxed."[68] Does the term "persons" in the fourteenth amendment include noncitizens, voters, or all residents regardless of legal status? As recently as 2009, attorneys with the Congressional Research Service, part of the Library of Congress, reported that no clear legal definition exists for who should be included in apportionment: "it does not appear that any court has decided the meaning of the term 'persons' for apportionment purposes."[69] Law professor Robert W. Bennett states, "avoidance by the Court of questions concerning the inclusion and exclusion of large groups in the apportionment base is truly stunning."[70] Apportionment is based on "persons," but we do not know to whom this refers.

When the fourteenth amendment was being drafted, some Republican representatives wanted apportionment to be based on voters.[71] These Republican representatives reasoned that freed male slaves were likely to vote Republican given that President Abraham Lincoln, who freed them, was Republican. Republicans in Congress feared southern states would count newly freed slaves in apportionment but deny them the right to vote. Such disenfranchisement is exactly what happened.

If the fourteenth amendment had limited apportionment to only voters when it was ratified in 1868, it would have benefited western states.[72] Only men could vote, and men outnumbered women in the West. Excluding women would have reduced the apportionment advantage of eastern states with their larger population of women. Northern states had large populations of nonvoting aliens who would have been excluded if apportionment had been based on voters. Southern states feared they would have to allow freed slaves to vote if representation were based on the number of voters. In 1868 it was not politically convenient to limit apportionment to only voters.

Illegal aliens did not exist when the fourteenth amendment was ratified. In some states noncitizen aliens could vote. The United States continued to expand westward and immigrants were welcomed. In 1868 it might have been the intent of Congress for the fourteenth amendment to include everyone in apportionment because the country was founded by immigrants and would continue to need immigrants to populate western lands. Circumstances are much different now. The United States is not adding new territory and current laws differentiate between citizens, legal foreign residents, and illegal aliens.

This sentence from the fourteenth amendment is often overlooked: "But when the right to vote . . . is denied . . . the basis of representation therein shall be reduced." This sentence requires the number of representatives to be reduced in states that have disenfranchised voters. This constitutional re-quirement of the fourteenth amendment has never been enforced. Southern states that disenfranchised African Americans and southwestern states that disenfranchised Mexican Americans did not have representatives taken away. Florida disenfranchised over 100,000 voters in the presidential election of 2000, but still obtained two additional representatives in reapportionment after Census 2000. Voter-count apportionment addresses the same fears of disenfranchisement that were present when the fourteenth amendment was being crafted, which the amendment has failed to remedy.

The population needs of the country and the legal standing of immigrant populations have changed dramatically since the fourteenth amendment was ratified in 1868. Furthermore, the clear wording in the fourteenth amend-ment to penalize states for violating voting rights has been ignored. Either Congress or the court should revisit the fourteenth amendment, which is equally behind the times as it is ineffective. Professors David Butler and Bruce Cain state "the practice of using the census lingers because of tradition and the Constitution, rather than a deliberate philosophical choice."[73] We use total population as the basis for apportionment because that is the way it has always been done, although it is not necessarily the best way.

Voter-count apportionment creates an incentive to enfranchisement. States will gain additional representation in the House only if voter participation increases. The appeal of voter-count apportionment is based on the premise that political parties will work harder to increase voter turnout to gain the maximum number of congressional representatives. Law professor Bradley Smith suggests that political parities could increase voter turnout if they wanted to: "We would expect turnout to be higher when candidates devote more resources, and we expect more voters to turn out where a race is close than when it is not."[74] Candidates will need to appeal to a broader range of voters to draw out the disillusioned middle-of-the-road Americans who do not vote. The result will be more districts that are competitive and less partisan representation.[75]

Utah's 2nd Congressional District provides a modern-day example of a truly competitive district. Since 1970 this district has had nine different representatives and five elections in which the opposing party won. In the 2000 congressional elections, the seat switched from Republican Merrill Cook to Democrat Jim Matheson. Utah state legislators later redrew the district's boundaries in 2001 and gave Republican voters a majority of about 60 percent of the districts. Republicans believed that manipulating the boundaries would give them an advantage among partisan voters in the 2002 election. However in 2002, Democrat Matheson won re-election by less than 2,000 votes of nearly 225,000 votes cast. The tone of the race was civil, and there was little negative campaigning. Democrat Matheson won re-election in 2004, 2006, and 2008 in the mostly Republican district. In the 2008 election, nearly 350,000 votes were cast, which was an increase of over 50 percent in voter participation from the 2000 election. Matheson was re-elected in 2010 by nearly 11,000 votes in contrast to a wave of anti-incumbent and anti-Democrat voting nationwide. The lesson may be that in competitive districts, voters connect more with the elected official than their party and vice versa.

Competitive districts such as Utah's 2nd provide an "open market" of political options instead of the current "boutique" or "specialty" politics that typify red and blue districts. Lawyers from the Association of the Bar of the City of New York argue for competitive elections: "Elections are about giving voters choices."[76] Just as important, former Illinois representative Rahm Emanuel argues that increasing competition will decrease political corruption: "There is a correlation between a lack of competition and cases of corruption. If we want true political and ethics reform, we need competition in the system, and politicians have to be truly accountable to the voters."[77]

There needs to be an incentive to increase the number of voters in congressional districts and thereby increase political competition. Voter-count apportionment will reward states for increasing voter participation. State legislatures will be induced into designing congressional districts so that disillusioned middle-of-the-road citizens start voting again; otherwise, states stand to lose congressional representation in the subsequent round of reapportionment. The re-emergence of moderate voters in large numbers will lead to a greater number of moderate congressional representatives not dependent solely on partisan voters to get re-elected. Voter-count apportionment will move America away from partisan politics and make elected officials primarily accountable to voters, not their political parties. The key is increasing voter participation so that moderate voters can "vote the bums out" when elected officials favor the wishes of their partisan supporters over the best interests of the communities they represent.

Illegal immigrants may fear that being excluded from apportionment will worsen their plight. However, there is no evidence that undocumented immigrants have any tangible representation in the House. The best illegal residents can hope for is that voters will be sensitive to their plight. If such empathy exists, it would be regardless of whether or not illegal residents are counted in apportionment. Pro-immigrant legislation requires support from voters nationwide, since a majority of congressional representatives are needed to enact immigration reform. The effect of a few congressional representatives who may be sensitive to illegal immigrants is inconsequential. At worst, voters in communities with large concentrations of undocumented residents will turn their added representation against the undocumented. Supporters of immigration reform should focus their efforts on influencing voters. Realistically, the undocumented receive no tangible advantage from being counted in apportionment. American history suggests it does more harm than good.

In contrast, voter-count apportionment will create an incentive for political parties to increase the number of voters among minorities and to turn noncitizens into voting citizens with an ownership stake in the country's future. In 1979 Democratic Sen. Birch Bayh, of Indiana, stated in discussions to reform the Electoral College: "What could assist black leadership more in increasing registration and voter participation in the Democratic process than efforts and resources of the national parties to go after every voter?"[78] The same holds true for Hispanics today.

The country that Abraham Lincoln sought to keep united is pulling apart politically, and largely along the same lines that defined Lincoln's election victory in 1860.[79] The red states get redder, the blue states get bluer, and the map of the United States takes on the divisions of the Civil War era.[80] In 1960 the three most populated states (New York, California, and Pennsylvania) held nearly 24 percent of House seats. In 2010 the three most populated states (California, Texas, and New York) will increase their control of the House to over 27 percent of representatives. If population trends that began in 1960 continue, by 2040 the three most populated states (California, Texas, and Florida) will hold one-third of House seats and the five most populated states (California, Texas, Florida, New York, and Georgia) will hold over 40 percent of House seats. Will the United States of America become the United States of "Caltexaflor"?

The Constitution provides two avenues for enacting amendments. Historically, constitutional amendments have been adopted by passing legislation in the House and Senate that is later ratified by the states. This requires two-thirds (290) of representatives and two-thirds (sixty-six) of senators to vote in favor of the amendment and three-in-four (thirty-eight) states to ratify it. The likelihood of enacting voter-count apportionment in this way is low, because the ten states that would lose seats have enough representation to block passage in the House. The biggest obstacles are California, Florida, and Texas, which combined will likely hold 115 seats (26 percent) after reapportionment in 2010.[81] The control these three states have over congressional legislation underscores the need to adopt voter-count apportionment to reduce the influence of "Super States." James Madison warned that states might intentionally increase their population in order to gain control of Congress.

The alternative method for enacting a constitutional amendment is for two-thirds (thirty-three) of state legislatures to call for a constitutional convention. Three-fourths (thirty-eight) of states would then have to ratify the legislation. Forty states would benefit from voter-count apportionment, and this is above the minimum needed to call a constitutional convention and ratify. A likely scenario would have seventeen states gaining seats and twenty-three states remaining unaffected. Unaffected states benefit from voter-count apportionment because the subsequent redistribution of seats would reduce the influence of the most populated states.

There is great irony in historical events. President Barack Obama is the most politically influential African American in U.S. history. Obama taught constitutional law at the University of Chicago. Might President Obama call for a constitutional convention of the states during his second presidential term? If so, it would be the first time a constitutional convention has taken place since the founding constitutional convention in 1787. A hypothetical second constitutional convention could amend the Constitution to expand the Bill of Rights to include the right to vote. The Electoral College could be eliminated. And congressional apportionment could be changed to include only voters. It would mark one of the most remarkable events in American history if an African American president oversaw the removal of the last vestiges of slavery from the U.S. Constitution. Future historians might call it the beginning of the Inclusionist Era of American politics.

Notes

Preface

1. Schmeckebier, Laurence F. *Congressional Apportionment.* Washington, DC: The Brookings Institution, 1941: 97.

Chapter 1. Apportionment

1. Feeney, Tom. "Immigration." Tom Feeney. http://feeney.tcvmedia.com/position-statements/immigration. May 17, 2010.
2. Ramos, Victor Manuel. "Immigrants May Boost Florida's Clout." *Orlando Sentinel.* October 4, 2007.
3. Goode, Virgil H. "H.RES.839." Library of Congress. http://thomas.loc.gov/cgi-bin/bdquery/D?d109:1:./temp/~bdn4lS:@@@L&summ2=m&|/bss/d109query.html| (May 20, 2010).
4. Nuñez-Neto, Blas. "Border Security: The Role of the U.S. Border Patrol." *Congressional Research Service* (2005): 27.
5. Zengerle, Patricia, and Tim Gaynor. "Obama Sending 1,200 Troops to Mexico Border." *Reuters,* May 25, 2010. http://www.reuters.com/article/idUSTRE64O5RE20100526 (May 25, 2010).
6. Conover, Ted. "Border Vigilantes." *New York Times.* May 11, 1997.
7. Ibid.
8. Southern Poverty Law Center "Leiva v. Ranch Rescue." Southern Poverty Law Center. http://www.splcenter.org/get-informed/case-docket/leiva-v-ranch rescue. May 17, 2010.
9. Yoxall, Peter. "Comment: The Minuteman Project, Gone in a Minute or Here to Stay? The Origin, History, and Future of Citizen Activism on the United States-Mexico Border." *University of Miami Inter-American Law Review* (Spring/Summer 2006): 5.
10. Walker, Christopher J. "Harvard Latino Law Review." *Article: Border Vigilantism and Comprehensive Immigration Reform* (Spring 2007): 153.
11. Yoxall, "The Minuteman Project," 6.
12. Vina, Stephen R. "Civilian Patrols Along the Border: Legal and Policy Issues." *Congressional Research Service* (April 7, 2006): 11.

13. Walker, Christopher J. "Harvard Latino Law Review." *Article: Border Vigilantism and Comprehensive Immigration Reform* (Spring 2007): 141.
14. Yoxall "The Minuteman Project," 3.
15. Ibid., 4.
16. Ibid., 4.
17. "Grisly '72 Massacre Still Haunts Texas Town." *The Victoria Advocate*. November 17, 2001, 5A.
18. Zakin, Susan. "The Hunters and the Hunted: The Arizona-Mexico Border Turns into the 21st Century Frontier." *High County News.* October 9, 2000.
19. Montejano, David. *Anglos and Mexicans in the Making of Texas, 1836–1986.* Austin: University of Texas Press, 1987: 127.
20. Ibid.
21. Webb, Walter Prescott. *The Texas Rangers: A Century of Frontier Defense.* Austin: University of Texas Press, 1965: 478.
22. U.S. Supreme Court. "Allee v. Medrano, 416 U.S. 802 (1974)." http://supreme.justia.com/us/416/802/index.html (May 21, 2010).
23. Walker, Christopher J. "Harvard Latino Law Review." *Article: Border Vigilantism and Comprehensive Immigration Reform* (Spring 2007): 167.
24. Vina, Stephen R. "Civilian Patrols Along the Border: Legal and Policy Issues." *Congressional Research Service* (April 7, 2006): 9.
25. Allen, Jennifer. "Jury Verdict Against Border Vigilante." ImmigrationProf Blog. http://lawprofessors.typepad.com/immigration/2006/11/jury_verdict_ag.html. May 17, 2010.
26. McGirk, Jan. "Private Posses Hunt Mexican Migrants for Sport." Asheville Global Report. http://www.theglobalreport.org/issues/70/nationalnews.html. November 4, 2010.
27. Nuñez-Neto, Blas. "Border Security: The Role of the U.S. Border Patrol." *Congressional Research Service* (2005): 2.
28. Cornelius, Wayne A. "Controlling 'Unwanted' Immigration: Lessons from the United States, 1993–2004." *eScholarship.* December 1, 2004. http://www.escholarship.org/uc/item/70c6g11d. January 24, 2010:14.
29. Walker, "Harvard Latino Law Review,"167.
30. Ibid., 153.
31. Jimenez, Maria. "Humanitarian Crisis: Migrant Deaths at the U.S.—Mexico Border." American Civil Liberties Union. http://www.aclu.org/files/pdfs/immigrants/humanitariancrisisreport.pdf. May 17, 2010.
32. Nuñez-Neto, "Border Security," 23.
33. Cornelius, "Controlling 'Unwanted' Immigration," 13.
34. Launius, Sarah. "Federal Judge Threatens NMD Volunteer with 25 Days Imprisonment." No More Deaths. http://www.nomoredeaths.org/index.php/Press-Releases/federal-judge-threatens-humanitarian-aid-worker-with-25-days-imprisonment.html (May 17, 2010).
35. "13 Humanitarians to Be Arraigned on "Littering" Charges." http://www.nomoredeaths.org/index.php/Press-Releases/13-humanitarians-to-be-arraigned-on-littering-charges.html (May 17, 2010).
36. Research and Innovative Technology Administration. "Border Crossing: Border Crossing/Entry Data." http://www.transtats.bts.gov/DL_SelectFields.asp?Table_ID=1358&DB_Short_Name=Border Crossing (May 17, 2010).

37. Office of Immigration Statistics. "Immigration Enforcement Actions: 2008." http://www.dhs.gov/xlibrary/assets/statistics/publications/enforcement_ar_08.pdf (May 17, 2010).

38. Nuñez-Neto, "Border Security," 9.

39. Walker, "Harvard Latino Law Review," 141.

40. Hayden, Grant M. "The False Promise of One Person, One Vote." *Michigan Law Review* (November 2003): 263.

41. Murphy, Dennis L. "Symposium: The Right to Privacy One Hundred Years Later: Note: The Exclusion of Illegal Aliens from the Reapportionment Base: A Question of Representation." *Case Western Reserve Law Review* (1991): 3.

42. Ibid., 10.

43. Garcia, F. Chris, and Gabriel R. Sanchez. *Hispanics and the U.S. Political System: Moving into the Mainstream.* Saddle River, NJ: Pearson Education, Inc., 2008: 146.

44. Keyssar, Alexander. *The Right to Vote: The Contested History of Democracy in the United States.* New York: Basic Books, 2000: 231.

45. Hall, Kermit L. *Major Problems in American Constitutional History Volume 1: The Colonial Era Through Reconstruction.* Lexington, MA: D.C. Heath, 1992: 137.

46. Library of Congress. "Federalist No. 54, The Apportionment of Members Among the States." http://thomas.loc.gov/home/histdox/fed_54.html (May 18, 2010).

47. Rowland, Kate Mason. *The Life of George Mason: 1725–1792.*

48. Levinson, Sanford. "Symposium: Baker v. Carr: A Commemorative Symposium: Panel II: One Person, One Vote: A Theoretical and Practical Examination: One Person, One Vote. A Mantra In Need of Meaning." *North Carolina Law Review,* 2002: 9.

49. Constitution Society. "Debates in the Convention of the State of North Carolina on the Adoption of the Federal Constitution." http://www.constitution.org/rc/rat_nc.htm (May 21, 2010).

50. Brutus. "Anti-Federalist Papers, Brutus III." November 15, 1787. http://teachingamericanhistory.org/library/index.asp?document=1670 (May 21, 2010).

51. U.S. Census Bureau, excluded Maine, Kentucky, S.W. Territory, and N. Territory

52. Ackerman, Bruce. *The Failure of the Founding Fathers.* Cambridge, MA: The Belknap Press of Harvard University Press, 2005: 17.

53. U.S. Census Bureau. "Apportionment of the U.S, House." http://www.census.gov/population/www/censusdata/apportionment/files/apportn.pdf (May 18, 2010).

54. Levinson, "Symposium," 9.

55. Remini, Robert V. *The House.* New York: Harper Collins Publishers, 2006: 115.

56. U.S. House of Representatives. "U.S. Constitution, Article IV, Section 3." http://www.house.gov/house/Constitution/Constitution.html (May 21, 2010).

57. *Chronicles of Oklahoma.* Vol. 38. Oklahoma Historical Society, 1960: 98.

58. Foreman, Grant. *Indian Removal: The Emigration of the Five Civilized Tribes of Indians.* Norman: University of Oklahoma Press, 1985: 115.

59. Ibid., 119.

60. Ibid., 121.

61. Ibid., 108.

62. Ibid., 124.

63. Ibid., 119.

64. Ibid., 134.

65. Jackson, Andrew. "Special Message February 15, 1832." The American Presidency Project. http://www.presidency.ucsb.edu/ws/index.php?pid=66841 (May 21, 2010).

66. Foreman, *Indian Removal*, 121.

67. Morais, Nina. "Sex Discrimination and the Fourteenth Amendment: Lost History." *Yale Law Journal*, May 1988: 1159.

68. Ibid., 1156.

69. Flack, Horace Edgar. *The Adoption of the Fourteenth Amendment*. Baltimore: Johns Hopkins Press, 1965: 98.

70. Gumbel, Andrew. *Steal This Vote: Dirty Elections and the Rotten History of Democracy in America*. New York: Nations Book, 2005: 127.

71. Flack, *The Adoption of the Fourteenth Amendment*, 123.

72. Amar, Akhil Reed. *America's Constitution: A Biography*. New York: Random House, 2005: 393.

73. Hamilton, Gail. *Biography of James G. Blaine*. Boston: Henry Bill Publishing Company, 1895: 194.

74. U.S. Census Bureau. "Apportionment of the U.S. House." http://www.census.gov/population/www/censusdata/apportionment/files/apportn.pdf (May 18, 2010).

75. Amar, Akhil Reed. *America's Constitution*, 392.

76. Flack, *The Adoption of the Fourteenth Amendment*, 116.

77. Schwarz, Frederick D. "How It Got that Way and Why We're Stuck with It." *American Heritage*, 2001: 43–49.

78. American Civil Liberties Union. "Voting Rights Act Timeline." http://www.aclu.org/voting-rights/voting-rights-act-timeline (May 18, 2010).

79. Valelly, Richard M. *The Two Reconstructions: The Struggle for Black Enfranchisement*. Chicago: The University of Chicago Press, 2004: 8.

80. Ibid.

81. Hayden. "The False Promise of One Person, One Vote," 232–233.

82. Anderson, Margo J., and Stephen E. Fienberg. *Who Counts? The Politics of Census-Taking in Contemporary America*. New York: Russell Sage Foundation, 1999: 42.

83. Ibid., 49.

84. U.S. Census Monitoring Board. "Final Report to Congress, September 1, 2001." http://govinfo.library.unt.edu/cmb/cmbp/reports/final_report/FinalReport.pdf (May 18, 2010): 114.

85. Hoeffer, Michael et al.,"Estimates of the Unauthorized Immigrant Population Residing in the United States: January 2009." Office of Immigration Statistics. http://www.dhs.gov/xlibrary/assets/statistics/publications/ois_ill_pe_2009.pdf (May 18, 2010): 4.

86. Lowenthal, Terri Ann. "Census News Briefs." Communications Consortium Media Center. http://www.thecensusproject.org/newsbriefs/cnb81-8nov2009.html (May 18, 2010).

87. Pew Research Center for the People & the Press. "Most View Census Positively, But Some Have Doubts." http://pewresearch.org/pubs/1468/survey-views-knowledge-of-census-likely-participation (May 2010).

88. Citro, Constance F., Daniel L. Cork, and Janet L. Norwood. eds. *The 2000 Census: Counting Under Adversity*. Washington, DC: The National Academies Press, 2004: 2.
89. Ibid., 11.
90. U.S. Supreme Court. "Utah et al. v. Evans, Secretary of Commerce et al— 536 U.S. 452 (2002)." http://supreme.justia.com/us/536/452/index.html (May 21, 2010).
91. Knutson, Ryan. "Republicans Send Out a 'Census' Form—That's Really a Fundraiser." ProPublica. http://www.propublica.org/article/republicans-send-out-a-census-form-thats-really-a-fundraiser-210 (May 18, 2010).
92. Simons, Meredith. "GOP Letter Invokes 'Census,' Sparks Controversy." *St. Louis Post-Dispatch*, January 30, 2010.
93. "Rescue The Census." *The New York Times*, December 4, 2008.
94. House Committee on Oversight and Government Reform. "Serial No. 109-119—Counting the Vote: Should Only U.S. Citizens Be Included in Apportioning Our Elected Representatives?." http://www.access.gpo.gov/congress/house/house07ch109.html (May 18, 2010): 5.
95. Ibid., 78.
96. Ibid., 122–23.
97. Ibid.
98. Ibid., 58.
99. Ibid., 20.
100. Library of Congress. "Federalist No. 54, The Apportionment of Members Among the States."

Chapter 2. Redistricting

1. Powe, Scot, and Steve Bickerstaff. "Anthony Kennedy's Blind Quest." *Michigan Law Review* 105, no. 63 (2006): 65. http://www.michiganlawreview.org/assets/fi/105/powe.pdf (May 23, 2010).
2. Toobin, Jeffrey. "Drawing the Line: Will Tom DeLay's Redistricting in Texas Cost Him His Seat?" *The New Yorker*, March 6, 2006 http://www.newyorker.com/archive/2006/03/06/060306fa_fact (May 23, 2010). Jeffrey Toobin quoting Stanford Professor Pamela Karlan.
3. Eilperin, Juliet. *Fight Club Politics*. Lanham, Maryland: Rowman & Littlefield, 2006: 112.
4. Menifield, Charles. ed. *Representation of Minority Groups in the U.S.: Implications for the Twenty-first Century*. Lanham, Maryland: Austin & Winfield, 2001: 57–75.
5. U.S. Census Bureau. "American Community Survey." http://factfinder.census.gov/servlet/DatasetMainPageServlet?_program=ACS&_submenuId=datasets_2&_lang=en.
6. Jost, Kenneth. "Redistricting Disputes: Should the Courts Limit Partisan Gerrymandering?" *The CQ Researcher*, March 12, 2004: 225.
7. Ibid., 225.
8. Ibid., 232.
9. U.S. Supreme Court. "Davis v. Bandemer, 478 U.S. 109 (1986)." http://supreme.justia.com/us/478/109/case.html (May 23, 2010).
10. Jost "Redistricting Disputes," 229.

11. Briffault, Richard. "Lulac on Partisan Gerrymandering: Some Clarity, More Uncertainty." *Michigan Law Review* 105, no. 58 (2006): 58. http://www .michiganlawreview.org/assets/fi/105/briffault.pdf (May 23, 2010).

12. Forest, Benjamin. "The Changing Demographic, Legal, and Technological Contexts of Political Representation." *Proceedings of the National Academy of Sciences* (2005): 15333. http://www.pnas.org/content/102/43/15331.full.pdf+html (May 23, 2010).

13. Jost, "Redistricting Disputes," 234.

14. Ibid., 236.

15. Ibid.

16. Ibid.

17. Moore, Allan B. "A 'Frightful Political Dragon' Indeed: Why Constitutional Challenges Cannot Subdue the Gerrymander." *Harvard Journal of Law & Public Policy* 13, no. 1 (1990): 949.

18. McDonald, Michael P., and John Samples. *The Marketplace of Democracy*. Washington, DC: Brookings Institution Press, 2006: 234.

19. Issacharoff, Samuel. "Collateral Damage: The Endangered Center In American Politics." *William and Mary Law Review*, 2004: 435.

20. U.S. Supreme Court. "Thornburg v. Gingles, 478 U.S. 30 (1986)."

21. Barreto, Matt A., Gary M. Segura, and Nathan D. Woods. "The Mobilizing Effect of Majority–Minority Districts on Latino Turnout." *American Political Science Review* 98, no. 1 (2004): 65.

22. Mayer, Kenneth R., and David T. Canton. *The Dysfunctional Congress? The Individual Roots of an Institutional Dilemma*. Boulder: Westview Press, 1999: 110.

23. Brunell, Thomas L. *Redistricting and Representation: Why Competitive Elections are Bad for America*. New York: Routledge, 2008: 72.

24. Office of the Clerk, U.S. House of Representatives. "Party Divisions of the House of Representatives (1789 to Present)." http://clerk.house.gov/art_history/ house_history/partyDiv.html.

25. Weber, Ronald E. "State Legislative Redistricting in 2003–2004: Emerging Trends and Issues in Reapportionment." The Council of State Governments. http:// csg-web.csg.org/knowledgecenter/docs/BOS2005-LegislativeRedistricting .pdf (May 23, 2010): 117.

26. Office of the Clerk, U.S. House of Representatives. "Party Divisions of the House of Representatives (1789 to Present)."

27. Tolson, Franita. "Increasing the Quantity and the Quality of the African-American Vote: Lessous for 2008 and Beyond." *Berkeley Journal of African American Law and Policy,* 10, no. 2 (2008): 333.

28. Hood III, M V., and Seth C. McKee. "Gerrymandering on Georgia's Mind: The Effects of Redistricting on Vote Choice in the 2006 Midterm Election." *Social Science Quarterly* (2008): 62.

29. Barreto et al, "The Mobilizing Effect of Majority–Minority Districts on Latino Turnout," 67.

30. Eilperin, *Fight Club Politics,* 6.

31. Ibid., 83.

32. Ibid., 71.

33. Ibid., 36.
34. Weber, Ronald E. "State Legislative Redistricting in 2003–2004: Emerging Trends and Issues in Reapportionment." The Council of State Governments. http://csg-web.csg.org/knowledgecenter/docs/BOS2005-LegislativeRedistricting.pdf (May 23, 2010): 118.
35. U.S. Census Bureau. "American FactFinder, Decennial Datasets." http://factfinder.census.gov/servlet/DatasetMainPageServlet?_program=DEC&_submenuId=datasets_1&_lang=en.
36. Hirsch, Sam. "The United States House of Unrepresentatives: What Went Wrong in the Latest Round of Congressional Redistricting." *Election Law Journal* 2, no. 2 (2003): 182.
37. Welch, Susan, and John R. Hibbing. "Hispanic Representation in the U.S. Congress." *Social Science Quarterly* 65 (1984): 334.
38. U.S. Census Bureau. "American Community Survey." http://factfinder.census.gov/servlet/DatasetMainPageServlet?_program=ACS&_submenuId=datasets_2&_lang=en.
39. Garcia, F. Chris, and Gabriel R. Sanchez. *Hispanics and the U.S. Political System: Moving into the Mainstream.* Saddle River, NJ: Pearson Education, Inc., 2008: 61.
40. Lublin, David. *The Paradox of Representation: Racial Gerrymandering and Minority Interests in Congress.* Princeton, N.J.: Princeton University Press, 1999: 72.
41. Bickerstaff, Steve. *Lines in the Sand: Congressional Redistricting in Texas adn the Downfall of Tom Delay.* Austin: University of Texas Press, 2007: 69–70.
42. Bickerstaff, *Lines in the Sand,* 346.
43. Office of the Clerk, U.S. House of Representatives. "Party Divisions of the House of Representatives (1789 to Present)."
44. Eilperin, *Fight Club Politics,* 4.
45. Bickerstaff, *Lines in the Sand,* 68.
46. Ibid., 176.
47. Kanelis, John. "Stand tall, Lt. Gov. David Dewhurst." *Amarillo Globe-News,* July 20, 2003.
48. Bickerstaff, *Lines in the Sand,* 179.
49. "Ruled Out: Texas Doesn't Need Costly, Contentious Redistricting Ploy." *The Houston Chronicle,* February 2, 2003. http://www.chron.com/CDA/archives/archive.mpl?id=2003_3623337.
50. Bickerstaff, *Lines in the Sand,* 299.
51. Eilperin, *Fight Club Politics,* 27.
52. Bickerstaff, *Lines in the Sand,* 252.
53. Ibid.
54. Jost, Kenneth. "Redistricting Disputes: Should the courts limit partisan gerrymandering?" *The CQ Researcher,* March 12, 2004: 223.
55. Bickerstaff, *Lines in the Sand,* 260–61.
56. Ibid., 215.
57. Ibid., 304.
58. "DeLay, Rove at Whip; Local Concerns Aren't Even Afterthought in Power Grab." *Waco Tribune Hearld,* September 7, 2003.
59. Bickerstaff, *Lines in the Sand,* 300.
60. Ibid., 5.

61. Jost, "Redistricting Disputes," 226.

62. Bickerstaff, *Lines in the Sand*, 144.

63. Ibid., 51.

64. Ibid., 197.

65. Kanelis, "Stand Tall, Lt. Gov. David Dewhurst."

66. Copelin, Laylan. "Travis Caught In Remap Crossfire." *Austin American-Statesman*, October 9, 2003.

67. Bickerstaff, *Lines in the Sand*, 2.

68. Andrews, Edmund L. "How Cafta Passed House by 2 Votes." *The New York Times*, July 29, 2005. http://www.nytimes.com/2005/07/29/politics/29cafta .html (May 23, 2010).

69. Office of the Clerk of the U.S. House of Representatives. "Final Vote Results for Roll Call 443." http://clerk.house.gov/evs/2005/roll443.xml (May 23, 2010).

70. U.S. Supreme Court. "League of United Latin American Citizens v. Perry - 05-204 (2006)." http://supreme.justia.com/us/548/05-204/index.html (May 23, 2010).

71. Lane, Charles, and Dan Balz. "Justices Affirm GOP Map for Texas." *The Washington Post*, 29 June 2006. http://www.washingtonpost.com/wp-dyn/ content/article/2006/06/28/AR2006062800660.html (May 23, 2010).

72. Katz, Ellen D. "From Laredo to Fort Worth: Race, Politics, and the Texas Redistricting Case." *Michigan Law Review* (2006): 42.

73. Bickerstaff, *Lines in the Sand*, 286.

74. Ibid., 293.

75. Ibid., 296.

76. Powe, Scot, and Steve Bickerstaff. "Anthony Kennedy's Blind Quest." *Michigan Law Review* 105, no. 63 (2006): 65. http://www.michiganlawreview.org/as-sets/fi/105/powe.pdf (May 23, 2010).

77. Lozano, Juan. "Tom DeLay Guilty." *Huffington Post*, November 24, 2010.

78. The Harvard Law Review Association. "An Interstate Process Perspective on Political Gerrymandering." *Harvard Law Review*, 2005–2006: 1578.

79. McGhee, Eric. *Redistricting and Legislative Partisanship*. San Francisco: Public Policy Institute of California, 2008: 8.

80. Ibid., 9.

81. Ibid.

82. Overton, Spencer. *Stealing Democracy: The New Politics of Voter Suppression*. New York: W.W. Norton, 2006: 20.

83. Eilperin, *Fight Club Politics*, 113.

84. Overton, *Stealing Democracy*, 20.

85. Ibid.

86. Hill, Steven. *Fixing Elections: The Failure of America's Winner Take All Politics*. New York: Routledge, 2002: 82.

87. Citizens for Responsibility and Ethics in Washington. "Family Affair." http:// www.citizensforethics.org/files/FINAL_FULL_REPORT.pdf (May 23, 2010): 11.

88. Overton, *Stealing Democracy*, 21.

89. Johnson, Kevin R. "Latinas/os and the Political Process: The Need for Critical Inquiry." *Oregon Law Review* 81, no. 4 (2003): 922. https://scholarsbank. uoregon.edu/xmlui/bitstream/handle/1794/4557/81_Or_L_Rev_917. pdf?sequence=1 (May 23, 2010).

90. U.S. District Court Central District of California. "Maria Cano, et al., Plaintiffs, vs. Gray Davis, et al., Defendants." http://swdb.berkeley.edu/resources/Court _Cases/california/Cano_v_Davis.pdf (May 23, 2010).
91. Jost, "Redistricting Disputes, 232.
92. Johnson, Douglas, Elise Lampe, Justin Levitt, and Andrew Lee. *Restoring the Competitive Edge.* Claremont: Rose Institute of State and Local Government, 2005: 13.
93. Eilperin, *Fight Club Politics,* 115.
94. Ibid., 102.
95. U.S. Supreme Court. "Vieth et al. v. Jubelirer, President of the Pennsylvania Senate, et al 541 U.S. 267 (2004)." http://supreme.justia.com/us/541/267/ case.html (May 23, 2010).
96. Eilperin, *Fight Club Politics,* 97.
97. Jost, "Redistricting Disputes," 240.
98. Ibid., 241.
99. Hood, "Gerrymandering on Georgia's Mind," 60.
100. Rarick, Ethan. "Learning to love gerrymandering." *Los Angeles Times,* October 2, 2005, M5.
101. Harvard Law Review Association. "An Interstate Process Perspective on Political Gerrymandering." *Harvard Law Review,* 2005–2006: 1588.
102. Dodd, Lawrence C., and Bruce I. Oppenheimer. *Congress Reconsidered.* 9th edition. Washington, DC: CQ Press, 2008: 429.
103. Garcia and Sanchez, *Hispanics and the U.S. Political System,* 205.
104. Ibid., 232.
105. McDonald, Michael P., and John Samples. *The Marketplace of Democracy.* Washington, DC: Brookings Institution Press, 2006: 241.
106. Jost, "Redistricting Disputes," 239.
107. Murray, Shailagh, and Lori Montgomery. "House Passes Health-Care Reform Bill without Republican votes." *Washington Post,* March 22, 2010. http:// www.washingtonpost.com/wp-dyn/content/article/2010/03/21/AR2010 032100943.html (May 23, 2010).
108. Eilperin, *Fight Club Politics,* 85.
109. Ibid., 13.

Chapter 3. Illegal Workers

1. Foley, Neil. *The White Scourge.* Berkeley: University of California Press, 1997: 21.
2. Kaiser, Robert G. *So Damn Much Money.* New York: Knopf, 2009: 46.
3. Ibid., 49.
4. Haines, David W., and Karen E. Rosenblum, *Illegal Immigration in America: A Reference Handbook.* Westport, CT: Greenwood Press, 1999: 236.
5. Haines and Rosenblum, *Illegal Immigration in America,* 32.
6. Newton, Lina. *Illegal, Alien, or Immigrant: The Politics of Immigration Reform.* New York: New York University Press, 2008: 75.
7. Ibid., 79.
8. Ibid., 82.
9. Ibid., 76.
10. Mazzoli, Romano L., and Alan K. Simpson. "Enacting Immigration Reform, Again." *The Washington Post,* September 15, 2006. http://www.washingtonpost

.com/wp-dyn/content/article/2006/09/14/AR2006091401179.html (May 21, 2010).

11. Newton, *Illegal, Alien, or Immigrant,* 87.

12. Calavita, Kitty. *Inside the State,* London: Routledge, Chapman and Hall, 1992: 8.

13. Grimm, Tyler. "Student Note: Using Employer Sanctions to Open the Border and End Undocumented Immigration." *Journal of Gender, Race & Justice,* 2009: 3.

14. Zuehlke, Eric. "Immigrants Work in Riskier and More Dangerous Jobs in the United States." Population Reference Bureau. http://www.prb.org/Articles/2009/usimmigrantsriskyjobs.aspx (May 21, 2010).

15. Tanger, Stephanie E. "Enforcing Corporate Responsibility for Violations of Workplace Immigration Laws: The Case of Meatpacking." *Harvard Latino Law Review.*2006.http://www.law.harvard.edu/students/orgs/llr/vol9/tanger.php #Heading171 (January 24, 2010).

16. Grimm, "Student Note," 3.

17. Cornelius, Wayne A. "Controlling 'Unwanted' Immigration: Lessons from the United States, 1993–2004." *eScholarship.* December 1, 2004. http://www.escholarship.org/uc/item/70c6g11d (accessed January 24, 2010): 11.

18. Cusack, Bob. "Dems May Take Hardline on Those Who Hire Illegal Immigrants." *The Hill,* December 5, 2006. http://thehill.com/business-a-lobbying/2328-dems-may-take-hardline-on-those-who-hire-illegal-immigrants (May 21, 2010).

19. "Tancredo Discusses Immigration Reform Bills." *Washington Post,* March 30, 2006. http://www.washingtonpost.com/wp-dyn/content/discussion/2006/03/29/DI2006032901468.html (May 21, 2010).

20. Haines and Rosenblum, *Illegal Immigration in America,* 152.

21. Grimm, "Student Note," 5.

22. Tanger, "Enforcing Corporate Responsibility for Violations of Workplace Immigration Laws: The Case of Meatpacking."

23. Ibid.

24. Lydersen, Kari. "Former CEO of Iowa Kosher Meatpacking Plant Is Arrested." *The Washington Post,* October 31, 2008. http://www.washingtonpost.com/wp-dyn/content/article/2008/10/30/AR2008103004617.html (May 21, 2010).

25. Waddington, Lynda. "Rubashkin Hope for New Trial Denied." *The Iowa Independent,* October 28, 2010. http://iowaindependent.com/46432/rubashkin-hope-for-new-trial-denied (November 6, 2010).

26. Ndulo, Nchimunya D. "Note: State Employer Sanctions Laws and the Federal Preemption Doctrine: The Legal Arizona Workers Act Revisited." *Cornell Journal of Law and Public Policy,* 2009: 3.

27. Cusack, "Dems May Take Hardline on Those Who Hire Illegal Immigrants."

28. Cornelius, Wayne A. "Controlling 'Unwanted' Immigration": 17.

29. "Tancredo Discusses Immigration Reform Bills." *Washington Post,* March 30, 2006. http://www.washingtonpost.com/wp-dyn/content/discussion/2006/03/29/DI2006032901468.html (May 21, 2010).

30. Ndulo, Nchimunya D. "Note: State Employer Sanctions Laws and the Federal Preemption Doctrine: The Legal Arizona Workers Act Revisited." *Cornell Journal of Law and Public Policy,* 2009: 3.

31. KEYTLaw. "Text of Arizona's Anti-Illegal Immigration Law–Part 4." http://

www.keytlaw.com/blog/2010/04/text-of-arizona%E2%80%99s-anti-illegal-immigration-law%E2%80%93part-4/ (May 21, 2010).

32. U.S. Department of Homeland Security. "E-Verify." http://www.dhs.gov/files/programs/gc_1185221678150.shtm (May 21, 2010).

33. Ndulo, "State Employer Sanctions Laws and the Federal Preemption Doctrine," 11.

34. Arizona Attorney General. "Frequently Asked Questions about the Legal Arizona Workers Act." http://www.azag.gov/LegalAZWorkersAct/FAQ.html#whatcando (May 21, 2010).

35. Arizona Department of Education. "Arizona October 1st Enrollment Figures." https://www.azcd.gov/researchpolicy/AZEnroll/ (May 21, 2010).

36. Kornman, Sheryl. "Sonoran Officials Slam Sanctions Law in Tucson Visit." *Tucson Citizen*, January 15, 2008.

37. Scerbo, Mike A. "First Employer Sanctions Case Filed." Maricopa County Attorney. http://www.mcaodocuments.com/press/20091118_a.pdf (May 21, 2010).

38. Slevin, Peter. "Arizona Law on Immigration Puts Police in Tight Spot." *Washington Post*, April 30, 2010. http://www.washingtonpost.com/wp-dyn/content/article/2010/04/29/AR2010042904970.html?wpisrc=nl_cuzhead (May 25, 2010).

39. Kornblut, Anne E., and Spencer S. Hsu. "Arizona Governor Signs Immigration Bill, Reopening National Debate." *Washington Post*, April 24, 2010. http://www.washingtonpost.com/wp-dyn/content/article/2010/04/23/AR2010042301441.html?wpisrc=nl_most (May 25, 2010).

40. Slevin, "Arizona Law on Immigration Puts Police in Tight Spot."

41. Steinhauer, Jennifer. "Arizona Law Reveals Split Within G.O.P." *The New York Times*, May 21, 2010. http://www.nytimes.com/2010/05/22/us/politics/22immig.html?nl=us&emc=politicsemailema1 (May 25, 2010).

42. Crockett, Davy. *A Narrative of the Life of David Crockett.* 7th ed. Philadelphia: E. L. Carey and A. Hart, 1834: 31.

43. Steinbeck, John. *The Portable Steinbeck.* Viking Press, 1971: 652.

44. Jaques, *Texan Ranch Life: With Three Months Through Mexico on a "Prairie Schooner,"* London: Horace Cox, 1894: 361.

45. Clay, Henry, and Melba Porter Hay. *The Papers of Henry Clay: Candidate, Compromiser, Elder Statesman January 1, 1844–June 29, 1852,* vol. 10. Lexington: University Press of Kentucky, 1991: 90.

46. Wheelan, Joseph. *Invading Mexico.* New York: Carroll & Graf, 2007: 85.

47. Foley, Neil. *The White Scourge.* Berkeley: University of California Press, 1997: 21.

48. Wheelan, *Invading Mexico,* 267.

49. Solnit, Rebecca. *Storming the Gates of Paradise: Landscapes for Politics.* Berkeley: University of California Press, 2008: 76.

50. Foley, *The White Scourge,* 21.

51. Montejano, David. *Anglos and Mexicans in the Making of Texas, 1836–1986.* Austin: University of Texas Press, 1987: 27.

52. Domenech, Emanuel. *Missionary Adventures in Texas and Mexico.* London: Longman, Brown, Green, Longmans, and Roberts, 1858: 228.

53. Meeks, Eric V. *Border Citizens: The Making of Indians, Mexicans, and Anglos in Arizona.* Austin: University of Texas Press, 2007: 36.

54. U.S. Supreme Court. "*Unites States v. Sandoval*, 167 U. S. 278 (1897)." http://supreme.justia.com/us/167/278/index.html (May 21, 2010).
55. Montejano, *Anglos and Mexicans in the Making of Texas*, 90.
56. Ibid., 183.
57. Ibid.
58. McWilliams, *Factories in the Field*, 126.
59. Calavita, *Inside the State*, 6.
60. Meeks, *Border Citizens*, 115.
61. McWilliams, *Factories in the Field*, 273.
62. Ibid., 126.
63. Hoefer, Michael, Nancy Rytina, and Bryan C. Baker. "Estimates of the Unauthorized Immigrant Population Residing in the United States: January 2009." *Publications*. January, 2010. http://www.dhs.gov/xlibrary/assets/statistics/publications/ois_ill_pe_2009.pdf (February 9, 2010).
64. Meeks, *Border Citizens*, 168.
65. Calavita, *Inside the State*, 37.
66. Ibid., 65.
67. Ibid., 217.
68. Ibid., 151.
69. Ibid., 64.
70. Garcia, *Operation Wetback*, 131.
71. Cornelius, Wayne A. "Controlling 'Unwanted' Immigration": 22.
72. Gonzalez, *Mexican Americans and the U.S. Economy*, 54.
73. Center for Science in the Public Interest. "Food-Disparagement Laws: State Civil & Criminal Statutes." http://www.cspinet.org/foodspeak/laws/existlaw.htm.
74. Hawkins, John. "An Interview with Congressman Tom Tancredo (R-CO)." Right Wing News. http://www.rightwingnews.com/interviews/tancredo.php (May 21, 2010).
75. The Democratic Party. "Bush's Immigration Plan Falls Flat." http://www.democrats.org/a/2006/05/bushs_immigrati_1.php (May 21, 2010).
76. Fears, Darryl. "Little Support for Bush Immigration Plan; Congress and Advocates Question Guest Worker and Return Proposals." *Washington Post*, October 22, 2005, A6.
77. CNN. "GOP Lawmakers Seek to Halt Immigration Reform Push." http://www.cnn.com/2010/POLITICS/04/25/immigration.reform/index.html?hpt=T2 (April 25, 2010).
78. Haines and Rosenblum, *Illegal Immigration in America*, 193.
79. Cornelius, "Controlling 'Unwanted' Immigration," 5.
80. Horsley, Scott. "Border Fence Firm Snared for Hiring Illegal Workers." NPR. http://www.npr.org/templates/story/story.php?storyId=6626823 (May 21, 2010).
81. Grimm, "Using Employer Sanctions to Open the Border and End Undocumented Immigration," 8.
82. Earls, Michael, and Jim Kessler. "Mission Accomplished II: The Bush Record on Immigration Enforcement." The Third Way. http://content.thirdway.org/publications/73/Third_Way_Report_-_Mission_Accomplished_II_-_The_Bush_Record_on_Immigration_Enforcement.pdf (May 21, 2010): 8.

Chapter 4. How the United States Disenfranchises its Citizens

1. U.S. Commission on Civil Rights. *Voting Irregularities in Florida During the 2000 Presidential Election*, chapter 9. Washington, DC: U.S. Commission on Civil Rights, 2001.
2. Ibid., chapter 1.
3. Ibid.
4. Gumbel, Andrew. *Steal This Vote: Dirty Elections and the Rotten History of Democracy in America*. New York: Nations Book, 2005: 205.
5. U.S. Commission on Civil Rights, *Voting Irregularities*.
6. Ibid.
7. Ibid.
8. Ibid., chapter 8.
9. Ibid., chapter 6.
10. Ibid., chapter 5.
11. Gumbel, *Steal This Vote*, 135.
12. Overton, *Stealing Democracy*, 168.
13. U.S. Commission on Civil Rights, *Voting Irregularities*, chapter 5.
14. Ibid.
15. Gumbel, *Steal This Vote*, 205.
16. Carter, Jimmy. "Still Seeking a Fair Florida Vote." *Washington Post*, September 27, 2004, A19. http://www.washingtonpost.com/wp-dyn/articles/A52800-2004Sep26.html (May 22, 2010).
17. Karlan, Pamela S. "Voting Rights and the Third Reconstruction." In *The Constitution in 2020*, Jack M. Balkin and Reva B. Siegel, 159. New York: Oxford University Press, 2009: 159.
18. Overton, *Stealing Democracy*, 91.
19. "Seven Ways to Compute the Relative Value of a U.S. Dollar Amount, 1774 to Present," MeasuringWorth.com. http://www.measuringworth.com/calculators/uscompare/index.php (May 22, 2010).
20. Valelly, Richard M. *The Two Reconstructions: The Struggle For Black Enfranchisement*. Chicago: University of Chicago Press, 2004: 202.
21. Valelly, *The Two Reconstructions*, 202.
22. Overton, *Stealing Democracy*, 97.
23. Gumbel, *Steal This Vote*, 146.
24. Karlan, "Voting Rights and the Third Reconstruction."
25. Overton, *Stealing Democracy*, 98.
26. U.S. Census Bureau. "Voting and Registration in the Election of November 2008– Detailed Tables." http://www.census.gov/hhes/www/socdemo/voting/publications/p20/2008/tables.html (May 22, 2010).
27. U.S. Census Bureau. "Voting and Registration in the Election of November 2000– Detailed Tables." http://www.census.gov/hhes/www/socdemo/voting/publications/p20/2008/tables.html (May 22, 2010).
28. Overton, *Stealing Democracy*, 118.
29. Ibid., 126.
30. Ibid., 128.
31. Ibid., 132.
32. Ibid., 130.

33. Ibid., 99.
34. Gumbel, *Steal This Vote,* 148.
35. Harris, Paul. "The Myth of Fair Elections in America." September 7, 2006. http://www.guardian.co.uk/world/2006/sep/07/usa.comment/print (May 22, 2010).
36. Edsall, Thomas B. "GOP Official Faces Sentence in Phone-Jamming." *The Washington Post,* May 17, 2006. http://www.washingtonpost.com/wp-dyn/content/article/2006/05/16/AR2006051601712.html (May 22, 2010).
37. U.S. Department of Justice. "Cases Raising Claims Under Section 2 of the Voting Rights Act." http://www.justice.gov/crt/voting/litigation/recent_sec2.php (May 22, 2010).
38. Overton, *Stealing Democracy,* 160.
39. U.S. Department of Justice. "Cases Raising Claims Under Section 2 of the Voting Rights Act." http://www.justice.gov/crt/voting/litigation/recent_sec2.php (May 22, 2010).
40. Ibid.
41. Ibid.
42. Ibid.
43. Overton, *Stealing Democracy,* 102.
44. Ibid., 158.
45. U.S. Commission on Civil Rights. *Voting Irregularities,* chapter 5.
46. The Massachusetts Historical Society. "Letter from John Adams to James Sullivan—May 26, 1776, Philadelphia." http://www.masshist.org/education/resources/wallingford/Unit-4-Voting-Rights.pdf (May 22, 2010).
47. Levinson, *Our Undemocratic Constitution,* 141.
48. Abbott, David, and James Levine. *Wrong Winner: the Coming Debacle in the Electoral College.* New York: Praeger Publishers, 1991: xi.
49. Ibid., 9.
50. Ingersoll, Charles. *Fears For Democracy Regarded from the American Point of View.* Philadelphia: J.B. Lippincott & Co., 1875: 25.
51. Slonim, Shlomo. "The Electoral College at Philadelphia," 40.
52. U.S. Commission on Civil Rights. *Voting Irregularities,* chapter 1.
53. University of Virginia Library. "Historical Census Browser." http://mapserver.lib.virginia.edu/ (May 22, 2010).
54. Slonim, "The Electoral College at Philadelphia," 40.
55. Ibid.
56. Ibid., 35.
57. Ibid., 52.
58. Amar, Reed, and Vikram David Amar, *History, Slavery, Sexism, the South, and the Electoral College*: Part One of a Three-Part Series on the 2000 Election and the Electoral College, November 3, 2001. http://writ.news.findlaw.com/amar/20011130.html.
59. Ibid.
60. Ibid.
61. League of Women Voters. "LWVUS Study on the National Popular Vote Compact Background Paper." http://www.lwv.org/AM/Template.cfm?Section=Home&template=/CM/HTMLDisplay.cfm&ContentID=12524 (May 22, 2010).

62. Smith, Bradley A. "Vanity of Vanities: National Popular Vote and the Electoral College." *Election Law Journal* 7, no. 3 (2008): 196.
63. CBS News. "Hillary Calls for end to Electoral College." http://www.cbsnews .com/stories/2000/11/10/politics/main248645.shtml (May 22, 2010).
64. The presidential election of 1824 resulted in John Quincy Adams as a wrong winner. However, it was the Three-fifths clause and the slave count that forced the election into the House of Representatives.
65. Phillips, Kevin P. "His Fraudulency the Second? The Illegitimacy of George W. Bush." *American Prospect.* http://www.prospect.org/cs/articles?article=his_ fraudulency_the_second (May 22, 2010).
66. "Benjamin Harrison." http://www.whitehouse.gov/about/presidents/ben-jaminharrison (May 22, 2010).
67. Wheeler, Sarah M. "Policy Point-Counterpoint: Electoral College Reform." *International Social Science Review* 82 (2007): 176–78.
68. Smith, Bradley A. "Vanity of Vanities: National Popular Vote and the Electoral College." *Election Law Journal* 7, no. 3 (2008): 208.
69. Schaffer, Frederic Charles, ed. *Elections for Sale: The Causes and Consequences of Vote Buying.* Quezon City, Philippines: Ateneo de Manila University Press, 2007: 2.
70. Carter, "Still Seeking a Fair Florida Vote."
71. National Popular Vote. "Question of Congressional Consent for the 'Agreement Among the States to Elect the President by National Popular Vote.'" http:// www.nationalpopularvote.com/resources/Cong-Consent-V7-2008-6-5.pdf (May 22, 2010).
72. FairVote.org. "2008's Shrinking Battleground and Its Stark Impact on Campaign Activity." http://archive.fairvote.org/?page=27&pressmode=showspecific&sh owarticle=230 (May 22, 2010).
73. Hendricks, Jennifer S. "Popular Election of the President: Using or Abusing the Electoral College?" *Election Law Review* 7, no. 3 (November 2008): 222.
74. Harvard Law Review Association. "Rethinking the Electoral College Debate: The Framers, Federalism, and One Person, One Vote." *Harvard Law Review* (2001): 2545.
75. National Popular Vote. "Explanation of National Popular Vote Bill." http:// www.nationalpopularvote.com/ (May 22, 2010).
76. Center for Women and Politics. "The Gender Gap and the 2004 Women's Vote Setting the Record Straight." http://www.cawp.rutgers.edu/research/topics/ documents/GenderGapAdvisory04.pdf (May 22, 2010).
77. National Popular Vote. "Explanation of National Popular Vote Bill." http:// www.nationalpopularvote.com/pages/explanation.php (May 22, 2010).
78. Raskin, Jamie. "Electoral College Organizers: The National Popular Vote Movement Rises, Part I." American Constitution Society. http://www.acslaw .org/node/13364 (May 22, 2010).
79. Jacobson, Arthur J., and Michael Rosenfeld. eds. *The Longest Night: Polemics and Perspectives on Election 2000.* Berkeley: University of California Press, 2002: 391–96.
80. Amar, Reed, and Vikram David Amar, *How to Achieve Direct National Election of the President Without Amending the Constitution.*
81. The Massachusetts Historical Society. "Letter from John Adams to James Sullivan —May 26, 1776, Philadelphia."

82. Berke, Richard L., and Janet Elder. "Counting the Vote; Americans Patiently Awaiting Election Outcome." *New York Times*, November 14, 2000. http://www.nytimes.com/2000/11/14/us/counting-the-vote-the-poll-americans-patiently-awaiting-election-outcome.html (May 22, 2010).

83. National Popular Vote. http://www.nationalpopularvote.com/

84. Hendricks, "Popular Election of the President," 220.

85. "2008's Shrinking Battleground and Its Stark Impact on Campaign Activity."

86. Schultz, David. "Less Than Fundamental: The Myth of Voter Fraud and the Coming of the Second Great Disenfranchisement." *William Mitchell Law Review*, 2008: 3.

87. U.S. Government Printing Office. "H. J. Resolution 28, Proposing an amendment to the Constitution of the United States regarding the right to vote." http://frwebgate.access.gpo.gov/cgi-bin/getdoc.cgi?dbname=111_cong_bills&docid=f:hj28ih.txt.pdf (May 22, 2010).

88. Keyssar, Alexander. *The Right to Vote: The Contested History of Democracy in the United States.* New York: Basic Books, 2001: 291.

89. Karlan, Pamela S. "Voting Rights and the Third Reconstruction." *The Constitution in 2020*, Jack M. Balkin and Reva B. Siegel, 161. New York: Oxford University Press, 2009: 161.

90. Word, David L., et al. "Demographic Aspects of Surnames from Census 2000." U.S. Census Bureau. http://www.census.gov/genealogy/www/data/2000surnames/surnames.pdf (May 22, 2010).

91. Library of Congress. "Federalist No. 68, The Mode of Electing the President." http://thomas.loc.gov/home/histdox/fed_68.html (May 22, 2010).

92. Amar, Akhil Reed. "The Electoral College, Unfair From Day One." *New York Times*, November 9, 2000. http://www.nytimes.com/2000/11/09/opinion/the-electoral-college-unfair-from-day-one.html (May 22, 2010).

93. Abbott, David, and James Levine. *Wrong Winner: the Coming Debacle in the Electoral College.* New York: Praeger, 1991: 117.

94. National Oceanic and Atmospheric Administration. "Hurricane History." http://www.nhc.noaa.gov/HAW2/english/history.shtml#katrina (May 22, 2010).

Chapter 5. Voter-Count Apportionment

1. Cohen, Richard E. "Broken Barometer." *National Journal Magazine*, July 12, 2003.

2. Library of Congress. "Federalist No. 52, The House of Representatives." http://thomas.loc.gov/home/histdox/fed_52.html (May 22, 2010).

3. "Electoral fusion." http://www.economicexpert.com/a/Electoral:fusion.html (May 22, 2010).

4. Karlan, Pamela S. "The Fire Next Time: Reapportionment After the 2000 Census." *Stanford Law Review*, 50 (1998): 739.

5. Besley, Timothy, Torsten Persson, and Daniel Sturm. "Political Competition and Economic Performance." *NBER Working Paper Series*, 2005: 34.

6. McDonald, Michael P., and John Samples. *The Marketplace of Democracy.* Washington, DC: Brookings Institution Press, 2006: 1.

7. Issacharoff, Samuel. "Collateral Damage: The Endangered Center in American Politics." *William and Mary Law Review* (2004): 428.

8. Will, George F. "An Election Breakwater?" *Newsweek*, February 27, 2006 http://www.newsweek.com/id/56887 (May 22, 2010).

9. "Money Wins Presidency and 9 of 10 Congressional Races in Priciest U.S. Election Ever." http://www.opensecrets.org/news/2008/11/money-wins-white-house-and.html (May 22, 2010).

10. Gersh, Mark. "The Republicans' Great Gerrymander." *Blueprint Magazine*, June 30, 2003 http://www.dlc.org/ndol_ci.cfm?kaid=127&subid=177&conte ntid=251791 (May 22, 2010).

11. Tumulty, Karen, and Dan Balz. "Democrats Pin Losses on Obama's Disconnect." *The Washington Post*, November 7, 2010 http://www.washingtonpost.com/ wp-dyn/content/article/2010/11/06/AR2010110604538.html?sub=AR (November 7, 2010).

12. Abramowitz, Alan I., Brad Alexander, and Matthew Gunning. "Incumbency, Redistricting, and the Decline of Competition in U.S. House Elections." *The Journal of Politics*, (2006): 79.

13. Fiorina, Morris. *Culture War? The Myth of a Polarized America*. New York: Pearson-Longman, 2005.

14. Putnam, Robert D. *Bowling Alone: The Collapse and Revival of American Community*. New York: Simon and Schuster, 2001: 342.

15. Abramowitz, et al., "Incumbency, Redistricting, and the Decline of Competition in U.S. House Elections," 81.

16. Ibid., 83.

17. Federal Election Commission. "Median Activity of House General Election Candidates." http://www.fec.gov/press/press2009/2009Dec29Cong/6medi ans08.pdf (May 22, 2010).

18. OpenSecrets.org. "Incumbent Advantage." http://www.opensecrets.org/over-view/incumbs.php (May 22, 2010).

19. Saad, Lydia. "Congress' Job Approval Ratings Grow More Polarized." Gallup. http://www.gallup.com/poll/122399/Congress-Job-Approval-Ratings-Grow-Polarized.aspx (May 22, 2010).

20. Pew Research Center for the People & the Press. "Independents Take Center Stage in Obama Era." http://people-press.org/report/517/political-values-and-core-attitudes (May 22, 2010).

21. Torry, Jack, and Jonathan Riskind. "Voters Feel Senator's Pain, Observers Believe; Moderate's Exit Underlines Squeezing of Center, Where Most Americans Stand." *The Columbus Dispatch*, February 17, 2010, A3.

22. Morgan, Bryson B. "Quantifying the Impact of Partisan Gerrymandering: Uncompetitive, Unresponsive, and Unaccountable American Democracy." *Hinckley Journal of Politics*, 8 (2007): 41.

23. Sabato, Larry. *A More Perfect Constitution: 23 Proposals to Revitalize our Constitution and Make America a Fairer Country*. New York: Walker & Company, 2007: 32.

24. Eilperin, *Fight Club Politics*, 97.

25. Rahm, "Roll Call."

26. Anderson, Nick. "GOP-Led House Will End Term Limits for Speaker." *Los Angeles Times*, January 7, 2003, http://articles.latimes.com/2003/jan/07/nation/ na-house7 (May 22, 2010).

27. Lee, Robert W. "Term Limits Tide Recedes: Support for Term Limits Has Steadily Declined as Voters Learn About the Danger This Deception Poses to the Constitution." *The New American*, March 11, 2002

28. U.S. Supreme Court. " *U.S. Term Limits. v. Thornton etal.*" http://supreme. justia.com/us/514/779/index.html (May 22, 2010).

29. Price, Deb. "Nation's Political Elite Honor Dingell." *Detroit News*, February 11, 2009. http://www.detnews.com/article/20090211/POLITICS/902110361/Nation-s-political-elite-honor-Dingell (May 22, 2010).

30. National Conference of State Legislatures. "Legislative Term Limits: An Overview." http://www.ncsl.org/default.aspx?tabid=14849 (May 22, 2010).

31. Broder, David S. "No Vote Necessary Redistricting is Creating a U.S. House of Lords." *The Washington Post*, November 11, 2004, A37. http://www.washington post.com/wp-dyn/articles/A41304-2004Nov10.html (May 22, 2010).

32. Goldfarb, Carl E. "Allocating the Local Apportionment Pie: What Portion for Resident Aliens?" *Yale Law Journal*, (1995).

33. Remini, Robert V. *The House*. New York: HarperCollins, 2006: 196.

34. Passel, Jeffrey S., and D'Vera Cohn. "A Portrait of Unauthorized Immigrants in the United States." Pew Hispanic Center. http://pewhispanic.org/files/reports/107.pdf (May 22, 2010).

35. Right Wing News.com. "An Interview With Congressman Tom Tancredo (R-CO)." http://www.rightwingnews.com/interviews/tancredo.php (May 22, 2010).

36. Nasser, Haya El. "Hispanic Groups Call for Census Boycott." *USA Today*, 15 April 2009. http://www.usatoday.com/news/nation/census/2009-04-15-census_N.htm (May 22, 2010).

37. Johnson, Kevin R, "Latinas/os and the Political Process: The Need for Critical Inquiry." *Oregon Law Review*. (September 30, 2003): 929.

38. Ludden, Jennifer. "Hispanics Divided Over Census Boycott." NPR. http://www.npr.org/templates/story/story.php?storyId=106555313 (May 22, 2010).

39. California Political News & Views. http://capoliticalnews.com/s/spip.php?breve3053.

40. U.S. House of Representatives. "Congressman Gene Green." http://www.house.gov/green/district/ (May 22, 2010).

41. Texas Secretary of State. "1992— Current Election History." http://elections.sos.state.tx.us/elchist.exe (May 22, 2010).

42. Coenen, Dan T. "Wesberry v. Sanders (1964)." New Georgia Encyclopedia. http://www.georgiaencyclopedia.org/nge/Article.jsp?id=h-2984 (May 22, 2010).

43. Levinson, Sanford. "Symposium: Baker v. Carr: A Commemorative Symposium: Panel II: One Person, One Vote: A Theoretical and Practical Examination: One Person, One Vote: A Mantra in Need of Meaning." *North Carolina Law Review*, (2002).

44. Hayden, "The False Promise of One Person, One Vote," 232.

45. Bennett, Robert W. "Should Parents Be Given Extra Votes on Account of Their Children? Toward a Conversational Understanding of American Democracy." *Northwestern University School of Law*, (2000): 557.

46. U.S. Census Bureau. "American FactFinder." http://factfinder.census.gov/home/saff/main.html?_lang=en (May 22, 2010).

47. Two districts in Louisiana had the fewest votes, which was likely due to the exodus of population from Louisiana after hurricane Katrina.

48. Goldfarb, "Allocating the Local Apportionment Pie."

49. In 1990, Miami-Dade County had the highest concentration of non-citizen adults at 33 percent.

50. Goldfarb, "Allocating the Local Apportionment Pie."
51. Murphy, Dennis L. "Garza v. County of Los Angeles: The Dilemma over Using Elector Population as Opposed to Total Population in Legislative Apportionment." *Case Western Reserve Law Review*, (1991).
52. Ibid.
53. Hayden, "The False Promise of One Person, One Vote," 217.
54. Cohen, Elizabeth F. "Neither Seen Nor Heard: Children's Citizenship in Contemporary Democracies." *Citizenship Studies* 9, no. 2 (2005): 229.
55. Ibid.
56. Bennett, "Should Parents Be Given Extra Votes on Account of Their Children?"
57. U.S. Census Bureau. "American FactFinder."
58. Prison Policy Initiative. "Prisoners of the Census." http://www.prisonersofthe census.org/legislation.html (May 22, 2010).
59. Schmeckebier, *Congressional Apportionment*, 97.
60. Hayden, "The False Promise of One Person, One Vote," 218.
61. The manuscript for *Vote Thieves* was completed before the reapportionment count was announced in December 2010.
62. Carter, Jimmy. "Still Seeking a Fair Florida Vote." *Washington Post*, September 27, 2004, A19. http://www.washingtonpost.com/wp-dyn/articles/A52800-2004Sep26.html (May 22, 2010).
63. Harris, "The Myth of Fair Elections in America."
64. U.S. Census Bureau. " Computing Apportionment." http://www.census.gov/population/www/censusdata/apportionment/computing.html (May 22, 2010).
65. Jost, "Redistricting Disputes," 241.
66. Miller, Candice. "H. J. Res. 11." http://www.govtrack.us/congress/bill.xpd ?bill=hj111-11 (May 22, 2010).
67. Abrams, Jim. "GOP: Only Legal Residents Should be Counted." Fox News. http://www.foxnews.com/wires/2008Sep02/0,4670,CVNGOPCensus,00 .html (May 22, 2010).
68. U.S. Senate. "Constitution of the United States, Amendment XIV (1868) ." http://www.senate.gov/civics/constitution_item/constitution.htm#amdt_14_ (1868) (May 22, 2010).
69. Lee, Margaret Mikyung, and Erika K. Lunder. *Analysis of Whether Unauthorized Aliens Must Be Included in the Census*. Washington, DC: Library of Congress, 2009: 2.
70. Bennett, "Should Parents Be Given Extra Votes on Account of Their Children?" 511.
71. Scarrow, Howard A. "One Voter, One Vote: The Apportionment of Congressional Seats Reconsidered." *Polity*, (1989): 256.
72. Ibid., 256–257.
73. Butler, David, and Bruce E. Cain. *Congressional Redistricting: Comparative and Theoretical Perspectives*. New York: Macmillan, 1992: 68.
74. Smith, Bradley A. "Vanity of Vanities: National Popular Vote and the Electoral College." *Election Law Journal* 7, no. 3 (2008): 210.
75. McDonald and Samples. *The Marketplace of Democracy*, 173.
76. *Dollars and Democracy: A Blueprint for Campaign Finance Reform*. Bronx: Fordham University Press, 2000: 91.
77. Rahm, "Roll Call."
78. *Direct Popular Election of the President and Vice President of the United States*.

Washington, DC: U.S. Government Printing Office, 1979: 181.

79. Dionne Jr., E. J. "One Nation Deeply Divided." *Washington Post,* November 7, 2003, A31. http://www.washingtonpost.com/ac2/wp-dyn?pagename=article &node=&contentId=A10319-2003Nov6¬Found=true (May 22, 2010).

80. Ibid.

81. The manuscript for *Vote Thieves* was completed before the official reapportionment count was announced in December 2010.

Selected Bibliography

Abbott, David, and James Levine. *Wrong Winner: the Coming Debacle in the Electoral College.* New York: Praeger, 1991.

Abramowitz, Alan I., Brad Alexander, and Matthew Gunning. "Incumbency, Redistricting, and the Decline of Competition in U.S. House Elections." *Journal of Politics,* 2006: 75–88.

Ackerman, Bruce. *The Failure of the Founding Fathers.* Cambridge, MA: The Belknap Press of Harvard University Press, 2005.

Allen, Gardner W. *Our Naval War with France.* Boston: Houghton Mifflin Company, 1909.

Amar, Akhil Reed. *America's Constitution: A Biography.* New York: Random House, 2005.

Amar, Akhil Reed, and Vikram David Amar. *A Critique of the Top Ten Modern Arguments for the Electoral College: Part Two of a Three-Part Series on the 2000 Election and the Electoral College.* December 14, 2001. http://writ.news.findlaw.com/amar/20011214.html (accessed December 16, 2009).

———. *History, Slavery, Sexism, the South, and the Electoral College: Part One Of A Three-Part Series on the 2000 Election and the Electoral College.* November 3, 2001. http://writ.news.findlaw.com/amar/20011130.html (accessed December 16, 2009).

———. *How to Achieve Direct National Elecction of the President without Amending the Constitution: Part Three of a Three-Part Series on the 2000 Election and the Electoral College.* December 28, 2001. http://writ.news.findlaw.com/amar/20011228.html (accessed December 16, 2009).

Ashbee, Edward, Helene Balslev Clausen, and Carl Pedersen. *The Politics, Economics, and Culture of Mexican-U.S. Migration: Both Sides of The Border.* New York: Palgrave Macmillan, 2007.

Babkina, A. M., ed. *Politics of Immigration.* Huntington, New York: Nova Science Publishers, Inc., 2001.

Balkin, Jack M., and Reva B. Siegel. *The Constitution in 2020.* Oxford: Oxford University Press, 2009.

Bennett, Robert W. "Should Parents be Given Extra Votes on Account of Their Children? Toward a Conversational Understanding Of American Democracy." *Northwestern University School of Law*, 2000: 503–565.

Bickerstaff, Steve. *Lines in the Sand: Congressional Redistricting in Texas and the Downfall of Tom Delay*. Austin, Texas: University of Texas Press, 2007.

The Big Buy: Tom DeLay's Stolen Congress. Directed by Mark Birnbaum and Jim Schermbeck. 2006.

Billias, George Athan. *The Federalists: Realists or Idealogues?* Lexington, MA: D.C. Heath, 1970.

Borjas, George J. *Heaven's Door*. Princeton: Princeton University Press, 1999.

Borneman, Walter R. *Polk*. New York: Random House, 2008.

The Braceros. Produced by Eric Cain. 2007.

Brady, David W., and Mathew D. McCubbins. *Party, Process, and Political Change in Congress*. Stanford, CA: Standford University Press, 2002.

Brown, Richard D. *Major Problems in the Era of the American Revolution, 1760–1791*. Boston: Houghton Mifflin Company, 2000.

Brown, Sarita E. "Making the Next Generation Our Greatest Resource." *Latinos and the Nation's Future*, edited by Henry G. Cisneros and John Rosales, 83–100. Houston: Arte Publico Press, 2009.

Brunell, Thomas L. *Redistricting and Representation: Why Competitive Elections are Bad for America*. New York: Routledge, 2008.

Bryson, Morgan B. "Quantifying the Impact of Partisan Gerrymandering: Un-competitive, Unresponsive, and Unaccountable American Democracy." *Hinckley Journal of Politics*, 2007: 35–44.

Cain, Bruce E. *The Reapportionment Puzzle*. Berkeley: University of California Press, 1984.

Calavita, Kitty. *Inside the State*. London: Routledge, Chapman and Hall, Inc., 1992.

Center for Science in the Public Interest. *State of Texas*. March 19, 1998. http://cspinet.org/foodspeak/laws/states/texas.htm (accessed September 17, 2009).

Christopher, J. Walker. "Border Vigilantism and Comprehensive Immigration Re-form." *Harvard Latino Law Review*, 2007: 1–44.

Cisneros, Henry G., ed. *Latinos and the Nation's Future*. Houston, Texas: Arte Publico Press, 2009.

Clay, Henry. "To Thomas M. Peters & John M. Jackson, Lexington, July 27th, 1844." *The Papers of Henry Clay Volume 10: Candidate, Compromiser, Elder Statesman*, edited by Melba Porter Hay and Carol Reardon, 89–90. Lexington: University Press of Kentucky, 1991.

Cohen, Richard E. "Broken Barometer." *National Journal*, 2003: 2240–2248.

Collins, Ronald K. L., and Jonathan Bloom. *Win or Lose, Dissing Food Can be Costly*. March 1, 1999. http://cspinet.org/foodspeak/oped/winorloss.htm (accessed September 17, 2009).

Cornelius, Wayne A. "Controlling 'Unwanted' Immigration: Lessons from the United States, 1993–2004." *eScholarship*. December 1, 2004. http://www.escholarship.org/uc/item/70c6g11d (accessed January 24, 2010).

Cornell, Saul. *The Other Founders*. Chapel Hill: The University of North Carolina Press, 1999.

Crockett, David. *A Narrative in the Life of David Crockett*. Philadelphia: E. L. Carey and A. Hart, 1834.

Daniels, Roger, and Otis L. Graham. *Debating American Immigration, 1882–Present.* Oxford, England: Rowman & Littlefield Publishers, 2001.

The Department of American Studies, Amherst College. *The Compromise of 1850.* Edited by Edwin C. Rozwenc. Boston: D.C. Heath, 1957.

DeRosier, Arthur H. Jr. *The Removal of the Choctaw Indians.* Knoxville: University of Tennessee Press, 1970.

The Descendents of Mexican War Veterans. *The U.S.-Mexican War.* August 7, 2007. http://www.dmwv.org/mexwar/mexwar1.htm (accessed July 4, 2009).

Domenech, Emanuel. *Missionary Adventures in Texas and Mexico.* London: Longman, Brown, Green, Longmans, and Roberts, 1858.

Eilperin, Juliet. *Fight Club Politics.* Lanham, Maryland: Rowman & Littlefield Publishers, 2006.

Fehrenbacher, Don E. *The Slaveholding Republic: An Account of the United States Government's Relations to Slavery.* New York: Oxford University Press, 2002.

Ferling, John. *Adams vs. Jefferson The Tumultuous Election of 1800.* Oxford, England: Oxford University Press, 2004.

Filler, Louis, and Allen Guttmann. *The Removal of the Cherokee Nation: Manifest Destiny or National Dishonor?* Boston: D.C. Heath, 1962.

Flack, Horace Edgar. *The Adoption of the Fourteenth Amendment.* Baltimore: The Johns Hopkins Press, 1965.

Foley, Neil. *The White Scourge.* Berkeley: University of California Press, 1997.

Foreman, Grant. *Indian Removal The Emigration of the Five Civilized Tribes of Indians.* Norman: University of Oklahoma Press, 1956.

The Harvard Law Review Association. "An Interstate Process Perspective On Political Gerrymandering." *Harvard Law Review,* 2005–2006: 1576–1597.

———. "Rethinking the Electoral College Debate: The Framers, Federalism, and One Person, One Vote." *Harvard Law Review,* 2001: 2,526-2,549.

Harvest of Shame. Directed by Fred W. Friendly. 1960.

Garcia, F. Chris, and Gabriel R. Sanchez. *Hispanics and the U.S. Political System: Moving into the Mainstream.* Saddle River, NJ: Pearson Education, Inc., 2008.

Garcia, Juan Ramon. *Operation Wetback.* Westport, CT: Greenwood Press, 1980.

Gay, Claudine. *The Effect of Minority Districts and Minority Representation on Political Participation in California.* San Francisco: Public Policy Institute of California, 2001.

Gimpel, James G., and James R. Edwards Jr. *The Congressional Politics of Immigration Reform.* Boston: Allyn & Bacon, 1999.

Goldfarb, Carl E. "Allocating the Local Apportionment Pie: What Portion for Resident Aliens?" *Yale Law Journal,* 1995.

Gonzales, Manuel G. *Mexicanos.* Bloomington: Indiana University Press, 1999.

Gonzalez, Arturo. *Mexican Americans and the U.S. Economy.* Tucson: The University of Arizona Press, 2002.

Grimm, Tyler. "Student Note: Using Employer Sanctions to Open the Border and End Undocumented Immigration." *Journal of Gender, Race & Justice,* 2009: 1–31.

Gumbel, Andrew. *Steal This Vote: Dirty Elections and the Rotten History of Democracy in America.* New York: Nations Book, 2005.

Gutzman, Kevin R. C. *The Politically Incorrect Guide to the Constitution.* Washington, DC: Regnery Publishing, 2007.

Haines, David W., and Karen E. Rosenblum. *Illegal Immigration in America: A Reference Handbook.* Westport, CT: Greenwood Press, 1999.

Hall, Kermit L. *Major Problems in American Constitutional History Volume 1: The Colonial Era Through Reconstruction.* Lexington, MA: D.C. Heath, 1992.

Hayden, Grant M. "The False Promise of One Person, One Vote." *Michigan Law Review*, 2003: 213–267.

Hendricks, Jennifer S. "Popular Election of the President: Using or Abusing the Electoral College?" *Election Law Review* 7, no. 3 (November 2008): 218–226.

Hietala, Thomas R. *Manifest Destiny.* Ithaca, NY: Cornell University Press, 2003.

Hoefer, Michael, Nancy Rytina, and Bryan C. Baker. "Estimates of the Unauthorized Immigrant Population Residing in the United States: January 2009." *Publications.* January 2010. http://www.dhs.gov/xlibrary/assets/statistics/publications/ois_ill_pe_2009.pdf (accessed February 9, 2010).

Issacharoff, Samuel. "Collateral Damage: The Endangered Center in American Politics." *William and Mary Law Review*, 2004: 415–435.

James, Smith Morton. *Freedom's Fetters.* Binghamton, NY: Vail-Ballou Press, 1956.

Jaques, Mary J. *Texan Ranch Life: With Three Months through Mexico on a "Prairie Schooner."* London: Horace Cox, 1894.

Jost, Kenneth. "Redistricting Disputes: Should the Courts Limit Partisan Gerrymandering?" *CQ Researcher*, March 4, 2004: 221–248.

Kaiser, Robert G. *So Damn Much Money.* New York: Knopf, 2009.

Katz, Ellen D. "From Laredo to Fort Worth: Race, Politics, and the Texas Redistricting Case." *Michigan Law Review*, 2006: 38–42.

Kimberling, William C. "The Electoral College." *Federal Election Commission.* May 1992. http://www.fec.gov/pdf/eleccoll.pdf (accessed December 17, 2009).

Kobach, Kris W. "Article: Reinforcing the Rule of Law: What States Can and Should Do to Reduce Illegal Immigration." *Georgetown Immigration Law Journal*, 2008: 1–28.

Kuffner, Charles. *New DA in Waller County.* September 26, 2004. http://offthekuff.com/wp/?p=9612 (accessed December 11, 2009).

Lee, Margaret Mikyung, and Erika K. Lunder. *Analysis of Whether Unauthorized Aliens Must be Included in the Census.* Washington, DC: Library of Congress, 2009.

LegalCasesDocs.com. *Texas Beef Group v Oprah Winfrey.* 2003. http://www.legalcasedocs.com/120/246/531.html (accessed September 17, 2009).

Leip, David. *1844 Presidential General Election Data—National.* 2005. www.uselectionatlas.org/RESULTS/data.php?year=1844&datatype=national&def=1&f=0&off=0&elect=0 (accessed July 2, 2009).

LeMay, Michael C. *Illegal Immigration.* Santa Barbara, CA: ABC-CLIO, Inc., 2007.

Levinson, Sanford. *Our Undemocratic Constitution.* New York: Oxford University Press, 2006.

———. "Symposium: Baker v. Carr: A Commemorative Symposium: Panel II: One Person, One Vote: A Theoretical and Practical Examination: One Person, One Vote: A Mantra in Need of Meaning." *North Carolina Law Review*, 2002.

The Library of Congress. *From Gold Rush to Golden State.* October 19, 1998. http://memory.loc.gov/ammem/cbhtml/cbrush.html (accessed September 5, 2009).

Lillian Goldman Law Library. *Inaugural Address of James Knox Polk.* 2008. http://avalon.law.yale.edu/19th_century/polk.asp (accessed July 4, 2009).

McDonald, Michael P., and John Samples. *The Marketplace of Democracy.* Washington, DC: Brookings Institution Press, 2006.

McGhee, Eric. *Redistricting and Legislative Partisanship.* San Francisco: Public Policy Institute of California, 2008.

McWilliams, Carey. *Factories in the Field.* Berkeley: University of California Press, 1966.

Microsoft Encarta Online Encyclopedia. *Henry Clay.* 2009. http://encarta.msn .com/encyclopedia_761566041/Henry_Clay.html (accessed July 4, 2009).

———. *Pennsylvania Dutch.* 2009. http://encarta.msn.com/encyclopedia_7615 60037/Pennsylvania_Dutch.html (accessed September 27, 2009).

———. *Texas Revolution.* 2009. http://encarta.msn.com/encyclopedia_761584400/ Texas_Revolution.html (accessed August 23, 2009).

Miller, John C. *Crisis in Freedom The Alien and Sedition Acts.* Boston: Little, Brown and Company, 1951.

Montejano, David. *Anglos and Mexicans in the Making of Texas, 1836–1986.* Austin: University of Texas Press, 1987.

Moore, Allan B. "A 'Frightful Political Dragon' Indeed: Why Constitutional Challenges Cannot Subdue the Gerrymander." *Harvard Journal of Law & Public Policy* 13, no. 1 (1990): 949–1015.

Morais, Nina. "Sex Discrimination and the Fourteenth Amendment: Lost History." *Yale Law Journal,* (May 1988): 1153–1172.

Murphy, Dennis T. "Case Comment: *Garza v. County of Los Angeles.* The Dilemma over Using Elector Population as Opposed to Total Population in Legislative Apportionment." *Case Western Reserve Law Review,* 1991.

———. "Symposium: the Right to Privacy One Hundred Years Later: Note: The Exclusion of Illegal Aliens from the Reapportionment Base: A Question Of Representation." *Case Western Reserve Law Review,* 1991.

Ndulo, Nchimunya D. "Note: State Employer Sanctions Laws and the Federal Preemption Doctrine: The Legal Arizona Workers Act Revisited." *Cornell Journal of Law and Public Policy,* 2009: 1–43.

Newton, Lina. *Illegal, Alien, or Immigrant: The Politics of Immigration Reform.* New York: New York University Press, 2008.

Nuñez Neto, Blas. *Border Security: The Role of the U.S. Border Patrol.* CRS Report for Congress, Washington, DC: Congressional Research Service, 2005.

Orndorff, Mary. "Alabama No Longer Needs Voting Rights Supervision, Gov. Bob Riley says," *The Birmingham News,* March 4, 2009. http://www.al.com/politics/ birminghamnews/index.ssf?/base/news/1236158279106560.xml&coll=2 (accessed December 11, 2009).

Overton, Spencer. *Stealing Democracy: The New Politics of Voter Suppression.* New York: W. W. Norton & Company, 2006.

Patterson, Kelly D. "'Nice Guys Finish Last'," and Other Possible Untruths about Congressional Elections," *Running On Empty? Political Discourse in Congressional Elections,* edited by L. Sandy Maisel and Darrell M. West, 71–83. Lanham, Maryland: Rowman & Littlefield Publishers, Inc., 2004.

PBS. The Compromise of 1850 and the Fugitive Slave Act. http://www.pbs.org/ wgbh/aia/part4/4p2951.html (accessed July 6, 2009).

Pennsylvania Historical and Museum Commission. *After the First Battle of Trenton: Washington Crosses the Delaware, Again.* http://www.ushistory.org/Washington Crossing/history/crossagain.htm (accessed December 8, 2009).

Pitkin, Hanna. *The Concept of Representation*. Berkeley: University of California Press, 1967.

Prucha, Francis Paul. *The Indian in American History*. New York: Holt, Rinehart and Watson, 1971.

Rakove, Jack N. *Original Meanings*. New York: Vintage Books, 1997.

Remini, Robert V. *The House*. New York: HarperCollins, 2006.

Ritchie, Mark. "The High Price of Cheap Food." In *It's Legal but It Ain't Right*, edited by Nikos Passas and Neva Goodwin, 178–193. Ann Arbor: University of Michigan Press, 2004.

Rivas-Rodriguez, Maggie, ed. *Mexican Americans & World War II*. Austin: University of Texas Press, 2005.

Rolle, Andrew. *California: A History*. Wheeling, IL: Harlan Davidson, Inc., 2003.

Samora, Julian. *Gunpowder Justice*. Notre Dame, IN: University of Notre Dame Press, 1979.

Santos, Adolfo, and Juan Carlos Huerta. "Representation of Minority Groups in the U.S.," *Representation of Minority Groups in the U.S.*, edited by Charles E. Menifield, 57–75. Lanham, MD: Austin & Winfield, Publishers, 2001.

Scarrow, Howard A. "One Voter, One Vote: The Apportionment of Congressional Seats Reconsidered." *Polity*, 1989: 253–268.

Schmeckebier, Laurence F. *Congressional Apportionment*. Washington, DC: The Brookings Institution, 1941.

Schuck, Peter H., and Rogers M. Smith. *Citizenship Without Consent*. New Haven, CT: Yale University Press, 1985.

Schultz, David. "Less than Fundamental: The Myth of Voter Fraud and The Coming of the Second Great Disenfranchisement." *William Mitchell Law Review*, 2008: 1–21.

Schwarz, Frederick D. "How It Got that Way and Why We're Stuck with It." *American Heritage*, 2001: 43–49.

Scott, Franklin D. "The Peopling of America: Perspectives on Immigration." *American Historical Association Pamphlets*, American Historical Association, 241 (1972).

Slonim, Shlomo. "The Electoral College at Philadelphia: The Evolution of an Ad Hoc Congress for the Selection of a President." *Journal of American History*, 1986: 35–58.

Smith, Bradley A. "Vanity of Vanities: National Popular Vote and the Electoral College." *Election Law Journal 7*, no. 3 (2008): 196–217.

Smith, James P., and Barry Edmonston, . *The New Americans: Economic, Demographic, and Fiscal Effects of Immigration*. Washington, DC: National Academy Press, 1997.

Southeast Asia Resource Action Center. *Southeast Asian Communities*. http://www.searac.org/commun.html (accessed October 4, 2009).

Steffen, Jerome O. *Hitchcock, Ethan Allen (1798–1870)*. http://digital.library.okstate.edu/encyclopedia/entries/H/HI020.html (accessed July 5, 2009).

Tanger, Stephanie E. "Enforcing Corporate Responsibility for Violations of Workplace Immigration Laws: The Case of Meatpacking." *Harvard Latino Law Review*, 2006. http://www.law.harvard.edu/students/orgs/llr/vol9/tanger.php#Heading171 (accessed January 24, 2010).

Texas State Historical Association. *Annexation*. January 8, 2008. http://www.tsha online.org/handbook/online/articles/AA/mga2.html (accessed July 4, 2009).

———. "Battle of San Jacinto." January 18, 2008. http://www.tshaonline.org/hand book/online/articles/SS/qes4.html (accessed August 23, 2009).

Texas State Historical Society. "Battle of The Alamo." January 8, 2008. http://www.tshaonline.org/handbook/online/articles/AA/qea2.html (accessed August 23, 2009).

———. "Emigrant Agent Acts." January 17, 2008. http://www.tshaonline.org/handbook/online/articles/EE/mleul.html (accessed September 6, 2009).

———. "Seguín, Juan Nepomuceno." February 10, 2009. http://www.tsha online.org/handbook/online/articles/SS/fse8.html (accessed August 22, 2009).

Texas State Library & Archives Commission. "Juan Seguin." March 6, 2009. http://www.tsl.state.tx.us/treasures/giants/seguin/seguin-01.html (accessed August 22, 2009).

Third Way. *Winning The Immigration Debate.* March 2008. http://www.thirdway.org/data/product/file/123/Third_Way_Immigration_Memo.pdf (accessed October 4, 2009).

U.S. Census Bureau. "2008 American Community Survey Table B01003." http://factfinder.census.gov/servlet/DTTable?_bm=y&-context=dt&-ds_name=ACS_2008_1YR_G00_&-CONTEXT=dt&-mt_name=ACS_2008_1YR_G2000_B01003&-tree_id=308&-redoLog=true&-geo_id=04000US42&-geo_id=NBSP&-search_results=01000US&-format=&-_lang=en&-Subject ID=174693 (accessed September 27, 2009).

———. "2008 American Community Survey Table B04003." http://factfinder.census.gov/servlet/DTTable?_bm=y&-context=dt&-ds_name=ACS_2008_1YR_G00_&-CONTEXT=dt&-mt_name=ACS_2008_1YR_G2000_B04003&-tree id=308&-redoLog=false&-geo_id=04000US42&-search_results=01000US&-format=&-_lang=en&-SubjectID=17469369 (accessed September 27, 2009).

———. "2008 American Community Survey Table C05002." http://factfinder.census.gov/servlet/DTTable?_bm=y&-geo_id=01000US&-ds_name=ACS_2008_1YR_G00_&-_lang=en&-_caller=geoselect&-state=dt&-format=&-mt_name=ACS_2008_1YR_G2000_C05002 (accessed September 27, 2009).

———. *Directors.* October 19, 2009. http://www.census.gov/history/www/census_then_now/director_biographies/directors_1790_-_1810.html (accessed March 20, 2010).

U.S. Census Bureau. *Measuring America: The Decennial Censuses from 1790 to 2000.* POL/2-MA, Washington, DC: U.S. Department of Commerce, 2002.

———. *Selected Historical Decennial Census Population and Housing Counts.* August 27, 2008. www.census.gov/population/www/censusdata/hiscendata.html (accessed July 3, 2009).

U.S. Census Monitoring Board. "Final Report to Congress." "U.S. Census Monitoring Board." September 1, 2001. http://govinfo.library.unt.edu/cmb/cmbp/reports/final_report/FinalReport.pdf (accessed March 20, 2010).

U.S. Commission on Civil Rights. *Voting Irregularities in Florida During the 2000 Presidential Election.* Washington, DC: U.S. Commission on Civil Rights, 2001.

U.S. Department of Homeland Security. "Immigration Enforcement Actions: 2008." "Immigration Statistics." July 2009. http://www.dhs.gov/xlibrary/assets/statistics/publications/enforcement_ar_08.pdf (accessed October 4, 2009).

U.S. Department of State. "The Immigration Act of 1924" *(The Johnson-Reed Act).* http://www.state.gov/r/pa/ho/time/id/87718.htm (accessed September 5, 2009).

U.S. Government. "About the White House Presidents." http://www.whitehouse. gov/about/presidents/jamespolk/ (accessed July 4, 2009).

———. "The Treaty of Guadalupe Hidalgo." April 16, 2009. http://www.loc.gov/ rr/hispanic/ghtreaty/ (accessed July 4, 2009).

———. "U.S. Electoral College." http://www.archives.gov/federal-register/elec-toral-college/votes/1837_1853.html (accessed July 4, 2009).

U.S. Government Accounting Office. *U.S. Department of Justice: Information on Employment Litigation, Housing and Civil Enforcement, Voting, and Special Litigation Sections' Enforcement Efforts from Fiscal Years 2001 through 2007.* Washington, DC: U.S. Government Accountability Office, 2009.

U.S. House of Representatives. "Election Statistics." http://clerk.house.gov/mem-ber_info/electionInfo/ (accessed January 9, 2010).

———. "Seasonal Agricultural Laborers from Mexico 1926." *Hearing Before the Committee on Immigration and Naturalization House of Representatives.* Washington, DC: Government Printing Office, 1926.

U.S. National Archives and Records Administration. "Chinese Exclusion Act (1882)." http://www.ourdocuments.gov/doc.php?flash=true&doc=47 (accessed Sep-tember 5, 2009).

Valelly, Richard M. *The Two Reconstructions: The Struggle For Black Enfranchisement.* Chicago: The University of Chicago Press, 2004.

Vigil, Maurilio E. *Hispanics in Congress: A Historical and Political Survey.* Lanham, Maryland: University Press of America, 1996.

Vina, Stephen R. *Civilian Patrols Along the Border: Legal and Policy Issues.* Con-gressional Research Service, Washington, DC: The Library of Congress, 2006.

Walker, Christopher J. "Border Vigilantism and Comprehensive Immigration Reform." *Harvard Latino Law Review,* 2007: 1–43.

Wallingford, Todd. "Classroom Tools at the MHS." *The Massachusetts Historical Society.* 2007. http://www.masshist.org/education/resources/wallingford/ Unit-4-Voting-Rights.pdf (accessed January 12, 2010).

The Washington Post Company. *Rights Commission's Report on Florida Election.* June 5, 2001. http://www.washingtonpost.com/wp-srv/onpolitics/transcripts/ccr draft060401.htm (accessed November 14, 2009).

Webb, Walter Prescott. *The Texas Rangers: A Century of Frontier Defense.* Austin, Texas: The University of Texas Press, 1965.

Weil, Gotshal & Manges LLP. "Prairie View Chapter of the NAACP." http://www. weil.com/industries/TransactionDetail.aspx?experience=10150&service=1920 (accessed December 11, 2009).

Wheelan, Joseph. *Invading Mexico.* New York: Carroll & Graf, 2007.

Yanek, Mieczkowski. *The Routledge Historical Atlas of Presidential Elections.* New York: Routledge, 2001.

Yoxall, Peter. "Comment: The Minuteman Project, Gone in a Minute or Here to Stay? The Origin, History and Future of Citizen Activism on the United States-Mexico Border." *University of Miami Inter-American Law Review,* 2006: 1–45.

Index

About the Author

Orlando J. Rodriguez is a geographer and former manager of the Connecticut State Data Center at the University of Connecticut, and was a Peace Corps volunteer in Ecuador. His reports on the impact of illegal immigration on apportionment have been widely covered by the media, and his knowledge of population issues has been used as expert testimony in federal court. Rodriguez is currently employed as a Senior Policy Fellow for a Connecticut nonprofit that advocates for families and children. He lives in Willington, Connecticut.

0524/4712